THE **BIG** BOOK OF
CITY

BY THE SAME AUTHOR

HISTORICAL/FACTUAL

From Maine Men To Banana Citizens (1989), Temple Press
The Pride of Manchester (with Steve Cawley, 1991), ACL & Polar
Manchester: The Greatest City (1997 & 2002), Polar Publishing
Farewell To Maine Road (2003), Polar Publishing
Manchester City Hall Of Fame (2005), Hamlyn
Manchester City The Complete Record (2006), Breedon Books
Manchester City: 125 Years Of Football (2006 & 2007), At Heart Publications
Manchester: A Football History (2008), James Ward

TELEVISION

The History Of Football (2007), Channel M

FICTION

Atkinson For England (with Mark Brown, 2001), Empire

BIOGRAPHY

Football With A Smile: The Authorised Biography of Joe Mercer, OBE
(1993 & 1994), ACL & Polar

THE **BIG** BOOK OF
CITY

GARY JAMES

PUBLISHED BY

First published in Great Britain in 2009 by
James Ward
PO BOX 822, HALIFAX, HX1 9FX

www.manchesterfootball.org

city@manchesterfootball.org

Designed by Trevor Hartley

ISBN 978-0-9558127-2-9

James Ward 729

Printed and bound in Great Britain by CPI
Antony Rowe, Chippenham, Wiltshire.

CONTENTS

INTRODUCTION

The idea of this book came on Christmas Day a few years back. I was sat looking at some of the presents and realised that for many people the ideal gift was a book that could be delved into when time allowed. This could be for long spells but more often than not would be for short spells. Basically I, like many other people, will pick up a book with the sole intention of reading a page or a couple of pages to while away a period of time.

Most of my books over the years have been detailed, in-depth histories or biographies and while I love writing those books and they have proved popular over the years, I have realised that most of us do not always get the right amount of time to dedicate to reading books of that type. Every so often we simply want to dive into a book for a few minutes.

"The Big Book Of City" developed out of a desire to provide a mix of entertaining information in an easy to read format. However, I was also keen to ensure that the book provided new or newly discovered information and within these pages you can read for the first time how Maine Road actually got its name. Previous books have guessed, but now "The Big Book Of City" provides the answer.

Similarly, I wanted to take some of the simple facts and provide the story behind those facts, so City's highly political visit to Berlin in 1938 is covered in more detail than ever before. Hopefully the story, as told in this book, explains why City's match in the Olympic Stadium is such a significant moment.

Alongside all of this was a desire to ensure the book was not simply a miscellany of information. I wanted it to provide valid, readable content alongside some of the more trivia based material. I decided there had to be a couple of key themes to the book. These are Europe – the 2008-09 season reminded us all of the stage City should be competing on – and Goalkeepers. City have a great reputation for producing talented 'keepers and within the pages of this book I have written profiles of every 'keeper to appear in the League for City up to date of publication.

If I am fortunate enough to write future editions of "The Big Book Of City" then I would like to ensure this approach continues with each book including two significant themes alongside more trivia based material.

I hope you enjoy this book and find it entertaining.

Best wishes,

Gary James
September 2009

ACKNOWLEDGEMENTS

As with every book I write there are many, many people who have helped during the production of this book. Some of the information has been gathered from interviews and in-depth research I have performed over many, many years into the Club's history. My first book was published in April 1989 and here, within the pages of *The Big Book Of City*, are snippets of information and research I gathered in the eighties but never managed to utilise in any of the books I've written. For this reason it is difficult to highlight everyone who has assisted me over the years. If I miss anyone I apologise.

I have received great support, assistance and inspiration from (listed in alphabetical order): Eric Alexander, Chris Bailey, Noel Bayley, Peter Barnes, Mike Barnett, Julian Baskcomb, Colin Bell, David Bernstein, Lawrence Bernstein, Chris Bird, John Bond, Tony Bugby, Jim Cassell, Dennis Chapman, Doug Cheeseman, Ian Cheeseman, Andy Cooke, Joe Corrigan, Kevin Cummins, Andy Dickman, Willie Donachie, Garth Dykes, Fred Eyre, Sir Tom Finney, Geoff Fisher, Steve Fleet, Jimmy Frizzell, Peter Gardner, Ray Goble, Peter Godkin, Bob Greaves, Bernard Halford, Frank Hannah, Trevor Hartley, Tony Heap, Mark Hodkinson, Brian Horton, Brian Houghton, David Johnson, Alan Jubb, Mark Kennedy, Francis Lee, Andy Lyons, John Maddocks, Jean-Francois Maille, David Mercer, Norah Mercer, John Motson, Tommy Muir, Ian Niven jnr, Mike Pavasovic, Simon Pearce, Roger Reade, James H Reeve, Stuart Renshaw, John Riley, Joe Royle, Steve Sayer, Ken Smallwood, Mike Summerbee, Gordon Taylor, Bert Trautmann, Richard Tucker, Dave & Sue Wallace, Andy Ward, John Wardle, Richard Whitehead, and Chris Williams.

The following museums, libraries and media organisations have provided support, imagery, and assistance: Action Images, the BFI, Channel M, Granada TV, Manchester Central Library, Manchester City Museum & Stadium Tour, Manchester County FA, Manchester Evening News, National Football Museum, the newspaper archive of the British Library at Colindale, the PFA, the Reporter Group, and Tameside Libraries. It is worth stating that this is not an official MCFC publication.

Inevitably, thousands of individual newspaper editions have been consulted during the production of this book, particularly those national and local editions produced in Manchester. These include:

Manchester Courier
Manchester Evening Chronicle
Manchester Evening News
Manchester Weekly Times
The Reporter (various locally branded versions)
Daily Dispatch
Athletic News
Sporting Chronicle

Plus of course all modern day national newspapers, football magazines, and club-based material.

Club historians and fellow members of the *Association of Football Statisticians* and *The Society of Authors* have assisted and, as always, I am grateful to them all. Similarly, I would like to thank all the journalists, photographers, and officials who have helped chronicle the game throughout the history of the Blues. The majority of photographs come from Action Images, Edward Garvey, Heidi James, Emma T Taylor, Richard Tucker, Cros Ward, Steve Worthington and the author. As always, thank you all.

Of course the staff at my publishers James Ward need thanking for their efforts in making this a great publication. As does Trevor Hartley who has, once again, performed miracles with the design of this book and its cover.

As always, I would like to say 'thanks' to my family for their continuing support. This book has been produced during a particularly difficult time for me. After almost seven years direct involvement with Manchester City creating the award winning museum & the Hall Of Fame, together with working on a variety of other significant projects, I left the Club in February 2009. Thanks to my family and those who have supported me through this difficult period.

One of the most positive elements of my research has been the support I have received from City fans. I am passionate about this Club and, as anyone who knows me will understand, I am obsessive about ensuring City's history is given the respect it deserves. It has been frustrating to read some of the media coverage of City during the last season or so. Many of the people commenting on the 'world's richest club', as they perceive the Blues, have little understanding of how the Blues have developed.

During my time at City I tried to ensure perceptions were changed. Throughout the twenty plus years of my writing and research I have demonstrated my willingness to prove that City have always been one of the game's most significant clubs. Every City fan knows this and, hopefully, in future years the media will recognise this as well.

In my final months at City I was enthused by the interest shown in City's history by the Chairman Khaldoon Al Mubarak. He personally asked me in-depth questions on the Blues' history and I was delighted with his clear determination to get to grips with what Manchester City is all about.

Finally, as we all know Manchester City is a special club and so my biggest acknowledgement of all is to the thousands of people who have contributed to the history and development of the Club over the years. Obviously, that includes the players, directors, Chairmen, and staff of the Club but more significantly it includes the fans. Supporters are the lifeblood of the Club. Fans love success but they also remember the low points. City's existence contains many highs and lows and as time moves on the media and others may forget the significance of certain moments, but the fans will always recognise them. Stoke 1934, Birmingham 1956, Swindon 1965, Rotherham 1966, Newcastle 1968, Vienna 1970, Newcastle 1976, Halifax 1980, Luton 1983, Charlton 1985, Stoke 1988, Bradford 1989, Gillingham 1999, Blackburn 2000, Old Trafford 2008 – not a comprehensive list but a variety of names and dates fans will recognise the significance of. Fans are the backbone of any club, but at City they have been the most positive aspect of the Club decade after decade, generation after generation. This book is dedicated to them all.

CITY'S NUMBER ONE

Did you know that between 3rd September 1892 when City (as Ardwick) played its first League game and the end of the 2008-09 season the Blues have had 69 goalkeepers play in League games?

How many can you name?

The full list appears on the next page, but to give some clues here are a few images of City keepers that may help jog the memory.

▲ Goalkeeper 35 **Who is this famous City 'keeper pictured with Joe Mercer and the ECWC?**

▲ Goalkeeper 65 **Another England international, but can you recall his name?**

▲ Goalkeeper 30 **Can you name the young 'keeper on the far right of this photo?**

▲ Goalkeeper 43 **This 'keeper became an England international and appeared in the 1970 ECWC, but can you name him?**

▼ Goalkeeper 40 **He may have welcomed Johnny Crossan to Maine Road in this photo, but do you recall his name?** *Hint – he won the FA Cup with City.*

CITY'S NUMBER ONE
THE FULL LIST

The following is a complete list of all goalkeepers in chronological order to have appeared for Ardwick/City in the League between 1892 and 2009.

1 - Billy Douglas

2 - Bert Stones

3 - F Steele

4 - Charlie Williams

5 - George Hutchinson

6 - Tom Chappell

7 - Walter Cox

8 - Frank Barrett

9 - Jack Hillman

10 - John Edmondson

11 - Frank Davies

12 - Bill Hall

13 - Walter Smith

14 - Herbert Broomfield

15 - Jack Lyall

16 - Jack Swann

17 - Gus Beeby

18 - Jim Goodchild

19 - Tom Blair

20 - Jim Mitchell

21 - Billy Harper

22 - Jack Phillips

23 - Dick Finnigan

24 - Bert Gray

25 - Lewis Barber

26 - Len Langford

27 - Cliff Walmsley

28 - Frank Higgs

29 - Jim Nicholls

30 - Frank Swift ▼

31 - Jack Robinson

32 - Alec Thurlow

33 - Ken Oxford

34 - Ron Powell

35 - Bert Trautmann ▼

36 - Derek Williams

37 - John Savage

38 - George Thompson

39 - Steve Fleet

40 - Harry Dowd ▲

41 - Alan Ogley

42 - Ken Mulhearn

43 - Joe Corrigan ▼

44 - Ron Healey

45 - Keith Macrae

46 - Alex Williams

47 - Eric Nixon

48 - Barry Siddall

49 - Perry Suckling

50 - Bobby Mimms

51 - Mike Stowell

52 - Andy Dibble

53 - Paul Cooper

54 - Tony Coton

55 - Martyn Margetson

56 - Simon Tracey

57 - John Burridge

58 - Eike Immel

59 - Tommy Wright

60 - Nicky Weaver

61 - Carlo Nash

62 - Peter Schmeichel

63 - David Seaman

64 - Kevin Stuhr Ellegaard

65 - David James ◄

66 - Joe Hart

67 - Andreas Isaksson

68 - Kasper Schmeichel

69 - Shay Given

CITY IN EUROPE

During 2008-09 City reached the quarter finals of the UEFA Cup for the second time in their history, while April 2010 marks the 40th anniversary of the Club's first European trophy success. To commemorate these two landmark moments *The Big Book Of City* highlights every season of European football the Blues have competed in. Spread throughout this book are features on each season to provide you with a handy record of every Blue Euro game.

1968-69

Competition: European Cup

Reason For Qualification: Reigning League champions

Manager: Joe Mercer

18th September 1968
Round 1 Leg 1
Attendance: 38,787

City 0-0 Fenerbahce

City: Mulhearn; Kennedy, Pardoe, Doyle, Heslop, Oakes. Lee, Bell, Summerbee, Young, Coleman

CITY LEAGUE CHAMPIONS
WEDNESDAY SEPTEMBER 18th 1968
Kick-off 7-45 p.m.
VERSUS
FENERBAHCE S.K. Champions of Turkey

MANCHESTER CITY FOOTBALL CLUB LTD.
European Champion Clubs' Cup
OFFICIAL PROGRAMME ONE SHILLING

The first European match involving City to be staged was this European Cup tie. The generally perceived view is that City underestimated the quality of the Turkish champions – neutrals had told the Blues Fenerbahce were equivalent to a mid-table Division Two side. But the truth is a little different and starts with concern over City's League form. Peter Gardner, writing for the *Manchester Evening News*, was the reporter closest to City at this time and pre-match he wrote: "Manchester City tonight twice step out into the great unknown. Unknown to them is the tension and highly skilled technique of top level European competition.

"Unknown to them, too, is the quality and standard of opposition on whom manager Joe Mercer has had to plan his first continental assault from second hand sources. But above all is the known fact that City are not playing anything like the powerful and punchy side that qualified for the European Cup so gloriously less than four months ago."

Leading up to the match City had only

won one League game (3-2 V Wolves back on 14th August) and had suffered four defeats and four draws, so Gardner's concern was justified. Of course the Blues were missing influential captain Tony Book through injury as well.

When it came to the first leg itself City were extremely impressive, however they simply could not break down a defensive minded Fenerbahce. Colin Bell had a header scooped off the line by defender Ercan while Mike Doyle had a full bodied attempt brilliantly saved by 'keeper Yavus Simack (above).

Glyn Pardoe, playing his first game in a fortnight, was impressive, while Alan Oakes made a perfect replacement for Book as captain.

Afterwards the headlines focused on Fenerbahce's strong defence: "Talented Turks give Blues lesson in tactics." Peter Gardner: "City commanded 90% of the play yet still could not break down the splendidly organised Fenerbahce defence."

The result was a shock 0-0 draw but manager Joe Mercer remained convinced that City could still progress: "I shall be very surprised if we don't beat Fenerbahce in Istanbul. I would have liked to have taken a lot of goals out there next month. But we don't go to Turkey with any fear; we go with a lot of confidence. Fenerbahce are a good team as I said before the match, but I don't know whether they can play any different than they did at Maine Road."

To help City with their preparation for the second leg, a Turkish friend of director Chris Muir called Malik Cin provided his view of what the Blues needed to do: "They would do well to throw flowers to the crowd before the match. Treat them with cheerfulness and courtesy and things will be okay. Disobey this code of conduct and you could be in trouble. The crowd gets angry. So do the players."

18th September 1968
Round 1 Leg 2
Attendance: 45,000

Fenerbahce 2-1 City

City Goalscorer: Coleman
City: Mulhearn; Connor, Pardoe, Doyle,
Heslop, Oakes. Lee, Bell, Summerbee,
Young, Coleman

As suggested, City captain Alan Oakes did take a bouquet of flowers on to the pitch and exchanged them with his opposite number, before the game started. Check footage of the moment on Youtube.

After the formalities, the second leg started with City performing exceptionally well. They managed to dominate the first half and went in at the break 1-0 in front. Tony Coleman (pictured) had taken advantage of a rare slip up from the impressive Erkan to score after twelve minutes. Peter Gardner recognised City's domination: "City did enough to earn a second round place on their opening 45 minute performance, but they carelessly threw it away in the second half when Fenerbahce should have been a spent force."

A minute into the second half Fenerbahce's Abdullah scored an equaliser. He was a half time substitute and scored with his first kick of the game. Captain Alan Oakes later admitted: "That really knocked the stuffing out of us."

Then twelve minutes from the end of normal time Ogun, who had been on loan to a side in Washington, USA, slid home the winning goal. Ogun also had two other efforts disallowed.

Fenerbahce Chairman Ilgaz was later credited as saying he was impressed with City's discipline: "We liked the gentlemanly manners of the Manchester players."

Joe Mercer told journalists the day after the game: "There can be no excuses. How can you expect to win matches when you make elementary defensive mistakes like we made last night? We lost the tie by failing to seal it up at Maine Road. Fenerbahce played no differently than I expected them to as they really possess few outstanding players. But I'm not grumbling. That fatal lapse after half time proved our down fall."

Malcolm Allison, Mercer's right-hand man, was not so talkative. For almost 48 hours after the game Allison remained silent. When he broke his silence he spoke to the trusted Peter Gardner: "'Defeat in Istanbul was the biggest disappointment of my

whole career. What made it so particularly frustrating was that in the first half at Fenerbahce we had conquered all the problems that go with playing abroad in the tense atmosphere of the European Cup. The players had silenced the hysterical crowd; they had overcome the different refereeing, poor pitch and the lighter, softer ball. I don't think the players realised the difficulties they would meet in this away leg with the result that there was not enough urgency in the first game at Maine Road."

Of course, the terrify Europe comment that Allison had made the previous May (see page 44) came back to haunt him, however Allison had the last laugh the following year when City won the European Cup Winners' Cup. Allison later laughed: "I said we'd terrify Europe, but I didn't say when!"

The Football Season Daily Reminder
August

Ever wondered what football anniversaries fall throughout the season? If you have take a look at the Big Book Of City's Football Season Daily Reminder. Spread throughout this book we have monthly snippets covering some memorable – and some not so memorable - moments in City's history. We don't highlight every anniversary, but we do provide one for every single date in the period 1st August through to 31st May. Let's start with August...

1st August 1970
Former City goalkeeper David James was born in Welwyn.

2nd August 1971
Wyn Davies signed from Newcastle for £50,000.

3rd August 1968
The Blues defeated FA Cup holders West Bromwich Albion 6-1 in the Charity Shield (right) watched by a Maine Road crowd of 35,510.

4th August 1987
The inaugural Manchester International Tournament was played over two days (4th & 5th) at Maine Road. City faced Manchester United (3-1 defeat) and beat PSV Eindhoven (3-1) to finish 3rd in the competition. Athletico Mineiro beat PSV on the first night and lost to United in the final.

Manchester International Football Tournament
at Maine Road, Manchester
Tuesday 4th and Wednesday 5th August 1987.

TOURNAMENT BROCHURE 60p

OFFICIAL CLUB SPONSORS
brother
The future at your fingertips.

5th August 1974
Antoine Sibierski was born in Lille, France.

6th August 1991
Keith Curle signed from Wimbledon for the then record fee of £2.5m.

7th August 1993
Former Sunday tabloid journalist John Maddock took on the role of General Manager. Supporters

saw this as being a rather unusual move at the time and it wasn't long before manager Peter Reid's role was being questioned.

8th August 1998

Nicky Weaver made his debut at home to Blackpool. City won their first match in the third tier of English football 3-0. The attendance was 32,134.

9th August 1969

Joe Mercer celebrated his 55th birthday with a 4-1 victory over Sheffield Wednesday on the opening day of the 1969-70 season.

10th August 1974

David Sommeil (below) was born at Ponte-a-Pitre, France.

11th August 2001

Goals from Shaun Goater, Eyal Berkovic and Stuart Pearce ensured a 3-0 victory over Watford at Maine Road in Kevin Keegan's first League game as manager.

12th August 1964

Barrie Betts joined Scunthorpe United after 117 first team appearances for the Blues.

13th August 1974

Asa Hartford signed from West Bromwich Albion for £210,000.

14th August 1991

Peter Reid's City headed the Football League after beating Crystal Palace 3-2 at Maine Road. The Blues had won their opening three matches, but poor form in September and March left them in 5th place at the season's end.

15th August 1963

Mancunian Peter Dobing joined Stoke City after scoring 31 goals in 82 City League appearances.

16th August 1906

Defender Bill Eadie signed for City from Greenock Morton.

17th August 1968

The League Champions (City) faced the European Cup holders (United) in the 79th Manchester League derby. The game ended goalless after an extremely defensive United employed spoiling tactics throughout. United's John Fitzpatrick performed several crunching tackles on City midfielder Colin Bell. Afterwards the media focused on United's

negative play with one 'paper claiming that United's defensive style proved their fear of the rather more attacking minded City. The game was watched by a Maine Road crowd of 63,052 and, for the first time, the Manchester derby was shown on the BBC's Match of The Day.

18th August 1971

Two goals from Francis Lee (below) helped City to a 4-0 victory over Crystal Palace at Maine Road but this was noteworthy as one of Lee's goals was scored from the penalty spot. This was the first of the record breaking 13 he netted that season.

19th August 1978

Brian Kidd scored on the opening day of the season at Derby County. The game ended 1-1 but Kidd went on to score in each of the first three games of the season.

19th August 1992

Injury in City's first Premier League away game brought a premature end to Paul Lake's career. The player (above) had been struggling against injury for some time, but this game at Middlesbrough ultimately became his last League match.

20th August 1949

Frank Swift was talked out of retirement following health problems with 'keeper Alec Thurlow. His return match ended in a 3-3 draw at home to Aston Villa, watched by 43,196.

21st August 1979

Colin Bell retired after a four-year fight to regain full fitness.

22nd August 1959

Popular striker Bobby Johnstone (right) scored his last League goal for City as the Blues defeated Nottingham Forest 2-1.

This opening game of the season was watched by a Maine Road crowd of 38,974.

23rd August 1947

Eddie McMorran made his League debut for City a good one. He scored as the Blues beat Wolves 4-3 before 67,782 at Maine Road (teamsheet above).

24th August 1994

The popular trio of Peter Beagrie, Uwe Rosler and Paul Walsh all netted to

August sunshine, which seemed more an invitation to cricket, welcomed the League football season which opened to-day. There you see a corner flag which looks so small but means so much going up on Manchester City ground for the match with Sheffield Wednesday

give City a decisive 3-0 win over West Ham United. The game was played in front of a sell-out 19,150 crowd the lowest for a City home game in the Premier League. The capacity had been restricted as the Kippax side of Maine Road was undergoing redevelopment.

25th August 1923

First match at Maine Road. Sheffield United were the visitors as the Blues won 2-1 before 58,159 spectators.

26th August 1994

After 96 (plus 22 as substitute) first team appearances Mike Sheron joined Norwich City.

27th August 1960

The only Manchester derby to be abandoned due to torrential rain was cut short with the scores at 2-2. A Maine Road crowd of 51,927 had witnessed City goals from Joe Hayes (left) and Denis Law, while Dennis Violet and Alex Dawson were on target for the Reds.

28th August 1998

Defender David Morley, a graduate from City's youth set up, joined Southend after making only one full appearance and two as substitute for the Blues. His debut game saw him score City's equaliser (against Bury in September 1997) from a Tony Scully corner.

29th August 1981

City beat West Bromwich Albion 2-1 on the opening

day of the season. Martin O'Neill made his City debut, while the game was also noteworthy as it was the first victory under the new 3 points for a win system.

30th August 1919

City's first League game played in August ended in a 3-3 draw with Sheffield United at Hyde Road.

31st August 1965

Defender Stan Horne (below) became a City trialist on this date. He went on to make 63 (plus 3 as substitute) first team appearances.

GOLDEN GOALS

1974

Rodney Marsh

Overhead kick v QPR

Many goals over the years are described as the greatest ever by a City player. Sometimes these become a talking point for a few days, sometimes for a few years but unless they happen to occur in a major trophy winning game goals tend to lose their significance as time moves on. This is especially true for games prior to the 1990s when television coverage was limited to, at best, a handful of top flight games.

The idea of this 'GOLDEN GOALS' feature is to remember a significant or spectacular goal from yesteryear. The Big Book Of City's hope is that modern day supporters will learn more about some of these goals. If you would like to nominate a goal for possible use in a future 'Big Book' then email: **city@manchesterfootball.org** with details of game, goalscorer and date.

The goal featured here is Rodney Marsh's overhead kick from the City-QPR Division One game of September 1974. For years this was perceived as the greatest overhead goal in City's history and, even for some time after Dennis Tueart's spectacular goal in the 1976 League Cup final, this was remembered as the best. It may not have been the most significant, but it was the one fans remembered.

Over time the goal has slipped from memory and so we've searched the archives of various newspapers and other sources to find as many images of the goal as possible. The images you see here show the goal stage by stage.

Match Stats

Date: 28th September 1974
Score: City 1-0 QPR
Scorer: Rodney Marsh (83mins)
Attendance: 30,647

City Team: Keith Macrae, Geoff Hammond, Willie Donachie, Mike Doyle, Colin Barrett, Alan Oakes, Mike Summerbee, Colin Bell, Rodney Marsh, Asa Hartford, Dennis Tueart.

Pre-Match

This was City's tenth game of the season and fifth at home. Apart from two defeats and a draw away from home the Blues were undefeated and looking likely to mount a serious challenge for the League title under manager Tony Book. Book had replaced Ron Saunders the previous April.

QPR were managed by Gordon Jago however the day before the game some journalists claimed that Jago had resigned and would not be manager for the match with City. Other journalists claimed he would be, so there was some confusion. Ultimately Jago officially left Rangers in October 1974 and so there must have been some truth in the pre-match rumours.

England manager Don Revie came to the game to watch a few City players. The media suggested this would be Colin Bell, Dennis Tueart and City captain Rodney Marsh.

The Game

The first half was a fairly tight affair with QPR adopting a highly defensive style. Blues did attack but attempt after attempt was snuffed out by QPR. Even when the Blues managed to break through the Rangers' defence they still had England international 'keeper Phil Parkes to contend with.

At half time manager Tony Book warned his side to adopt a patient approach. He argued that QPR would be broken down sooner or later and that the Blues had enough fire power to find the net.

As the second half progressed Colin Bell and Dennis Tueart shone. Writing in the *Manchester Evening News*, Peter Gardner talked of a spell of relentless City pressure: "For ten minutes Bell turned Rangers inside out... then Tueart took over to provide a dazzling performance. The willingness of Marsh to graft as well as turn on the tricks was another feature for the England manager to consider deeply."

Despite the pressure the game remained goalless until the 83rd minute. That's when something out of the ordinary managed to break the deadlock. Gardner: "The Blues skipper provided that flash of genius with an overhead kick to which even the brilliant Phil Parkes had no answer. Up to that point England goalkeeper Parkes had defied all City's attempts to score."

The overhead strike was described as: "A spectacular Marsh goal" and "A Rod gem for City."

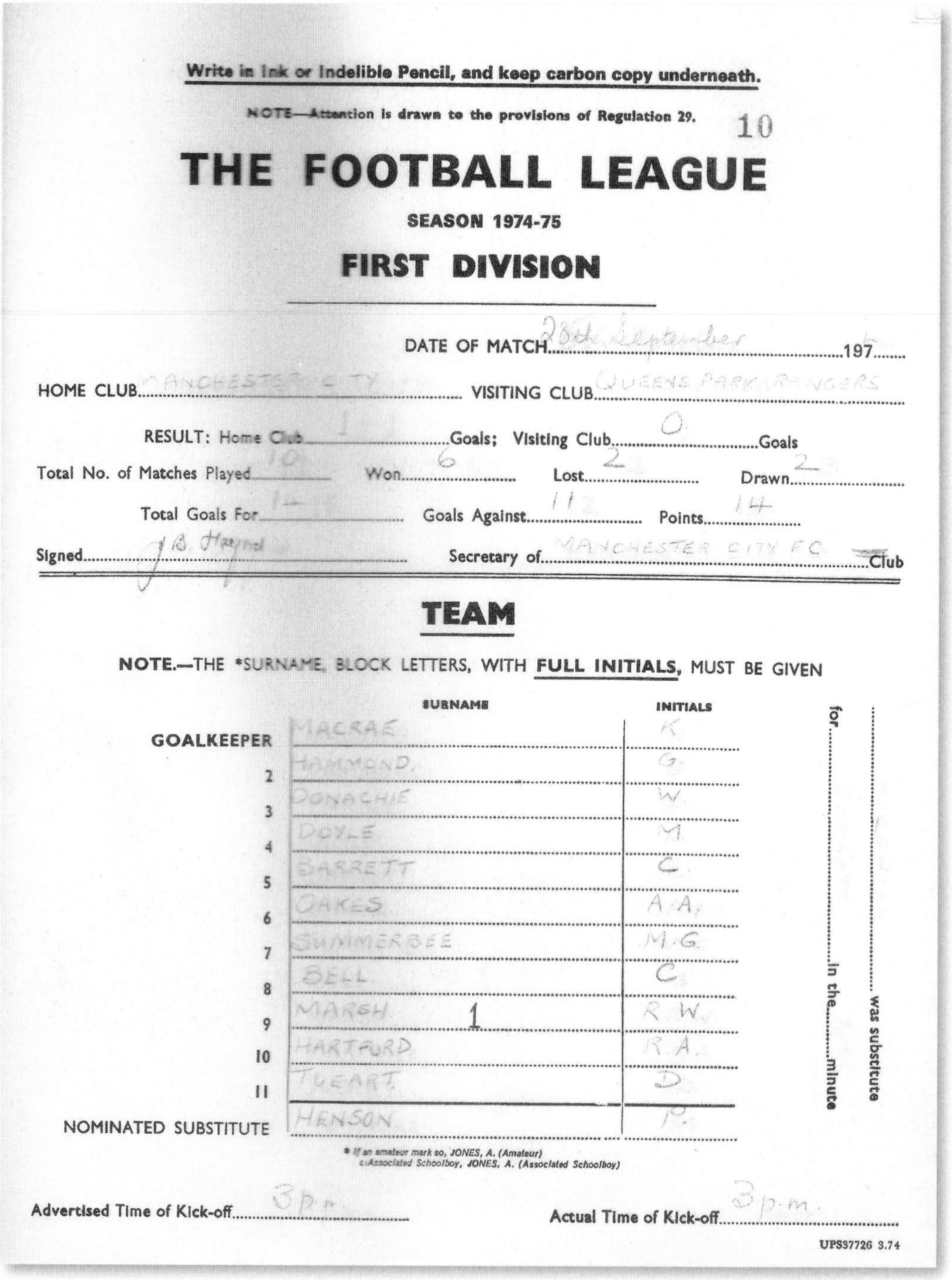

Write in Ink or Indelible Pencil, and keep carbon copy underneath.

NOTE—Attention is drawn to the provisions of Regulation 29.

10

THE FOOTBALL LEAGUE

SEASON 1974-75

FIRST DIVISION

DATE OF MATCH........28th September........197....

HOME CLUB........MANCHESTER CITY........ VISITING CLUB........QUEENS PARK RANGERS

RESULT: Home Club........1........Goals; Visiting Club........0........Goals

Total No. of Matches Played........10........ Won........6........ Lost........2........ Drawn........2

Total Goals For........14........ Goals Against........11........ Points........14

Signed........J.B. Hayward........ Secretary of........MANCHESTER CITY FC........Club

TEAM

NOTE.—THE *SURNAME, BLOCK LETTERS, WITH **FULL INITIALS**, MUST BE GIVEN

	SURNAME	INITIALS
GOALKEEPER	MACRAE	K
2	HAMMOND	G
3	DONACHIE	W
4	DOYLE	M
5	BARRETT	C
6	OAKES	A.A.
7	SUMMERBEE	M.G.
8	BELL	C
9	MARSH 1	R.W.
10	HARTFORD	R.A.
11	TUEART	D
NOMINATED SUBSTITUTE	HENSON	R

for........in the........minute........was substitute

* If an amateur mark so, JONES, A. (Amateur)
c Associated Schoolboy, JONES, A. (Associated Schoolboy)

Advertised Time of Kick-off........3 p.m........ Actual Time of Kick-off........3 p.m.

UPS37726 3.74

Above: **The official Football League teamsheet.**

Previous page and right: **Rodney Marsh's amazing overhead kick beats Phil Parkes. City players celebrating with Marsh are Colin Barrett and Geoff Hammond**

Man Of The Match

Manchester Evening News City reporter declared that Asa Hartford was the real star of the match: "He is the perfect foil to Bell and Doyle in a midfield department the likes of which City have not possessed for years. Hartford is the complete player in this role and has already paid back much of that £250,000 fee."

Post Match

"Rodney Marsh and Dennis Tueart turned on the style for England boss Don Revie and the outcome should be a certain European Nations Cup call for both players when Revie picks his squad to face Czechoslovakia in the first qualifying match at Wembley next month. They dazzled in a second half when the Blues ended a game of patience with an explosive burst that preserved a 100% home record and maintained their title challenge."

Despite those great words from journalist Peter Gardner there was no place in the England side that ultimately appeared against Czechoslovakia. It is worth noting that Tueart was injured for much of October and would not have been fit enough to play. Colin Bell did play – and scored twice as England won 3-0 at Wembley.

Geoff Hammond, who had been on a month's trial, was signed from Ipswich for £40,000 four days after his performance in this match with QPR.

The victory over QPR placed City second, two points behind leaders Ipswich Town and manager Tony Book had nothing but praise for his captain Rodney Marsh. Book claimed that regardless of the goal, this was Marsh's best ever start.

Book: "Rodney has made his best-ever start to a season while at City, and while I will not put this down solely to the captaincy he has been given I am sure it is a valuable contributory factor. The prime reason is, I believe, Rodney's own frame of mind and his determination to be involved' in a successful team. His overall mood as this season started could not have been bettered I think it has reflected in the team's performance. The difficulty I faced after the opening weeks was the return of Mike [Summerbee] from his F.A. ban. It was important that I was fair to Mike, who had thrown himself heart and soul into the task of being City's captain and had set a fabulous example off the field as well as on the field with his enormous spirit."

"When Mike came back I felt he was entitled to be in a similar position to myself in my playing days. Whenever I was missing from the team through injury I was always restored to leading the team when I returned to the senior side. There were no explanations or apologies. I told Mike that he could resume being the club captain and he could pick up from where he left off if he felt he wanted to. 'You are the skipper of the club and I have only made changes temporarily in your absence' I told him."

"Mike had his own views. He normally does in situations like this. He said that he did not wish to be re-instated and that the duties should be left with Rodney. Mike maintained that he could still play an important part in the future without being titled as captain.

And to show how unselfish his approach was, he told me that all the evidence pointed to Rodney having found something from being skipper. I am sure he is right."

Elsewhere

Earlier in the month Brian Clough had left Leeds United after only 44 days in charge and, at the time of the City-QPR game, newspapers were still delving in to the story of Clough's departure.

The BBC's Match of the Day for the Saturday of the game had two matches – Everton 3 Leeds 2 (First Division) & Southampton 0 Aston Villa 0 (Second Division). City had been on the programme two weeks earlier (City 2 Liverpool 0) while QPR had been on the week before their meeting with City and also the week after.

The BBC's Saturday night viewing included Kojak at 9.10, Match of the Day at 10.20 and Parkinson at 11.20; while Granada's schedules included Upstairs Downstairs and Russell Harty (interviewing Rod Stewart). The following Monday's Coronation Street had a familiar feel as TV listings said: "Deirdre's mum is on the warpath."

Colin Bell, Rodney Marsh and Dennis Tueart are put through their paces by Tony Book. When this photo was taken all three players were tipped to be picked by Revie for the next England game – in the end only Bell managed to play.

Managers
Their First Season

No, no, the other side!
Where it says
'WELCOME'

Mark Hughes completed his first season as manager in May 2009 by taking the Blues to the quarter-finals of the UEFA Cup for the first time in thirty years. This seems a great achievement for a manager in his first season at the Club, but how does it compare to previous managers?

Here we take a look at some of our other managers and try to identify which manager achieved most in his first season at the Club. As managerial changes often come (but not always!) after a period of failure, success has to be measured differently from times when a manager is well established in his role. In terms of actual trophy winning success, none of our managers have won a major trophy in their first season, however four have won the Divisional title in their first season which, to be frank, has to be the greatest success anyone could have hoped for.

Have a look at the following records and see which achievement you work out to be the most significant. Incidentally, Tony Book

Previous page: **John Bond.**

This page (clockwise from top left): **Wilf Wild, Sam Cowan, Joe Mercer and Malcolm Allison, Ernest Mangnall, Tom Maley.**

Facing page: **Peter Reid with his team.**

(the League Cup), Wilf Wild (the FA Cup), and Tom Maley are the only managers to date to have won a major trophy in their second season, while Ron Saunders, Sven Goran Eriksson and Sam Cowan had all left without managing another season.

Highest placed side after a manager's first season

MALCOLM ALLISON	4th	1971-72 (became Team Manager on 7th October 1971, and missed the title by a solitary point)
PETER REID	5th	1990-91 (became manager in November 1990)
ERNEST MANGNALL	6th	1912-13
TONY BOOK	8th	1974-75 (became manager in April of previous season)
SVEN GORAN ERIKSSON	9th	2007-08
DAVID ASHWORTH	10th	1924-25
MARK HUGHES	10th	2008-09
JOHN THOMSON	10th	1947-48
JOHN HART	11th	1972-73 (replaced Malcolm Allison on 30th March 1973)
JOHN BOND	12th	1980-81 (became manager in October 1980)
HOWARD KENDALL	14th	1989-90 (replaced Mel Machin on 8th December 1989)
STUART PEARCE	15th	2005-06 (became manager in March of previous season)
BRIAN HORTON	16th	1993-94 (became manager on 28th August 1993)
WILF WILD	16th	1932-33
HARRY NEWBOULD	17th	1906-07
ALAN BALL	18th	1995-96
JOHN BENSON	20th	1982-83 (became manager on 5th February 1983)
JIMMY FRIZZELL	21st	1986-87 (became manager on 20th September 1986)

Although Malcolm Allison achieved the highest finish in the top division of any City manager in his first season, it has to be remembered that Allison had played a major part in City's direction since 1965.

Mercer takes City back to top in 295 days

MANCHESTER CITY are back in Division One. With a win at Rotherham last night they made sure of promotion after three seasons of Second Division Soccer at Maine Road.

And for manager Joe Mercer this magic night of fulfilment came just 295 days after taking on the tough job of leading them back.

An elated Mercer said last night: "I'm thrilled for everybody associated with the club . . . and that includes all the supporters who have rallied to our cause."

"I saw this as a long-term job," said Mercer. "But it has come rather quicker than any of us dared to hope. Now we must all be sensible and bear in mind that there's still a long-term job to carry through.

"Now we've got to establish ourselves as a First Division club, so we must get the rejoicing over quickly and look forward rather than backwards. We've got to get down straight away to the next stage of the job."

Asked to name the factors that had brought such swift results, Mercer said: "This has been a team effort right down from the chairman and the boardroom to the field of play.

"I asked for three things—enthusiasm, honesty, and effort. These we have had in abundance.

"It would be wrong to try to pin-point any one thing, but our formula has been founded as much as anything on co-ordination. This is the trend in football. Liverpool, Burnley, and other clubs have set this example.

"I think our formula is right and we hope to make it operate successfully in the top table. But now is the moment for me to thank everybody concerned for their loyalty and their wholehearted effort. I am grateful, and I am sure they all know it."

A jubilant Johnny Crossan interrupted the celebrations in the Millmoor dressing-room to say: "This is just great. It is a fitting reward for a lot of hard work and flat-out effort. I am pleased most of all for Mr. Mercer and his assistant Malcolm Allison.

"All their planning, patience, and perseverance has paid off."

But Crossan added: "It wasn't the real City tonight. There was too much tension. We couldn't be proud of our performance, but the real trouble was that everybody in the team was afraid of making any mistakes. That is the way it is when promotion success is so near and yet so far away.

"But now, thank goodness, the heat is off. We will be a far better side in the remaining matches."

Colin Bell, the player signed by City in a £45,000 pre-deadline deal, said of the goal that clinched promotion: "This was the most exciting goal I've ever scored."

Managers who achieved promotion as champions in their first season

TOM MALEY – 1902-03

SAM COWAN – 1946-47 (managed City from 2nd December)

JOE MERCER – 1965-66

KEVIN KEEGAN – 2001-02

Most successful manager in the FA Cup during his first season

WILF WILD – FA Cup finalists 1932-33

JOHN BOND – FA Cup finalists 1980-81 (became manager in October 1980)

Most successful manager in the League Cup during his first season

RON SAUNDERS – League Cup finalists 1973-74 (became manager on 24th November)

Most successful manager in Europe during his first season

MARK HUGHES – UEFA Cup quarter-finalists 2008-09

Left: **Ron Saunders**   *Above:* **Kevin Keegan**

CITY'S NUMBER ONE

THE PROFILES

Earlier in The Big Book of City we listed all the 'keepers who have appeared in League games for the Blues. But what do we know about them? Throughout this book we provide brief biographies, in chronological order, of each 'keeper. We start with our first twelve League 'keepers....

1 – WILLIAM DOUGLAS

Goalkeeper for our first League game, Scotsman Billy Douglas originally joined Ardwick AFC in May 1890. He was an ever-present for the Club's first season in the Alliance League and also appeared in Ardwick's first ever FA Cup tie (City 12 Liverpool Stanley 0 on 4th October 1890).

Douglas stayed with the Blues until 26th January 1894, making 36 League appearances, before signing for Newton Heath. In August 1899 when Douglas returned to Dundee the Scottish Sport described him as one of the three best 'keepers ever produced within the city. One of the others, Frank Barrett also played for the Blues.

Appearances: League: 36 FAC: 4

2 – HERBERT STONES

Goalkeeper for his debut game on 25th March 1893, Bert Stones appeared in some reserve games as a half-back. All his first team appearances for City were in goal but in 1894 he transferred to Newton Heath and they record that he was a half back in each of his 7 first team appearances.

Sadly, Bert's time in nets saw him concede 10 goals in the 10-2 thrashing by Small Heath on 17th March 1894. Perhaps he really was a half-back! The following summer he went to Newton Heath and had a spell at Ashton North End in 1895.

Appearances: League: 12

3 – F STEELE

Sadly, research has failed to identify Steele's first name to date. He joined Ardwick on 11th October 1892 and played a variety of roles during his 18 first team appearances. He made his League debut at full back. His next appearance at centre half. His third game saw him play at centre forward.

In 1893-94 after playing in both attack and defence again he finally made his first League appearance in goal. He ultimately played only two League games in nets.

Appearances: League: 17 (1 goal) FAC: 1

4 – CHARLIE WILLIAMS

The first player to keep goal for the Blues in the League under their new name of Manchester City, Charlie Williams was a cult hero following his arrival from Woolwich Arsenal. He was a highly entertaining if somewhat erratic 'keeper. Of the 23 games he played during his opening season only three ended with clean sheets, and one game saw the Blues defeated 8-0 by Burton Wanderers. The situation improved dramatically the following season with Williams appearing in every League game as the Blues finished second in Division Two.

In November 1897 he appeared for the Football League against the Irish League at Hyde Road – this was a major honour at the time – and in 1898-99 Williams helped City to the Second Division Championship. On 14th April 1900 against Sunderland he became the first Ardwick/City 'keeper to be credited with a City goal (while keeping goal!). According to legend the wind caught one of his goal kicks and the opposing 'keeper (the famous Scottish international Ted Doig) fumbled the ball into the net.

Williams remained City's first choice until January 1902 after 10 of the 15 games he played ended in defeat, and the following summer he returned to London to play for Spurs. A spell at Brentford followed before he moved into coaching. He led the Danish Olympic team to the 1908 Olympic final, had spells with French side Olympique (Lille) and Dutch team Le Havre, and eventually he settled in Brazil where he worked with Rio Grande Do Sol. In May 1910 he helped guide the Blues across Germany and Denmark during the Club's first continental tour.

Appearances: League: 221 (1 goal) FAC: 7 Test Matches: 4 apps

5 – GEORGE HUTCHINSON

George Hutchinson joined the Blues on 7th December 1893 and made his debut against Woolwich Arsenal in September 1894 – a 4-2 defeat. He went on to play in the following six games only two of which ended in victory.

In his seven matches he conceded a total of 23 goals and was soon replaced by Charlie Williams. His whereabouts after the 1894-95 season are unknown but it's clear he did not appear in the Football League for any other side.

Appearances: League: 7

6 – THOMAS CHAPPELL

Never on the losing side Tom Chappell would really have had more games under his belt had it not been for the popularity of regular 'keeper Charlie Williams. In a role similar to that of Steve Fleet over fifty years later, Chappell was a perfect understudy just as Fleet was to Trautmann.

Chappell made his debut in December 1897 (Williams was injured) but despite both his appearances ending in victory the regular 'keeper returned as soon as he was fit.

By the Summer of 1900 (when Williams ended the season as an ever present) Chappell decided the time was right to move on and he went to local side Fairfield on 18th December that year.

Appearances: League: 8

7 - WALTER COX

As with Chappell the form and popularity of Charlie Williams meant opportunities for Walter Cox to replace him were few and far between. Only one came (February 1901) during his 10 months at Hyde Road and, even though the game ended in victory, the player had to stand down for the next match.

Cox was a fairly useful 'keeper after previously playing for Millwall. He joined Bury in March 1901 and also had spells at Preston and Dundee.

Appearances: League: 1

8 - FRANCIS BARRETT

Former Newton Heath 'keeper and Scottish international Frank Barrett was signed by City from Arbroath in September 1901. He had only been with the Scottish side for a month and was keen on a return to England (previously he had been a member of the New Brighton Tower side that had to resign from the League). On Boxing Day 1901 the absence of Williams allowed Barrett the opportunity to impress. Sadly, his first game ended in defeat. With Williams still absent, Barrett was given an extended run, but the five games he played saw City collect only two points. He had more success in the FA Cup that season – appearing in a draw (that game often appears recorded as being abandoned but it actually ended after 90 minutes as a goalless draw) , a win, and a defeat. In November 1902 he joined Dundee after he became City's third choice goalkeeper.

Sadly, he passed away in August 1907 at the age of 35. Both City and Newton Heath sent contributions to his widow to help ease her financial burden.

Appearances: League: 1 FAC: 3

Right: **Big Jack Hillman pictured at John McMahon's funeral.**

9 - JACK HILLMAN

The 'keeper for City's first FA Cup final, Tavistock born Jack Hillman was regarded as a giant of a goalkeeper at the time due to his height (6 feet) and bulk (he weighed 14 stone). Although his size would not be noteworthy today it was often commented on in match reports. His name also made it into the 'papers when he was accused of taking part in a bribery scandal while with Burnley – it resulted in him receiving a year long ban.

In January 1902 he joined City, bringing to an end Frank Barrett's run in the first team shortly afterwards, and he appeared in the final 14 games of the season. From that point on he replaced Williams as the Club's regular number one. In 1903 he helped City to the Second Division title then topped this with the FA Cup success and runners up spot in the League.

Controversy followed him again in 1905 when he was a member of the City squad that was investigated as part of the illegal payments scandal that rocked the Blues. He

was fined £50 and suspended. Ultimately he transferred to Millwall in the Southern League where his career was cut short with an injury to his elbow.

A spell as trainer to Burnley followed and at the time of the 1934 FA Cup final it was reported that he was running a shop in the town and had on display the 1904 FA Cup final ball in his shop window. The whereabouts of the ball today are a mystery – if you have any information on what happened to the ball then please contact *The Big Book Of City*. We're desperate to track down this item and believe Hillman would have kept it until his death at the age of 85 in 1955.

Appearances: League: 116 FAC: 8

10 – JOHN EDMONDSON

As with Hillman, John Edmondson was fined and suspended as part of the illegal payments scandal. Transferred to Bolton when his ban was lifted (the FA made it a condition that the players had to leave City and Edmondson had almost signed for United), Edmondson had really been Hillman's understudy throughout his four year career with the Blues.

Edmondson had joined City in May 1902 and made his first appearance the following December. One of his two FA Cup appearances came in the 1904 quarter final replay when Middlesbrough were defeated 3-1.

Appearances: League: 38 FAC: 2

Edmondson has no chance with Lindsay's penalty kicks.

11 – FRANK DAVIES

Birkenhead born Frank Davies joined City in June 1906 from near neighbours Glossop North End where he had kept goal for two seasons in the League.

It was a daunting task for Davies to replace the experienced – but suspended - Hillman and Edmondson, but his City debut was made much worse by the conditions. His debut was the highly unusual 1st September meeting with Woolwich Arsenal – unusual because the temperature (recorded as 90 degrees in the shade) had caused several players to collapse. At one point City only had 7 players on the pitch. That match ended in a 4-1 defeat and then two days later Everton beat City 9-1 at Goodison. It was no surprise that Frank was dropped for the next match.

Occasional appearances followed with his last coming in September 1909 (a 3-2 defeat), but he was never really given enough of a run to see whether he could regain his Glossop form or not. He left in 1910.

Appearances: League: 6

12 – WILLIAM HALL

 City were experiencing a goalkeeping crisis when Bill Hall signed on 6th September 1906. Hillman & Edmondson were banned, Davies seemed unsuitable and another 'keeper, Walter Smith, had been injured in the pre-season public practice match. In desperation the Blues signed Hall from Bristol Rovers where the 'keeper had made one appearance (a 2-1 defeat to Millwall) in the Southern League.

He made 11 consecutive appearances for City (5 defeats, 4 draws and 2 wins), keeping one clean sheet, before Walter Smith regained his fitness. In May 1907 he was transferred to Southern League side Crystal Palace.

Appearances: League: 11

CITY IN EUROPE

1969-70

Competition: European Cup Winners' Cup

Reason For Qualification:
Reigning FA Cup winners

Manager: Joe Mercer

17th September 1969
Round 1 Leg 1
Attendance: 45,000

Atletico Bilbao 3-3 City

City Goalscorers: Young, Booth,
Echebarria (og)
City: Corrigan; Book, Pardoe, Doyle, Booth,
Oakes, Summerbee, Bell, Lee, Young,
Bowyer

Years later Tony Book commented about this
tie with Bilbao: "The newspapers had said that
I'd done well, but all this European football was
new to me. I'd never played in Europe before
so it was a fresh challenge, and I enjoyed it.
After each of our successes I told myself 'I'll
never have to go back to bricklaying now'. I
just couldn't believe it. It was just like a dream
and I didn't want to wake up. I just wanted it to
go on. Success was the great thing about it and
it kept me going."

1st October 1969
Round 1 Leg 2
Attendance: 49,665

City 3-0 Atletico Bilbao

City Goalscorers: Oakes, Bell, Bowyer
City: Corrigan; Book, Pardoe, Doyle, Booth,
Oakes, Summerbee, Bell, Lee, Young,
Bowyer

As time progressed Tony Book talked
positively about these games but on 1st
October 1969 itself the local newspapers
carried interviews with the City captain
where he claimed to be nervous of European
football: "From a personal point of view I
am scared of Europe because I find it means
so much to the Club. It means a lot to me
as well as the rest of the players especially
after last year and the tragic blow of going
out in the first round. But most of all is what
it means to Manchester City and this is the
bit that scares me."

"I believe we have at last got the feel of

European football and what it is all about. Everyone is in the right frame of mind and we are determined to keep the flag of Manchester flying in Europe."

After the game Book's confidence had grown further: "I believe that victory saw us smash through a psychological barrier that had existed since we failed against Fenerbahce. There was a genuine fear on my part before we tackled Atletico and it existed until Alan Oakes put us ahead in the second leg at Maine Road.

"I was scared we might fail again, but the 6-3 aggregate win worked away all the fear that had hung over me. The pressure has eased since then and now I am positive we are going to do well in Europe this season."

The game ended in a 3-0 City win. Alan Oakes started the scoring with a terrific shot from 30 yards out – the best goal of the night – that beat the impressive Bilbao 'keeper Jose Iribar. After 67 minutes Colin Bell scored the second from close range, then after 85 minutes Ian Bowyer scored the third from a Neil Young shot that rebounded to him.

12th November 1969
Round 2 Leg 1
Attendance: 18,000

SK Lierse 0-3 City

City Goalscorers: Lee 2, Bell
City: Corrigan; Book, Pardoe, Doyle (Heslop), Booth, Oakes, Summerbee, Bell, Lee, Young, Bowyer

Francis Lee scored the opening goal in the seventh minute and by the 44th minute the Blues had raced to a 3-0 lead. Lee's second came in the 35th minute and Bell ended the scoring a minute before half time.

Joe Mercer said it was a thoroughly deserved victory and that the Belgians had little to offer. He added: "Conditions were ideal for us in Lierse."

26th November 1969
Round 2 Leg 2
Attendance: 26,486

City 5-0 SK Lierse

City Goalscorers: Bell 2, Lee 2, Summerbee
City: Mulhearn; Book, Pardoe, Doyle, Booth, Oakes (Towers), Summerbee, Bell, Lee, Jeffries, Bowyer

A powerful City performance jettisoned the Blues into the quarter finals. Derek Jeffries performed well in the first half and then in the second half a dominant City managed to score three goals between the 48th minute and the 60th.

This scoreline meant that City were the leading scorers in the competition with 14 goals in four games and only three against.

4th March 1970
Round 3 Leg 1 (Quarter-final)
Attendance: 8,000

Academica Coimbra 0-0 City

City: Corrigan; Book (Heslop), Mann, Doyle, Booth, Oakes, Pardoe, Bell, Summerbee, Lee, Young

This first leg took place only three days before the League Cup final. The press expected City to rest their key players, especially as their opponents were allegedly rather inexperienced students, but Mercer and Allison were keen to ensure a good result.

Malcolm Allison stunned tabloid journalists with some outspoken comments about the importance of European football in comparison with the domestic game. He admitted: "I'd rather beat Academica than West Brom in the League Cup final on Saturday."

The general view at the time was that domestic football was always the main aim for English clubs, however Allison pointed out that no matter how important the League Cup was (and it was very important in 1970, the first year that all 92 League clubs entered it) it was only on the European stage that sides would be recognised as being truly great. He wanted City to be a great side known – and feared – across Europe and argued that beating West Bromwich Albion would not bring that attention but progressing to the ECWC semi-final would.

Talking specifically about Coimbra, Allison commented: "They will be hard to beat but I shall be terribly disappointed if we don't return with at least a draw. A one goal victory would make me absolutely delighted."

In the match, City's defence was outstanding as the Blues kept a clean sheet for their fourth consecutive European game. *Manchester Evening News*: "Apart from Summerbee, City's heroes were in defence where everyone played as a tightly knit unit. Book, until his ankle injury, was once more the inspiring leader."

A whole host of travel problems followed, disrupting preparations for the League Cup final.

18th March 1970
Round 3 Leg 2
Attendance: 36,338

City 1-0 Academica Coimbra

City Goalscorer: Towers
City: Corrigan; Book, Mann, Booth, Heslop (Towers), Oakes, Doyle, Bell (Glennon), Lee, Young, Pardoe

City reached the semi-finals of the ECWC for the first time when Neil Young provided a cross from which 'keeper Carduso dropped the ball for Tony Towers to score his first senior goal late in extra time.

According to Peter Gardner: "After 209 minutes stalemate the Blues finally cracked the resistance of Academica – a team of tough guy students – and it took a sub to finally sink the Portuguese men of war when Tony Towers, with almost the last kick of extra time, scored the goal that gave City victory when a play off in Amsterdam next week seemed a certainty."

Gardner later added that Academica displayed: "negative football at its worst."

Right: **Malcolm Allison congratulates match winner Tony Towers after the home leg with Academica Coimbra.**

1st April 1970
Semi-Final Leg 1
Attendance: 38,000

Schalke 04 1-0 City

City: Corrigan; Book, Pardoe, Doyle, Jeffries, Oakes, Booth, Bell, Lee, Young, Summerbee

Potentially the best and most important European victory ever at Maine Road came with the visit of Schalke '04 of West Germany. Schalke had been a major side pre-war, winning many titles, and had a great history. They were still a formidable side, and in the first leg at Gelsenkirchen they defeated City 1-0.

Nineteen year old defender Derek Jeffries performed exceptionally well, while Joe Corrigan played one of his best games of his first full season, although even his fine performance had no chance of saving Reinhard Libuda's magnificent goal in the 78th minute. Libuda, incidentally, had been described by journalists as the German Tom Finney. Their view was that he was Schalke's most complete player and the man to watch in both games.

In attack City had several opportunities with Bell, Young, and Lee all coming close at one stage or another. In fact, Lee could quite easily have scored an hat trick had luck been on his side. This gave City hope for the second leg.

15th April 1970
Semi-Final Leg 2
Attendance: 46,361

City 5-1 Schalke 04

City Goalscorers: Doyle, Young 2, Lee, Bell
City: Corrigan; Book, Pardoe, Doyle (Heslop), Booth, Oakes, Towers, Bell, Lee, Young, Summerbee (Carrodus)

The confidence the players felt after the first leg proved justified as City dominated the match, playing irresistible football. As early as the ninth minute Mike Doyle gave the Blues their opening goal – "as cool a goal as you could see" according to one report. Five minutes later Alan Oakes and Colin Bell combined to provide an opening for Neil Young, who controlled the ball superbly before sending home his first goal since the January F.A. Cup tie with Hull. In the 27th minute he scored his second – a trademark screaming left foot shot - and then seven minutes into the second half Doyle passed to Francis Lee who curved in from the left to shoot past the 'keeper for City's fourth of the night.

Colin Bell made it five in the 81st minute, and in the final minute or so Libuda gave Schalke a consolation goal. This was the first real effort to trouble Corrigan, who was playing with a broken nose, all night.

Peter Gardner was enthusiastic with his reporting of the match for the *Manchester Evening News*: "It wasn't so much a match... more like a massacre! Mean and magnificent Manchester City routed Schalke 04 with a dazzling display that charged Maine Road with an atmosphere that has rarely been generated before.

"No side in Europe could have lived with them as they outfought, outsmarted and completely outplayed the German side, who reeled in a three goal blitz in 19 sensational minutes of the first half."

Left: **City skipper Tony Book exchanges souvenirs with his Schalke counterpart in Germany.**

Right: **Mike Doyle celebrates his opening goal in the return leg... and fans invade the pitch in celebration at the final whistle.**

"I am delighted City have got through and naturally I hope they win the trophy." Leeds manager Don Revie, who lined up his players to applaud City's European exploits prior to City's 3-1 victory at Elland Road 18/4/70

"Good luck and best wishes to you and the lads"... telegram sent to Joe Mercer and Malcolm Allison in Vienna from England captain Bobby Moore

29th April 1970
European Cup Winners' Cup Final
played at Prater Stadium, Vienna
Attendance: Variously reported as
anything from 7,968 to 12,000
Cup Final Referee: P Schiller (Austria)

City 2-1 Gornik Zabrze

City Goalscorers: Young, Lee (pen)
Gornik Goalscorer: Oslizlo
City: Corrigan; Book, Pardoe, Doyle
(Bowyer), Booth, Oakes, Heslop, Bell, Lee,
Young, Towers
Gornik Zabrze: Kostka, Latocha, Oslizlo,
Gorgan, Florenski (Deja), Szoltysik, Wilczek
(Skowrone), Olek, Banas, Lubanski,
Szarinski

Reaching the 1970 ECWC final was a major triumph although, incredibly, the game was not shown live on British television. Typically, even in 1970, any European final would be broadcast, but the FA Cup final between Leeds and Chelsea had gone to a replay, at Old Trafford, and as that was being played on the same night the BBC covered it. ITV, the only other television channel at the time, were unable to broadcast the game live, and so only highlights late in the evening were shown.

In addition to the lack of television coverage there were issues with the venue itself. The Prater Stadium was highly honoured to have been awarded the final and investment was made to improve the facilities. New floodlights were erected for the game and other improvements made. Despite this investment, the stadium was more or less totally open without shelter even for the directors, press and officials. As torrential rain came in bursts throughout the game it was not a pleasant night to either play or watch the game. In spite of the conditions, City were the first to make an impression.

Ronald Crowther described the action for the *Daily Mail*: "When Young scored his goal it was only the culmination of 12 minutes of absolute dominance, and his breakthrough was the just reward for intelligent anticipation. Lee, playing with all the fire and fervour that will serve England well in Mexico, shook off three defenders out on the left and hammered in a shot of fearsome power. It struck the foot of the post and then cannoned off the legs of goalkeeper Kostka straight to Young, whose flick into goal was the merest of formalities."

The Austrian newspaper *Die Presse* reported: "City played as if the Cup was already theirs. The British side took a 1-0 lead when the Polish goalkeeper Kostka was only able to Parry a surprise shot from Lee, and Young streaked in to score as a matter of course. Although Manchester were in a position to improve upon this lead immediately, they preferred for the moment to rest upon the security of this goal and at the same time to demonstrate a further strength: the English side had the Poles so much under control that they never allowed Gornik to become dangerous."

Francis
Lee

Four minutes after the goal, Mike Doyle badly damaged an ankle tendon in a collision with Florenski and was left in agony on the pitch for two minutes as play went on around him. A reluctant referee eventually allowed trainer and former City star Dave Ewing on, and Doyle was carried off the pitch on his shoulders. City played on for six minutes with only ten men as they tried in vain to get Doyle back to fitness. He was eventually replaced by Ian Bowyer.

Despite the loss of Doyle, City continued to dominate and three minutes before the interval Young broke free in the centre. Die Presse: "Quite of itself and without having been in any way contrived, a second goal fell Manchester City's way in the 43rd minute. It resulted from a dreadful mistake by the otherwise memorable Gornik stopper, Oslizlo, on a surface now slippy from the downpour. He lost the ball midway inside his own half to Manchester City's Young, who was left completely free to advance on Kostka and was fouled by the 'keeper as he attempted to round him with the ball. Lee converted the resultant penalty kick, though not without understandable anxiety: he simply let fly from the spot and the ball rebounded from Kostka into the net."

Thirty years later Les Saul, a senior official in the Supporters' Club, gave his memories of what followed: "As it got near half time with a lead of 2-0 we were highly contented, the lights had gone on as it started to get dark. We thought that we could feel rain drops but it got gradually heavier until it became a downpour. As there was no cover we just had to stay where we were. The second half started and the pitch started to churn up and become waterlogged. City found it hard going in the second half and after Gornik pulled one back we started to have doubts."

Gornik's goal came in the 68th minute when a free kick led to Oslizlo cutting in from the left. He sent a left foot drive past Corrigan, but City remained in overall control despite an effort from Banas that went slightly wide moments after the goal.

In the 75th minute Wilczek was forced to leave the field with a broken leg and the Polish side lost the momentum.

At the final whistle the City fans, who numbered some five thousand in a crowd variously reported as anything from 7,968 to around 12,000, invaded the pitch. As Gornik were a side from behind the Iron Curtain

Francis Lee's penalty in the final.

only around 300 club officials, players' wives, and fans were allowed to travel to the final.

Inevitably, the English media focused on the qualities of City but it is interesting to note how the Austrian press viewed the Blues: "Manchester City possessed every type of English footballer, who are first and foremost model athletes, who can be bone crushingly hard and sometimes were, players who spare themselves and their opponents nothing. Their star man was called George Heslop. Lubanski, who was easily the Poles' best forward, suffered ninety minutes under this Heslop.

"In the Manchester ranks, though, were several players of that 'extra' class. The sturdy Francis Lee, for example, who in the eighth minute provided the finest move of the game when, taking a pass from Book, he swivelled to shoot, bringing an instinctive and spectacular leap from Kostka to keep his goal intact. Though such finesse was a rarity, Oakes, Bell and Young were also

players who particularly distinguished themselves."

Afterwards the City players and management focused on the support they had received. Mercer: "Our supporters, about 4,000 of them, stood in the pouring rain in Vienna to cheer us on. We are only sorry the rest of them were unable to watch on television." Lee: "We were all thrilled with the fans. But for them there would have been no game at all."

Mike Summerbee: "It was not so bad having to sit it out. We won easily. There was never any danger. We could have had six."

Tommy Booth: "Gornik were very disappointing, I was expecting a much harder game. It was a bit upsetting to play in front of so few people, but our fans made all the difference. They were marvellous."

Die Presse also praised the City fans: "Manchester City justified their role as favourites. They controlled the game as effectively as their supporters controlled the scenery. With flags, scarves, banners and

A good night in Vienna.

painted steel helmets which clearly indicate the dangers of being a fanatical soccer fan, the English brought with them a whiff of every possible footballing emotion – which was proper, they having reached the final of a European competition. The fervour was released into a dead stadium – a pity. With sudden chants of 'Cit-ty! Cit-ty!' they urged their team on, certain of success. Some had even attached a replica of the Cup to their banners long before the game got under way."

Despite the positivity, vice-chairman Frank Johnson announced that the Blues were thinking about pulling out of Europe the following season as they were disgusted with the choice of venue: "This was an absolute scandal. Our fans had to travel a thousand miles to be soaked to the skin. It came close to ruining the whole thing. A European final played before such a handful of people is ridiculous. And we're in the mood to pull out of Europe altogether if we do not get any satisfaction from UEFA.

"We could have packed 60,000 into Maine Road for this match. But as it is we have lost money on the tie."

Manchester Evening News photographer Eric Graham gave his memories of the day, thirty years later: "I worked for 37 years as a photographer for the MEN - and that was one game I will never forget, there was torrential rain throughout the game, and they only turned on two of the four floodlights for some reason (probably because there were only about 9000 fans in the stadium). The sports writers, in their posh sheepskin coats and expensive mohair suits were falling about laughing in the coach on the way to the stadium in the heavy rain, about how wet us poor 'snappers' were going to get - until they arrived at the ground and discovered that it had no roof! Still, the result was right, for a lifelong Blue - and completely unbiased journalist!"

Malcolm Allison was at his boastful best. He announced that City would go out and win the League title next, then the European Cup and then: "We shall win the World Club Championship just to show how great we really are."

No one doubted him. He also went on to explain that City's European success had to be seen in perspective and compared with all the other English successes: "Only Spurs have come out to the Continent and taken home the bacon. West Ham won the Cup Winners' Cup at Wembley and Manchester United played there too when they took the European cup. You can't count the Fair's Cup because that is played on a home and away basis, so our victory here is all the more meritorious. I have always maintained that to be great you have to win a major European trophy. Perhaps people will begin to take notice of us."

At the homecoming Allison continued in this style. After hearing the supporters at Manchester's Ringway airport welcoming the team with a chant of "We won the cup" he responded with: "We won another cup!" Later he told the fans in Albert Square: "We are the greatest club in Manchester. I am only sorry ladies & gentlemen that we were unable to win more than 2 cups this year. We decided to let a London club (Chelsea, FA Cup) win something for a change!"

In 1993 Malcolm Allison talked of his greatest success at City: "It's always been difficult picking the greatest success. Winning the League – and for that matter winning the Second Division title – proved our consistency week in week out so that is significant, but winning the ECWC is also a major success. I'm sure we scored more goals in Europe that year than anybody else and we really did 'terrify Europe'. Actually when I said we'd be the first to play on Mars, and that we'd murder everybody in Europe, I did believe it. I also knew it'd get the headlines – remember we'd won the Championship but United were still getting the attention, so I had to do something. I was right... I was just a year late that's all!"

Manager Joe Mercer boards the homecoming bus at Manchester Airport.

The Football Season Daily Reminder
September

1st September 1906

A remarkable heat wave caused City to end their 4-1 home defeat by Woolwich Arsenal (see below) with only seven men. Several players were affected with sunstroke – it was 90 degrees in the shade!

2nd September 1982

Joey Barton was born at Huyton, Merseyside.

3rd September 1892

Under the name of Ardwick, the Blues played their first ever League game. Bootle were defeated 7-0 at Hyde Road on 3rd September, and City headed the first official Second Division table that evening on goal average.

4th September 1935

Future City captain and manager Tony Book was born in Bath.

5th September 1979

Stuart Lee signed for City from Stockport County.

6th September 1986

After gaining first team experience the previous season (and a place in the *Guinness Book of Records* for his goalscoring) Paul Moulden signed professional forms for City. He ended the season as the Club's second highest goalscorer.

7th September 1949

Despite announcing his retirement the previous season, ever-popular goalkeeper Frank Swift finally played his last match for City. Appropriately, he kept a clean sheet as City drew with Everton on.

8th September 1962

City were defeated 6-1 by West Ham at Maine Road and - incredibly - the season was to end

MANCHESTER CITY v. WOOLWICH ARSENAL,
The Gunners' second goal.

eight months later with exactly the same result at Upton Park (Oakes scored the consolation goal). Colin Barlow scored the consolation in the September meeting.

9th September 1978

Two goals from future Oldham cult hero Roger Palmer and an effort from Dave Watson brought a comfortable 3-0 victory at home to Leeds.

10th September 1966

A goal from Glyn Pardoe helped City achieve a 1-1 draw with Arsenal at Maine Road. This match was also the first of the season for Stan Horne (seen wearing 4, below). He went on to appear in 29 (plus 1 as substitute) that season.

11th September 1993

Brian Horton's first match at Maine Road as manager of the Blues ended in a 3-0 victory. Ten days earlier he started his City reign with a 3-1 victory at Swindon.

12th September 1925

The first Maine Road Manchester derby ended 1-1 in front of a crowd of 62,994 (see cutting, right). City had moved to the stadium in 1923 but as United were a Second Division outfit at the time, Manchester had to wait until the ground's third season for a derby match. The return derby ended 6-1 to the Blues.

13th September 1972

The Blues drew 2-2 at

WOMEN FANS IN BIG MATCH RUSH.

Start the Queue at 11-30 a.m.

HUGE INVASION.

Thousands of Rosettes for Keen Rivals.

If anyone mentioned the word "match" in Manchester to-day there was only one meaning of it—"Maine-road, City v. United."

Moss Side was first invaded about 1-30 this morning, and the dauntless "foothe" enthusiasts who were first to arrive at the City ground were two women, who placidly seated themselves on the steps of the stand entrances, and opening novels read away the time of waiting.

They were soon reinforced by others, of the fair sex and a number of youths. These were the outposts of the vast army that later was to pass through the numerous turnstiles.

When the gates were opened at 12-50 p.m. five ladies had the honour of being the first spectators on the ground for the famous encounter of the Manchester clubs.

In a few minutes about a thousand spectators clicked through, following in the feminine steps. There was a steady in-pouring of spectators until 1-30, when suddenly the human stream became a torrent.

home to Valencia in City's first UEFA Cup tie. The City scorers were Ian Mellor and Rodney Marsh.

14th September 2003

Two penalties from Anelka helped the Blues to their first League victory at the City Of Manchester Stadium. The match with Aston Villa ended 4-1 and it also saw Anelka score the first hat-trick at the new stadium and the first penalty.

15th September 1976

City defeated Italian giants Juventus 1-0 at Maine Road in the UEFA Cup. A crowd of 36,955 watched Brian Kidd net the only goal.

16th September 1967

Stan Bowles scored twice on his League debut as City beat Sheffield United 5-2 on 16th September 1967. Three days earlier he also scored twice as the Blues defeated Leicester

4-0 in the League Cup – Bowles came on as substitute in his debut game. Despite this tremendous start, Bowles never scored again for City and only made a total of 16 (plus 4 sub) appearances.

17th September 1983

Derek Parlane limped off after scoring a hat-trick for the Blues in the 6-0 defeat of Blackburn.

18th September 1968

City's first European Cup fixture ended goalless at Maine Road against Fenerbahce.

19th September 1981

Tommy Booth made the last of his 382 League appearances for City in the 3-0 defeat by Birmingham City. When all first team appearances are taken into consideration, Booth ended his career ninth in the list of all-time City appearance holders.

20th September 1947

A crowd of approximately 78,000 witnessed the first post-war Manchester derby (see teamsheet, left). A tense match ended goalless before the derby's record crowd. The return fixture, also played at Maine Road, was watched by 71,690.

21st September 1979

Richard Dunne was born in Dublin.

REGULATION 29.—Clubs must send the results of League Matches with the names of the Players Competing therein to the League Secretary within 3 days of each match. In case of default, Clubs must pay a fine of 10/-.

THE FOOTBALL LEAGUE
FIRST DIVISION

SEASON 1947-48

Date of Match 20 SEP 1947 194

Home Club MANCHESTER CITY. Visiting Club MANCHESTER UNITED.

Result :—Home Club 0 Goals ; Visiting Club 0 Goals.

Total No. of Matches Played 9

Won 5 Lost Drawn 3

Total Goals for 11 Goals Against 9 Points 9.

Signed W. Vera Secretary of Manchester City Club

TEAM.

Notes.—The Surname, Block Letters, with Full Initials, must be given.

Goal H.C.F.THURLOW.

Backs (Right) B.SPROSTON.

" (Left) E. WESTWOOD.

Half-Backs (Right) W.WALSH.

" (Centre) J.FAGAN.

" (Left) A.T.EMPTAGE.

Forwards (Outside Right) J.E.WHARTON.

" (Inside Right) G.B.SMITH.

" (Centre) E.McMORRAN.

" (Inside Left) T.A.CAPEL.

" (Outside Left) R.CLARKE

Advertised Time of Kick-off 3-0.

Actual Time of Kick-off 3-0.

REPORT ON OFFICIALS

REGULATION 30.—Reports on the conduct of the game must be sent by both Clubs to the League Secretary within six days of each match. Such Reports should be the considered Reports of the Club Board of Directors.

So that the Management Committee can keep an accurate record of the value of each Referee's work will you please insert in your Report the index figure which in your opinion most fairly assesses the value of his work.

Index Figure 0 indicates Bad, Incompetent.
" " 1 " Poor.
" " 2 " Moderate.
" " 3 " Satisfactory.
" " 4 " Very Good.

Date of Match 20 SEP 1947 194

Home Club Manchester City Visiting Club Manchester United

Result : Home Club 0 Goals ; Visiting Club 0 Goals

Referee C.FLETCHER Index Figure 3

Comments (if any)

H.C. DENHAM

22nd September 1959

Cup final hero Bobby Johnstone returned to his former club Hibernian after 50 goals in 137 first team appearances.

23rd September 1989

City defeated United 5-1 in the 111th Manchester League derby. A makeshift City side proved dominant against Alex Ferguson's multi-million pound side. The Reds were the most expensive side in England at the time, while City were missing influential players Clive Allen, Neil McNab and regular first choice 'keeper Andy Dibble.

24th September 1984

Defender Kevin Bond left City for a new career at Southampton.

25th September 1956

Late 70s defender Paul Futcher was born at Chester.

26th September 1946

Goalkeeper Alec Thurlow signed for City with the hope that the young 'keeper would be a permanent replacement for Frank Swift.

27th September 1997

Swindon Town, then top of the First Division, were beaten 6-0 at Maine Road. Paul Dickov (right) could have scored a hat-trick but instead chose to

set the expensive Lee Bradbury up for a much needed morale boosting goal.

28th September 1928

After making 306 first team appearances for the Blues - including the 1926 FA Cup final - Sam Cookson joined Bradford.

29th September 2007

Goals from Petrov (38 mins), Mpenza (47) and Elano (87) helped City to a 3-1 victory over Newcastle United. Elano's goal came from a truly outstanding free kick and was his first goal for the club.

30th September 1977

Jihai Sun was born in Dalian, China.

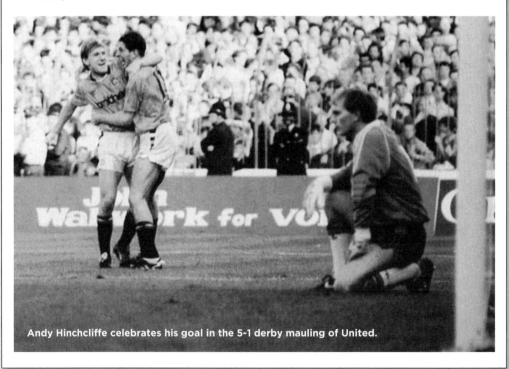

Andy Hinchcliffe celebrates his goal in the 5-1 derby mauling of United.

CITY'S NUMBER ONE

THE PROFILES

13 – WALTER SMITH

Walter Smith was signed for the relatively high fee of £600 with a reputation for being one of the best 'keepers in the Second Division. Manager Newbould signed him in 1906 as the Blues sought a permanent replacement but misfortune struck when he was injured in the pre-season public practice match. He made his debut on 24th November 1906 – the 14th game of the season – and soon became established as the Club's undisputed number one. The following season he was an ever-present – playing in 44 League and Cup games. He was loved by fans and was a 'keeper of immense quality throughout the pre-war period, often described as the 'hero of Hyde Road' in important matches.

Smith spent 14 years with City and during the First World War he guested for his old club Leicester. After the war he started the first post war League season as City's first choice, but after only 9 games he was dropped and then transferred. His last game came in October 1919, the first post war League meeting with United. The Reds took the lead three times before the Blues levelled at 3-3. Smith had an absolutely appalling game. For much of his City career Smith had saved the Blues with a consistently high standard of play, but for this match it seems he could do nothing right. He was heavily criticised for two of United's goals - for one he hesitated, for the other he was dispossessed while bouncing the ball in his area oblivious to the presence of United's goal poaching star of the period Joe Spence. One newspaper report mentioned his name three times - twice for the

Smith, the new idol at Ardwick.

goals and then once in the final summary: "The City played a greatly improved game all round, and apart from Smith's mistakes, the defence was most faultless".

Inevitably, Smith left Hyde Road for Port Vale (£250 fee) where the nightmare of the Manchester derby was rapidly eclipsed by accusations of assault on the morning of his debut. It seems that he was falsely accused of assaulting a hotel chambermaid at the Regent Hotel, South Shields prior to his first game for Vale. He was bailed in time to play, but went through the match knowing that he was constantly being watched by a police detective who had been sent to keep tabs on him throughout the match. The tabloids would love that today! Smith was acquitted at Durham Assizes.

At Hyde Road, despite his final appearance Smith was remembered as a hero. Like all 'keepers he was a little eccentric - the *Athletic News* once called him: "the only first class goalkeeper in the Country who disdains training" - but he had been a superb player for the Blues.

Appearances: League: 232 FAC: 23

14 – HERBERT BROOMFIELD

At 6ft 1.5 inches Herbert Broomfield was regarded as a very tall goalkeeper when he made his City debut in November 1908. Prior to City Broomfield had played briefly for Manchester United in their first title winning season and also had a near five year career with Bolton. During his Bolton days he was recorded as being: "A man who does not waste words, unassuming and a loyal clubman."

While with City he was also enjoying another career as a painter and decorator, and had been a gardener when he first made it into Bolton's League side.

Broomfield only made four League appearances for the Blues, including a 3-1 defeat against his former club United in January 1909. Interestingly, he rejoined the Reds in October 1910.

Away from actually playing, Broomfield's place in football history is assured as he was one of the founding fathers of the players' union, the PFA. He became the first PFA secretary.

Appearances: League: 4

15 – JACK LYALL

Scottish international John Lyall, known as Jack to City fans and players, had already found great success when he joined the Blues in September 1909. Two League titles and a FA Cup winners medal with Sheffield Wednesday had really secured his place in football history.

Another 6ft 1.5 inch 'keeper, Lyall was brought in as replacement for Walter Smith who, the City management felt, was nearing the end of his Hyde Road career. Lyall made his debut ten days after signing for the Blues and City were undefeated in his first 8 games.

Lyall's quality and consistency helped the Blues win the Second Division title in his first season and he kept 13 clean sheets in 33 appearances – at the time this was second only to Jack Hillman's record in 1903 of 13 clean sheets in 31 appearances.

Surprisingly however Lyall struggled in 1910-11 and was dropped after conceding nine goals in two games. Walter Smith returned and Lyall never played for the Blues again. He moved to Dundee in April 1911. He emigrated to North America in the inter-war period and passed away in the States in 1944.

Appearances: League: 40 FAC: 4

16 – JOHN SWANN

Another 'Jack', Salford born Swann appeared in only one game for the Blues' first team – a 2-1 victory at Stockport County on 16th October 1909. His debut was a typically City scenario and came as a result of injury to Lyall. Other problems with Davies and Smith meant that City simply did not have a fit and able 'keeper on their books. Jimmy Broad, brother of Tommy Broad and son of trainer Jimmy Broad senior, had played reserve games in nets but he was not suitable for first team football. So City's management and directors had to think long and hard about a possible replacement. Albert Alexander senior, who spent much time with reserve football, is believed to have brought up the name of the Northern Nomads goalkeeper Swann. Swann had faced City reserves about six weeks earlier and so a City official was sent to find the 'keeper. According to legend the City official tracked down Swann, who was preparing to play for Nomads, and persuaded him and the club to release him to appear for the Blues.

The player arrived at the ground shortly before kick off and City won the game 2-1. Lyall returned to fitness for the next match and, apart from three reserve appearances, Swann's chance to shine never came again. Ultimately, Swann's fairytale story ended with the 'keeper moving back to Nomads.

Appearances: League: 1

17 – AUGUSTUS BEEBY

Augustus Beeby, known as Gus to the Blues, arrived at City on 26th May 1911 from Liverpool. At Anfield Beeby made 16 League appearances – including 24th September 1910 when Liverpool beat City 2-1 at Hyde Road and the player impressed the Blues – but was never likely to be the Merseysiders' regular 'keeper due to the form of Sam Hardy.

He had been signed because City were struggling to find a permanent replacement for Smith, who many believed had reached the end of his career, and the recently

departed Lyall. Smith kept goal for the opening three fixtures of 1911-12, but after a 6-2 defeat at home to Aston Villa it was inevitable Beeby would make his debut on 23rd September 1911. That match ended in a 1-0 defeat at Newcastle but Beeby's form looked much better than Smith's and the player kept his place.

Sadly, Beeby's performances were somewhat erratic and after a total of nine consecutive games he was dropped. Only one of the matches had ended in victory, and Beeby conceded four in two separate games.

Smith, despite his own performance issues, was brought back into the side, while the Club searched for a permanent replacement. Then in February injury to Goodchild (who became City's number one) gave Beeby another chance to impress. Sadly, after two games – the last of which ended in a 6-2 defeat at Sheffield United – Beeby was dropped again. The following August he moved to Tranmere Rovers.

Appearances: League: 11

18 – JIM GOODCHILD

After a spell of 'keepers of over 6ft in height, 5ft 11 inches Jim Goodchild was viewed suspiciously by some fans at first. However, he soon proved to be a quality 'keeper and a reassuring presence in City's goal.

Goodchild initially failed to impress. He joined Southern League side Southampton in 1909 and made his debut in their last match of the 1909-10 season (a 3-1 win), but he only managed four games the following season. He kept clean sheets in two of those games, but his final couple of games both ended in 5-1 defeats. Inevitably, the Southampton management felt that he was never likely to be good enough to oust their regular number one, and so at the end of the season he was released.

He found employment on the Southampton docks, before Southampton scout and ex-1892-3 season Ardwick League player Jimmy Yates called his former club and told them of Goodchild's availability. The following January he made his debut and became City's first choice for the next couple of seasons. Surprisingly a return to form by former first choice Walter Smith saw the older 'keeper return to first team action in 1913, but by the start of the 1915-16 wartime season Goodchild was back in goal.

After the war 'naughty boy' Goodchild as he was nicknamed by fans became a popular player and had a distinguished career. He was not a thrilling 'keeper in the mode of Trautmann, nor was he an entertainer like Swift, but he was safe and a consistent performer. He was ever-present when City finished second in 1920-21 and he was 'keeper for the 1926 FA Cup final, although by that time he was nearing the end of his career and was under immense competition. The following year he left the Blues, moved back to Southampton and became licensee of the Royal Albert Hotel, playing part-time for Guildford City. In 1941 he took over the Cricketers Arms at Eastleigh, and he remained there until his death in 1950.

Two popular stories from the early 1920s focussed on his large woollen cap that he always tried to wear and of what lay underneath. According to one story he dived to make a save in one match, his cap fell off and Goodchild quickly dived away from the ball to get his cap and replace it before the fans could see his bald head! Similarly when the King visited in 1920 Goodchild was reluctant to remove his cap when the King came on to the field to meet the players. Eventually he did and his lack of hair became a major talking point.

Goodchild was loved by supporters and, alongside Walter Smith and Charlie Williams, helped establish the tone and style of 'keeper the Blues loved. In essence those three 'keepers paved the way for Swift, Trautmann and Corrigan.

Appearances: League: 204 FA Cup: 13

19 – TOM BLAIR

Glaswegian Tom Blair was Kilmarnock's captain when they won the Scottish Cup in 1920. He joined City on 15th July 1920 and made his debut on 7th September 1921 when City drew 1-1 at home to Liverpool. This was the first of 41 consecutive League and Cup appearances during which Blair received much praise.

He chose to emigrate in the summer of 1922, robbing the Blues of a good 'keeper, and spent most of the next decade in Canada and the United States. While there he played for sides in Edmonton, Vancouver and Boston amongst other locations.

He returned to Scotland in 1931 and played for Ayr United before moving on to Linfield in 1932. By the summer of 1937 he was Dundee United's player-coach and he passed away in Dundee in 1961 at the age of 69.

Appearances: League: 38 FA Cup: 3

The HATTON Connection

For many years the boxer Ricky Hatton has talked of his family connections with City. This has included the fact that his father Ray used to be on City's books. This 1970 team photo shows Ray lining up with the great Mercer-Allison side of the period. Can you spot Ray?

Ray is actually on the front row. Third from left (second player after coach Johnny Hart). Ray joined City as an apprentice in July 1966. So now you've seen the proof.

While we're on the subject of the Hatton family, here's a shot of Ricky walking with City on their lap of honour following promotion in 2002. He's next to Nicky Weaver.

RAY HATTON
winger
signed App. 22.7.66

In 1977 a spin off comic from the Beano was produced called Plug. It followed the story of 'Percival Proudfoot Plugsley', the Bash Street Kids character Plug, and included lots of new characters. It also included features such as the one illustrated here.

Although the article includes a mistake – City had also won the League Cup in 1976! – it was significant that the Blues were one of the first sides to appear in Plug. This page is from issue five.

Plug also featured a team of insects called Antchester United and one of those players was Mike Summerbee (the only genuine name included, amongst the others was Francis Flea!). Inevitably, in issue 7 United played Antchester City (wearing Sky Blue) in the derby match. Bizarrely City played on horseback and their star player was Gerd Mule-er.

Snippets from the 1940s...

Conjuring Tricks?

It looks like a nice balancing act by Manchester City's left-back Westwood—but isn't there some rule in soccer about not using your hands ?

There is only $\frac{1}{4}$ inch difference in height between the two players on the right, but Walsh of Manchester City just beat Chelsea's Len Goulden for the ball because he jumped a fraction earlier.

Note that each player has gone up with his body fully stretched and tensed.

1970-71

Competition: European Cup Winners' Cup

Reason For Qualification:
Reigning ECWC winners

Manager: Joe Mercer

16th September 1970
Round 1 Leg 1
Attendance: 25,184

City 1-0 Linfield

City Goalscorer: Bell
City: Corrigan; Book, Pardoe, Doyle, Booth,
Oakes, Summerbee. Bell, Lee, Young,
Towers

City qualified for this competition as winners
of the ECWC, however by winning the League
Cup in March 1970 the Blues had qualified
for the European Inter-Cities Fairs Cup, the
predecessor of the UEFA cup. Interestingly,
that competition only allowed one entrant
from each city, causing Mike Doyle to joke that
qualification had helped him achieve an aim:
"That's not bad for my new campaign and car
stickers – 'Keep United out of Europe'."

Joe Mercer joked: "If we can win the ECWC
and so qualify to defend it next season, maybe
the authorities will let us flog our Fairs Cup
place to the highest bidders!"

In the end Mercer's wish was not granted,
but the Blues did enter the ECWC instead of
the Fairs Cup as UEFA's order of significance
stated that the ECWC was more important
than the Fairs Cup.

Linfield, managed by former Everton winger
Billy Bingham (also the man who guided

Northern Ireland to the 1982 World Cup), were
a confident outfit and gave City a bit of a shock
with their style and determination in this match.

This was a tense match and reminded many
fans of the home game against Fenerbahce
in the European Cup a couple of years earlier.
Fortunately, a late winner from Colin Bell gave
City the edge and the Blues were confident
that the return leg would see them through.

30th September 1970
Round 1 Leg 2
Attendance: 21,000

Linfield 2-1 City

(City won on away-goals rule)
City Goalscorer: Lee
City: Corrigan; Book, Pardoe, Doyle, Jeffries,
Oakes, Summerbee, Bell, Lee (Bowyer),
Young, Towers

In between the two legs of this round the Blues
suffered several crippling injuries. Tommy
Booth suffered a damaged left knee which
needed an operation and kept him out of
action for three months, while George Heslop
and Francis Lee were also struggling to regain
fitness. In the end Lee made it, but Heslop was
replaced by Derek Jeffries.

Lee's selection proved to be very important as
he scored early on to put City into a deserved
two goal lead, but Linfield were not prepared
to roll over and, playing in front of a noisy
Windsor Park, they fought back. The Irish side
scored twice to make the tie 2-2 on aggregate
and, in the dying minutes, they almost scored
a third.

The match ended with the Blues progressing

via the away goals rule. An Irish journalist accurately recorded: "Linfield are out, but this is one of the greatest moments in the footballing history of this country."

21st October 1970
Round 2 Leg 1
Attendance: 10,000

Honved 0-1 City

City Goalscorer: Lee
City: Corrigan; Book, Pardoe, Doyle, Heslop, Jeffries, Summerbee, Bell, Lee, Hill, Towers

When he heard the draw Malcolm Allison was delighted. He told journalists: "Some managers prefer a home tie initially to build a commanding lead. I would rather go away first and then face the second leg knowing exactly the task that faces you."

This was City's first visit behind the Iron Curtain for a competitive fixture and saw the Blues face the former Hungarian masters Honved. Everyone expected the home side to be extremely tough, but Honved actually offered little.

Derek Potter, writing in the *Daily Express*, believed this was one of City's best performances: "Glimpses of high quality skill allied to aggressive running saw Manchester City probe and pound Honved into submission in the Kispest Stadium. It could have been five following one of City's best ever displays."

Tony Book felt Honved had just experienced an off-day: "I'm sure that they can be a much better side. Just because we are leading by one goal it would be a mistake to assume that it is all over. It's not over yet by a long chalk."

4th November 1970
Round 2 Leg 2
Att: 28,770

City 2-0 Honved

City Goalscorers: Bell, Lee
City: Corrigan; Book, Pardoe, Doyle, Heslop, Oakes, Summerbee, Bell, Lee, Hill, Towers

In appalling conditions the Blues had control from the start, but there were some potentially bleak moments. Shortly before the half time break Colin Bell and Honved's Sandor Pinter leapt together for the ball, and the City star fell to the ground injured. He was stretchered off but fortunately returned for the second half.

After City's 2-0 victory much was made of

DAILY MAIL, Thursd

Bell wouldn't lie down

CITY STAR BOUNCES BACK AFTER BEING STRETCHERED OFF

THERE was just one moment of hope, strange though it may seem, for the Hungarian Army side Honved at Maine Road last night.

That was immediately before the interval when their arch - tormentor— Manchester City and England star Colin Bell— was carried off.

Fans groaned as City's first-half scorer went off on a stretcher after a collision. But they cheered when he returned unexpectedly after the interval.

Bell dismissed his injury as 'trivial' and stormed back to master-mind his side in appalling conditions.

And that ended Honved's one hope. The Hungarians conceded another goal to Lee and were sunk without trace as City's all - weather experts ploughed through the mud and rain to one of their most brilliant European victories.

Left: Bell is carried off after the collision. Below: The scourge of Honved is back at his best.

Pictures by
MIKE HOLLIST and
PETER PITTILLA.

MANCHESTER CITY

NEWS 1/- 5p

VERSUS

HONVED

OF HUNGARY

EUROPEAN CUP WINNERS' CUP
8th FINALS—2nd LEG
WEDNESDAY
4th NOVEMBER 1970
Kick-off 7-45 p.m.

HATS OFF TO CITY: A smiling Joe Mercer returns to Manchester after that victorious first leg. *Picture: Daily Mirror*

the poor weather. The media seemed to be looking for an angle and they pumped Honved's manager Kalman Preiner hoping he would say that the conditions were too poor and that the game should have been called off. Instead Preiner stated that the conditions were poor but added that City were able to adapt superbly whereas Honved struggled. Commenting about Mercer's side he added: "If they go on playing like this they must surely be favourites for the trophy."

Captain Tony Book admitted that he had been worried: "I'd been scared right from the start that the referee might call off the game. The rain was getting heavier. That really was our only worry. Of course, we adapted ourselves to the conditions better than they did, but even in the first 15 minutes, when conditions were comparatively good, we were hitting them with everything. If the ground had stayed reasonably firm I am sure we would have murdered them."

Book laughs off secret fear

For ten minutes last night Manchester City skipper **Tony Book** sat in the dressing-room fearing that the next knock on the door would rob his side of a certain place in the quarter-finals of the Cup-Winners' Cup.

When Book and his team squelched off at half-time with a goal lead and victory already in their grasp, Maine Road was already water-logged and still the rain came down.

Heavies

'I'd been scared right from the start that the referee might call off the game,' admitted Book afterwards.

'The rain was getting heavier and I knew that if he intended to stop it he would do it during the interval.

'And that really was our only worry. Of course, we adapted ourselves to the conditions better than they did, but even in the first 15 minutes, when the conditions were comparatively good, we

By PETER JOHNSON

were hitting them with everything.

'If the ground had stayed reasonably firm I am sure we would have murdered them.

'It was pretty hard work out there, but I don't think the pace of the side ever slackened.

And in a disconsolate Honved dressing-room, manager **Kalman Preiner** almost admitted as much.

'The side lost a lot of their spirit when they found their football was not working in conditions like this,' he said.

Should it have been allowed to go on ? 'That,' said Preiner, with an expressive Continental shrug, 'was up to the referee. The conditions were terible, but Manchester City were able to play superbly in them.

'If they go on playing like

this they must surely be favourites for the trophy.'

For City manager **Joe Mercer** the result should have read: Manchester City 2, The Pitch 0.

'There was no one else out there to beat,' he said. 'We never gave them a look-in and it proves what I've always said—there's no more adaptable animal than the British footballer.'

After the game, **Colin Bell** was limping only slightly after the incident that led to his being carried off on a stretcher a minute before the interval.

Bell, who made a late and theatrical reappearance as the teams lined-up for the restart, said: 'I don't think it is anything serious. When I collided with Pinter I felt a blow on the leg just below the knee, and my whole leg went dead.

'It seems I got a knock on a nerve, but the feeling began to come back as I reached the dressing-room.'

59

10th March 1971
Round 3 Leg 1 (quarter-final)
Att: 100,000

Gornik Zabrze 2-0 City

City: Corrigan; Book, Towers, Doyle, Booth, Oakes, Summerbee, Bell, Lee, Young, Jeffries

When Joe Mercer heard the draw he admitted: "'It will be tough. . . but we can do it."

City took their own food supplies – steaks, butter and tea! – to Poland, while an 800 strong army of workers toiled hard to keep the pitch free of snow. It was a bitterly cold day and the kick off was scheduled to be 5.30pm to ensure the game could be played before temperatures dropped too low.

The City players took to the pitch wearing sweaters under their shirts and Francis Lee later remarked about the Gornik players: "I knew they had been on a sunshine tour to Spain, but I thought their legs could not be as brown as that until it dawned on me that they were wearing tights."

Gornik's aluminium studs had also been sharpened, enabling them to get a better grip on the frozen surface. It must have worked as the home side put in a terrific performance. Polish international Lubanski was in blistering form and scored one and made the other before going off injured after 60 minutes.

Allison was disappointed but recognised that Gornik had been the better side: "We didn't play too badly, but nothing went right for us. We were all right at the back but there was nothing coming up front. That was a great goal by Lubanski. The second one was a bit unfortunate."

"I know how good this Polish side is... they are much better than probably the general public appreciate. I would rate Lubanski as a world class player ... one of the best three in the world in his role. He likes to play just behind the centre-forward and go through all the time."

Facing page: **How the win in Copenhagen was featured in the City programme.**

24th March 1971
Round 3 Leg 2
Attendance: 31,950

City 2-0 Gornik Zabrze

City Goalscorers: Mellor, Doyle
City: Healey; Connor, Towers, Doyle, Booth, Donachie, Jeffries, Bell, Lee, Young (Mann), Mellor (Bowyer)

The weather played a significant part in this game, as it did the earlier leg, the City pitch was absolutely soaked as Manchester's rain played its part in creating conditions that the Blues could excel in.

There had been some real selection issues however. Three significant stars – Tony Book, Alan Oakes and Mike Summerbee – were out through injury. They were replaced by Dave Connor, Willie Donachie and Ian Mellor. It should be noted that both Donachie and Mellor were debutants in the Coventry game only four days earlier.

Despite their inexperience Donachie and Mellor performed well. In fact it was Mellor who scored first with a great header shortly before half time. Mellor: "Four days after making my debut I played in the second leg of the

MANCHESTER CITY

NEWS 5p

VERSUS
GORNIK ZABRZE
OF POLAND

EUROPEAN CUP WINNERS' CUP
QUARTER FINALS 2nd LEG
WEDNESDAY
24th MARCH 1971
Kick-off 7-45 p.m.

DANGER MAN . . . *the Gornik star who sets Soccer alight wherever he plays . . . Lubanski, pride of all Poland.*

European Cup Winners' Cup and managed to score, so it was a great start really."

Mike Doyle added a second goal to send the match into extra time, during which City went on to hit the crossbar and the post. The game ended 2-2 on aggregate.

31st March 1971
Round 3 Replay in Copenhagen
Att: 12,100

City 3-1 Gornik Zabrze

City Goalscorers: Young, Booth, Lee
City: Healey; Connor, Towers, Doyle, Booth, Donachie, Jeffries, Bell, Lee, Young, Hill

Prior to the advent of penalty shoot-outs in European football, drawn games were decided based on the away goals rule and, if sides were still level, then there would be a replay at a neutral venue. The venue would typically be midway between the two

competing clubs and so Copenhagen was selected for this match.

Controversy surrounded the game with Gornik's President, Ernest Wyra, demanding that City's players be tested for drugs after the replay. He claimed that they'd taken drugs during the second leg and wanted to see the Blues punished. Mercer became angry and accused the Poles of trying to put the City players off their game. Nevertheless, UEFA listened to Gornik's gripes and City were forced to accept the tests.

Journalist Peter Gardner: "The submission to tests, however, was firmly pushed to the backs of City players' minds as they once more fairly ripped into Gornik and the vital break came when Neil Young ended a personal lean spell without scoring to explode a shot that Gornik goalkeeper Kostka allowed to slip through his grasp and into the back of the net. Later

FLAT OUT . . . Gornik's goalkeeper beaten by Francis Lee. *Pictures: Daily Mirror*

TAKE THAT . . . Mike Doyle lets everyone know how he feels!

SO EASY . . . for Tommy Booth with this header against Gornik

ONE FOR NEIL . . . Gornik defenders beaten by Young's shot.

THREE OF A KIND . . . our Copenhagen goalscorers Tommy Booth, Frannie Lee and Neil Young.

centre-half Tommy Booth advanced to meet a free kick and City were two-up at the break. Gornik pulled one back through Lubanski early into the second half, but any threat of a comeback by the Poles was quickly squashed. For Colin Bell, with a brilliant dribble in which he beat five defenders, laid on an easy third goal for Francis Lee. So City were home and dry."

Then came the dope testing fiasco. Colin Bell, David Connor and Derek Jeffries, the three players whose names had been drawn out of a hat, were unable to provide Urine samples. Orange juice was given to the men, but still no luck. Then Allison tried to lighten the atmosphere a little. He picked up a bottle of champagne, demanded entry into the medical room, then returned a few seconds later laughing: "They won't allow them to have this!"

Eventually, samples were produced and the tests were negative, but the whole affair seemed scandalous. Despite the controversy City were now through to the semi-finals for the second year in succession. Their opponents would be F.A. Cup winners' Chelsea.

Facing page: **(top) Corrigan punches clear from Webb. (bottom) An anxious moment.**

14th April 1971
Semi-Final Leg 1
Attendance: 45,595

Chelsea 1-0 City

City: Corrigan; Book, Connor, Towers, Booth, Donachie, Johnson, Hill, Lee, Young, Mann

Immediately prior to the first leg the Blues suffered with an incredible number of injuries. By the time of the match Summerbee, Oakes, Heslop, Bell and Doyle were all on the injury list alongside long term invalid Pardoe. It was always going to be difficult to prepare for the match against such a strong English side, but with so many injuries Manager Joe Mercer had to hope for a bit of luck. In addition to those out of action, other players were suffering. Goalkeeper Joe Corrigan was particularly brave, and actually played against Chelsea with his left eye half-closed and badly bruised.

Understandably, City were forced to play a defensive game and managed to keep the score down to a 1-0 defeat away from home. Mercer was pleased: "We had to play it in a negative way to some extent and it was a very difficult match, but it went more or less as we planned it, and Joe Corrigan in particular was magnificent. We made one mistake and we lost, but we showed that we know a bit about defensive football, and you don't learn it all on the Continent."

(top) Arthur Mann watches as Corrigan saves from Webb.
(bottom) Francis Lee makes life difficult for Ron Harris and John Phillips.

Malcolm Allison had been in trouble once again with the F.A. during this period and was banned from all football activity for a couple of months, which had left Joe Mercer in total control of the side. This caused some friction between the two men as Allison felt players should have been rested in the League games immediately prior to the European tie.

28th April 1971
Semi-final Leg 2
Attendance: 43,663

City 0-1 Chelsea

City: Healey; Book, Connor, Towers, Heslop, Jeffries, Summerbee (Carter), Lee, Bowyer, Young, Johnson (Donachie)

Further injuries affected team selection for the second leg, played 48 hours after a 2-2 draw with Liverpool in the League. It is worth pointing out that Liverpool, also due to play a European tie two days later, fielded a reserve team. This was against League rules and Joe Mercer, being a firm believer in playing the game in the right spirit and always keen to play the strongest side possible, insisted on playing the best City side available.

In the end injuries against Liverpool seriously impacted the European game. Joe Corrigan and Tommy Booth were both out with

Ron Healey taking the goalkeeper's place. Unfortunately, two minutes before half-time, Healey turned an in-swinging free kick from Chelsea's Keith Weller into his own net. It was the only goal and Chelsea won 2-0 on aggregate, ending City's dream of becoming the first side to retain the trophy - a feat no side ever managed. Chelsea went on to defeat Real Madrid in the final.

Ron Healey felt responsible: "There was a hunger for us all in those days. The win bonus would double your wage so we always went out fully determined. That bonus would truly change your week, and so you did all you could to win. Losing in Europe was bad because we wanted to progress, but I also felt guilty for losing the guys their win bonus."

Mercer was disappointed with the result, while Allison was angry. He felt that Mercer should have approached the European games differently. In an interview for "Football With A Smile" in 1992 he admitted: "The worst moment was when I was suspended and we were playing Chelsea in the Cup Winners' Cup semi. I said to Joe when we play Newcastle don't play Doyley, and don't play Colin Bell. In fact I told him to leave out three players for this League match, which wasn't a very important game. Remember I was suspended and Joe was in complete control of the team. In the

Mascot Paul Todd leads out Tony Book and Ron Healey for the Chelsea home leg.

end Joe played them all because he wanted to win the match. Two of them got injuries and they couldn't play in the semi-final, and I was really, really annoyed at him. Really angry. He wanted to win it without my advice because, well, we've all got egos and he perhaps wanted to prove he could do it without me. I told him that he was foolish, but now thinking about it I probably would have done the same thing. Even so, at the time I was really annoyed because those players wouldn't be playing

in the semi-final... and it probably cost us the game. It was the blackest moment for me."

City still received much positive coverage – "It's another super show from those Mercer minors" – but it was a major blow to the club at the time.

Tony Book summed it up nicely though: "We fought hard in both games but we lost by a single goal both times."

Photographer Alan Jubb's image of Neil Young taking to the field V Chelsea.

The Football Season Daily Reminder

October

1st October 1969

City's first home tie in the ECWC ended 3-0 (6-3 on aggregate) as the Blues defeated Atletico Bilbao on 1st October 1969.

2nd October 1976

Dennis Tueart (2), Asa Hartford, and Gary Owen shared the goals as West Ham were beaten 4-2 before 37,795 fans.

3rd October 1987

Paul Stewart & Imre Varadi both scored twice as the Blues beat Leicester City 4-2 at Maine Road. The game was also noteworthy as it was goalkeeper Bobby Mimms last game and it also saw the City players take to the field carrying large inflatable bananas which they then threw into the crowd. This was not a regular occurrence!

4th October 1930

City 4 United 1 with two goals each from Tait and Marshall. It was the Reds' ninth straight defeat of the season and they were relegated at the end of it.

The Athletic News claimed: "City obviously grew sympathetic and declined to rub it in."

5th October 1968

City played for the first time in the red & black stripes chosen by Malcolm Allison. The game at Everton ended in a 2-0 defeat and the result brought a lot of complaints from fans about the use of the colours. Inevitably, by the time of City's FA Cup win later in the season most fans had accepted Allison's inspired choice.

6th October 1966

Niall Quinn (left) was born and on this day in 1990 he scored in a 2-0 win against Coventry.

7th October 1996

Steve Coppell arrived as City manager at Maine Road on this day.

8th October 1975

The Blues defeated Swansea 2-1 with goals from Duncan Davidson (his only goal for the Club) and Derek Parlane. Parlane later became an employee of Reebok and worked with the Blues on their Reebok merchandise following the move to Eastlands.

MANCHESTER City VERSUS SWANSEA CITY
THE CANON LEAGUE SECOND DIVISION
MATCH MAGAZINE 40p
SAAB & CITY
SATURDAY 8th OCTOBER, 1983
KICK-OFF 3.00 p.m. AT MAINE ROAD MANCHESTER
TODAY'S MATCH IS SPONSORED BY KITCHENS DIRECT

game at Maine Road. A crowd of 41,683 witnessed the City win with future Spanish TV presenter Michael Robinson wearing the number 9 shirt for the Blues that day.

14th October 1953

The first game under floodlights at Maine Road took place - City 6 Hearts 3.

15th October 1996

The second League game under new manager Steve Coppell ended in a 2-0 defeat at Reading.

16th October 2004

Eventual champions Chelsea were defeated 1-0 at Eastlands. City were the only side to beat the champions during 2004-5 and managed to draw the return fixture 0-0.

17th October 1919

Following the collapse of Leeds City, Defender Thomas Lamph was bought in an auction of Leeds' players by the Blues. A little over six years after joining City Lamph died in Leeds at the age of 33.

9th October 1967

Francis Lee (above) signed for the Blues from Bolton after a protracted transfer which only 3 days earlier had been called off due to issues registering Lee as a City player.

10th October 1985

Chelsea forward Gordon Davies joined the Blues. Davies made 3 Welsh international appearances while at City.

11th October 1993

Winger Ricky Holden rejoined Oldham Athletic after 14 months with the Blues.

12th October 1965

80s City 'keeper Perry Suckling was born in Hackney.

13th October 2002

Kaziu Deyna scored the only goal of the City-Nottingham Forest League

18th October 2003

Although the game was 1-1 at half-time, City defeated Bolton 6-2 at the City of Manchester stadium. The sixth was scored by Claudio Reyna in the 84th minute.

19th October 1996

Goals from Paul Dickov and Nigel Clough helped City to a 2-1 win over Norwich City. Clough's was the last of four League goals he scored for the Blues.

20th October 2007

A 37th minute goal from Elano gave City a 1-0 victory over Birmingham City

21st October 1953

The second game under floodlights at Maine Road occurred with Turkish side Fenerbahce (later famous for being City's opponents in the Blues' first European cup match) defeated 5-1.

22nd October 1994

Brian Horton's Blues defeated Ossie Ardiles' Spurs 5-2, with goals from Walsh (2), Quinn, Flitcroft, and Lomas. This was a very memorable and popular match and when it was shown on Match of the Day that evening the BBC also chose to

re-screen highlights from the December 1967 'Ballet on Ice' meeting between the sides. The game was later described by BBC commentator John Motson as one of his all-time top three classic Maine Road matches.

23rd October 2005

Famous City supporter Helen 'the bell' Turner (above) passed away.

24th October 1925

City 8 Burnley 3 with Tommy Browell scoring five.

25th October 1968

Mancunian and highly popular Blue Paul Lake was born on this day. He went on to captain the Blues, played in several memorable matches, and brought much excitement during a brief injury plagued career.

26th October 1986

The Manchester derby was televised live for the first time. Mick McCarthy netted as the relegation-bound Blues, managed by Jimmy Frizzell (left) earned a 1-1 draw at Maine Road. Shortly after this match United dismissed Ron Atkinson.

27th October 1965

City drew 0-0 with Norwich at Maine Road. City were on top of Division Two and heading for promotion, and a crowd of 34,091 watched the match. Despite the score Malcolm Allison was delighted. The attendance had won him ten pounds off United's Paddy Crerand who had told the City coach that City were a "dying club" and bet him the Blues would never get above 30,000 at Maine Road. Later that season 63,034 watched City play Everton – an attendance greater than any domestic crowd at Old Trafford that season.

28th October 1978

Goals from Mike Channon and Asa Hartford helped City to a 2-2 draw at home to West Bromwich Albion before 40,521. Cyrille Regis & Bryan Robson netted for Albion.

29th October 1980

Dennis Tueart netted four against Notts County in the League Cup. The Blues won 5-1.

30th October 1973

The 2nd round League Cup tie with Walsall went to a second replay. City won the game 4-0 with a hat-trick for Francis Lee, but a pitiful crowd of 13,646 witnessed the match at Old Trafford. City fans didn't mind playing a 2nd replay, but they did object to it being played at United's ground.

31st October 1913

Tommy 'Boy' Browell signed. Browell (right) went on to become a major City star and appeared in 247 first team games, scoring 139 goals.

CITY'S NUMBER ONE

THE PROFILES

20 – JIM MITCHELL

Born in Prestwich, Jim Mitchell was a former Manchester University and Northern Nomads 'keeper. He also had spells at Blackpool and at Preston where he gained an extremely good reputation. He earned several significant honours and was the Great Britain goalkeeper at the 1920 Olympics. He also kept goal for Preston in the 1922 FA Cup final (the last played at Stamford Bridge before Wembley Stadium opened) against Huddersfield and hit the headlines by leaping around while a penalty was being taken against him – this caused the rules to be changed.

He joined City shortly after the final and replaced Goodchild as City's number one the following September, making his debut on 9th September 1922 at home to Birmingham. Despite wearing glasses – on the pitch as well as off it – Mitchell was an agile 'keeper and made 22 appearances in his first season.

Always an amateur, Mitchell made history by being City 'keeper for the first game at Maine Road (25th August 1923) and was generally recognised as a quality 'keeper by neutrals. He was certainly known nationwide and was capped at both an amateur level and for the full England side.

He later had a spell at Leicester, though he never appeared in their first team, and joined the footwear firm Stead & Simpson. He went on to become their Managing Director. He passed away in 1975.

Appearances: League: 99 FA Cup: 10

21 – BILLY HARPER

Nineteen year old Billy Harper's League debut came for Sunderland against City on 14th January 1922. The Blues won 3-2 but there was something about Harper which caused someone at the Club to make a note of his name. Fourteen months later City signed him, ostensibly as cover for Mitchell and Goodchild.

Harper's City debut came on 13th February 1924 as City were defeated 3-1 by Nottingham Forest. He kept his place for the next game – a 2-2 draw with Burnley – but was replaced as soon as first Mitchell then Goodchild were fit enough to play.

Two further appearances followed (both defeats) and it became inevitable that the Blues would release Harper when the opportunity came. He moved to Crystal Palace in May 1924. A brief spell at Luton followed before he moved to Weymouth in 1927.

Appearances: League: 4

22 – JACK PHILLIPS

An injury to Jim Mitchell in September 1925 gave Jack Phillips his first City game on 23rd September 1925. City were defeated 4-1 by West Bromwich Albion and Welsh Youth international Phillips never played a first team game again.

In the reserves though Phillips excelled, earning a Manchester Cup medal for the Blues. Sadly, just as he was starting to be considered for first team duty again a wrist injury in a reserve match against Bolton on 18th December 1926 forced him to quit the game. The Blues settled his compensation claim in 1929 and Phillips took a job in the insurance business. By the end of World War Two he was a trainer with Oswestry.

Appearances: League: 1

23 – RICHARD FINNEGAN

Welsh international Dick Finnegan was apparently discovered by Wrexham while performing at a circus and, according to the "Who's Who of Welsh International Soccer Players", was "of Gypsy extraction" – the reason he moved around so much, apparently!

Finnegan joined City in May 1926 and had already been with four Welsh sides and, by the time his career ended, he seemed to average a move roughly every twelve months.

He made his City debut in a 2-0 win at Port Vale on 23rd October 1926, but by the end of that season he was on his way to Accrington Stanley. At Stanley he had a dispute with a director and his contract was cancelled.

Appearances: League: 8

24 – ALBERT GRAY

Another Welsh international 'keeper Albert Gray was 6ft 3 inches tall. He signed for City on 6th January 1927 from Oldham Athletic and made his debut nine days later against Fulham (City won 5-2).

He was a very capable 'keeper and appeared in 42 consecutive League appearances before injury caused him to miss a couple of matches. His performances helped the Blues come close to promotion in 1927 (they missed promotion on goal average) and win the Second Division title in 1928.

A move away from City came towards the end of the decade when Gray became one of the star players for Manchester's third side Manchester Central (Central had aspirations to be a League side and they seriously threatened United's existence until City & United worked together to thwart their ambitions).

In August 1930 Gray moved to Coventry before becoming an established member of the Tranmere Rovers side from 1931 to 1936. In later life he became a bookmaker at Cleveleys, near Blackpool.

Appearances: League: 68 FA Cup: 2

25 – LEWIS BARBER

Former miner Lewis Barber made his City debut in October 1927 following the absence of Bert Gray. City beat Reading 4-1 but inevitably first choice Gray returned for the following match. Occasional appearances followed then on Christmas Day 1928 Barber replaced Gray as City's regular number one and went on to make 82 consecutive League appearances. Without doubt Barber was a quality 'keeper by this time but injury against Chelsea on 15th November 1930 brought him significant problems. As he struggled to regain fitness due to the knee injury City later acknowledged that they treated him appallingly during this time.

In 1932 he was released by the Club while still hobbling on crutches following two unsuccessful operations – the story hit the media around forty years later, during the time of Joe Mercer's managerial reign, as the City manager was made aware of the story by other former players. Mercer invited Barber into the Club to meet Joe Corrigan (below) and other members of the City squad.

Barber passed away at Halifax in June 1983.

Appearances: League: 92 FA Cup: 7

26 – LEN LANGFORD

Barber's injury had a positive impact on the career of 31 year old Len Langford. Langford had been Nottingham Forest's 'keeper between 1925 and 1930 and had made 144 first team appearances, so he was obviously experienced when he arrived at Maine Road in June 1930 as cover. Whether Langford expected to become City's first choice is not clear but he did seem satisfied with his role as understudy to Barber initially.

When Barber's injury gave Langford the chance to make his debut the player shone. He performed exceptionally well and became recognised as one of the reasons why the Blues became defensively strong during the early 1930s.

In 1932 he helped the Blues reach the FA Cup semi-final – Cinema footage shows he stood no chance of saving the last minute Arsenal winner that knocked City out – and then in 1933 he was City's first choice as City reached their first FA Cup final for 7 years. Everton won the game, but Langford was not faulted.

Len Langford (right of photo) with Sam Cowan and Matt Barrass.

By the time of City's next Cup final in 1934 Langford had lost his place as first choice. Injury had given young Frank Swift his chance and Langford became Swift's understudy, though the younger 'keeper made it clear throughout his life that Langford had been very supportive.

In 1934 he joined Second Division Manchester United and made 15 appearances for the Club. He passed away in 1973 at Stockport.

It's worth noting that in his earlier life he was a noted boxer, particularly during his time with the Coldstream Guards during World War One. While at Maine Road he helped introduce boxing training methods to the Blues – at that time City seemed keen to try anything that might give them an edge.

Langford was also a noted high-jumper and wicket-keeper.

Appearances: League: 112 FA Cup: 13

27 – CLIFF WALMSLEY

Former Burnley amateur Cliff Walmsley only made two first team appearances for City and they came over a three day period in March 1932 when Langford was injured. City won one and lost one with Walmsley conceding three goals.

He did find success at a lower level for the Blues when he kept goal in the Manchester Cup final against Oldham in 1932 – City won 1-0.

On 30th May 1932 he moved to Reading and stayed there a year before he joined Rochdale in August 1933. He made 59 League appearances for 'Dale before joining Stalybridge Celtic in May 1935.

Appearances: League: 2

CITY IN EUROPE

1972-73

Competition: UEFA Cup

Reason For Qualification: Finished fourth (one point behind champions Derby County)

Manager: Malcolm Allison

13th September 1972
Round 1 Leg 1
Attendance: 21,698

City 2-2 Valencia CF

City Goalscorers: Mellor, Marsh
City: Corrigan; Jeffries, Donachie, Doyle, Booth, Oakes, Mellor, Bell, Marsh, Lee, Towers

The first European game played following the departure of Joe Mercer was also the Club's first in the UEFA Cup. The UEFA Cup evolved out of the Inter-Cities Fairs Cup which ran from 1958 to 1971. Although City qualified for the competition in 1970 by winning the League Cup, the Blues had to compete in the European Cup Winners' Cup instead (City were ECWC holders and in prestige terms the ECWC was viewed as being more significant than the Fairs Cup at the time). The UEFA Cup replaced the Fairs Cup for the 1971-72 season.

This was a fairly tense game with Allison's City keen to ensure a home victory to take over to Spain, however by half time the game was 1-1 with Ian Mellor scoring the first historic City goal in the UEFA Cup. Rodney Marsh, who had signed the previous March, scored a second for City but a score draw (Valencia's goals came from Valdez & Adorno) was all the Blues could manage.

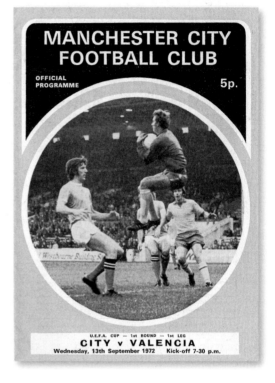

MANCHESTER CITY FOOTBALL CLUB

OFFICIAL PROGRAMME

5p.

U.E.F.A. CUP — 1st ROUND — 1st LEG
CITY v VALENCIA
Wednesday, 13th September 1972   Kick-off 7-30 p.m.

27th September 1972
Round 1 Leg 2
Attendance: 54,000

Valencia CF 2-1 City

City Goalscorer: Marsh
City: Healey; Book, Barrett, Doyle, Booth (Mellor), Oakes, Summerbee, Bell, Marsh, Lee, Towers

The Blues knew it would be tough after the 2-2 draw had given Valencia the advantage of two away goals, however Allison's City fought hard. Ultimately, home advantage shone through and, despite a Rodney Marsh goal, Valencia

Rodney Marsh – on target in both legs against the Spaniards.

won 4-3 on aggregate. Incidentally, Valencia were managed by the former Real Madrid star Alfredo Di Stefano.

A week after this defeat the Blues were also knocked out of the League Cup by Fourth Division Bury, prompting some to suggest City were too quick to allow Mercer to move on.

Date Quiz 1

Dates are almost everywhere in Manchester. Have a look at many of the older buildings and you'll see date stones and plaques commemorating the official opening of buildings and so on.

Whenever I see a date in Manchester I automatically think of it from a City perspective. For example, every time I see anything that shows that Granada TV first started broadcasting in 1956 I immediately think of City winning the FA Cup.

So, to see if you've got this particular form of Citydate-itis the Big Book Of City has taken photographs of some Manchester buildings – and a bridge in Yorkshire that was made by a Manchester company – and used these images to form our first Date Quiz.

Take a look at these photographs and see if you can identify what moment in City's history these dates tie in with. Of course some of the dates may have more than one significance and so to help steer you towards the answer we're looking for we've given you three options. For each image, only one of these options is correct.

Answers can be found on page 80.

IMAGE A

The date this bridge was built is noteworthy because:

A Ardwick AFC (City) joined the Football League

B Ardwick AFC changed their name to Manchester City FC

C Ardwick AFC moved to Hyde Road

IMAGE B

Look carefully and there are two dates on this image of the base of the Victoria monument in Piccadilly Gardens. The earliest date is significant because:

A Welsh international Billy Meredith made his debut that year

B The first Manchester derby was played at Hyde Road

C Cult hero Billy Gillespie made his debut that year

IMAGE C

In Piccadilly Gardens, next door to the Gardens Hotel, is this building. It was built in a year that's more famous to City fans as:

A The year City won the League for the first time

B The year City won the Second Division title for the first time

C The year City won the FA Cup for the first time

IMAGE D

On the other side of the Gardens Hotel is this building, but what significance does the date have to City?:

A It's the year City moved to Maine Road

B It's the year City's players banned as part of the illegal payments scandal were told to sign for other clubs

C It's the year City wore blue for the first time

IMAGE E

The Royal Exchange was enlarged in this year, but what relevance does it have to City?:

A The Blues won the League Championship on the last day of the season

B Future City manager Joe Mercer was born in this year

C A devastating fire caused City to seriously consider moving out of their old Hyde Road ground

IMAGE F

The year the Shakespeare Inn was being rebuilt in Manchester was important to City because:

A The Blues won the Second Division title

B The Blues missed promotion on the last day of the season by the narrowest goal average margin in history

C The Blues had four points deducted for fielding an ineligible player and missed promotion as a result

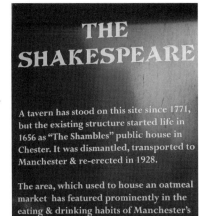

THE SHAKESPEARE

A tavern has stood on this site since 1771, but the existing structure started life in 1656 as "The Shambles" public house in Chester. It was dismantled, transported to Manchester & re-erected in 1928.

The area, which used to house an oatmeal market has featured prominently in the eating & drinking habits of Manchester's populace for many years.

IMAGE G

The year King George V opened Manchester Central Library was significant to City because

A The League title was won by City

B A controversial goal caused City to be relegated on the final day of the season

C Frank Swift fainted as City won the FA Cup at Wembley

IMAGE H

This plaque, added to the Royal Exchange, lists two dates with significance to City. The dates cover a period in City's history that saw some significant lows and highs in the Club's history. So what does this four year period represent? Is it:

A the period when City were out of the Premier League for the first time since it was formed

B The years Kevin Keegan managed the Blues

C The full length of Shaun Goater's City career

IMAGE I

This plaque, added to a bench in Market Street, lists a date with a rather unpleasant significance to City, but what was it?:

A The Blues finished third bottom in the Premier League and were relegated

B The Blues missed qualification for the UEFA Cup by missing a penalty on the last day of the season

C The Blues were knocked out of the FA Cup at the quarter final stage

DATE QUIZ – THE ANSWERS

Here are the answers to our first Date Quiz

Image A – The date this bridge was built is noteworthy because: (a) Ardwick AFC (City) joined the Football League.

Image B – Look carefully and there are two dates on this image of the base of the Victoria monument in Piccadilly Gardens. The earliest date is significant because: (c) Cult hero Billy Gillespie made his debut that year.

Image C – In Piccadilly Gardens, next door to the Gardens Hotel, is this building. It was built in a year that's more famous to City fans as: (c) The year City won the FA Cup for the first time.

Image D – On the other side of the Gardens Hotel is this building, but what significance does the date have to City?: (b) It's the year City's players were banned as part of the illegal payments scandal were told to sign for other clubs.

Image E – The Royal Exchange was enlarged in this year, but what relevance does it have to City?: (b) Future City manager Joe Mercer was born in this year.

Image F – The year the Shakespeare Inn was being rebuilt in Manchester was important to City because: (a) The Blues won the Second Division title.

Image G – The year King George V opened Manchester Central Library was significant to City because; (c) Frank Swift fainted as City won the FA Cup at Wembley.

Image H – This plaque, added to the Royal Exchange, lists two dates with significance to City. The dates cover a period in City's history that saw some significant lows and highs in the Club's history. So what does this four year period represent? It is: (a) the period when City were out of the Premier League for the first time since it was formed.

Image I – This plaque, added to a bench in Market Street, lists a date with a rather unpleasant significance to City, but what was it?: (a) The Blues finished third bottom in the Premier League and were relegated.

SWALES' AIMS

City director Peter Swales didn't waste much time in stating his ambition. This article from 1973 was the first, but by no means the last, in which Swales compared the Blues to the Reds. By the end of the year he was City's Chairman but despite the hyperbole the Blues only managed to win one major trophy during his twenty year reign as Chairman. The focus on United proved to be unhealthy for the Club. It could have been so much better if the Blues had focused on their own dreams and not on the competition.

Old Trafford ... the best thing that's happened to Maine Road

UNITED ARE NOT MEMBERS OF A MAGIC CIRCLE

SAYS CITY DIRECTOR SWALES

THE TRAUMATIC events of recent weeks at Manchester United will be to the long-term benefit of—Manchester City. That is the provocative viewpoint expressed by a man with a powerful voice in affairs at Maine Road, recently-elected vice-chairman Peter Swales.

Swales admits that City have struggled to achieve their cherished ambition of matching

RODNEY MARSH—he's a crowd puller

United, stride for stride, when it comes to recognition. City have collected cups, in recent seasons, but United, although struggling, have still cornered the crowds.

"But the events of the past few weeks have equalised the situation. The mystique of Manchester United has been torn aside, and the frailties of the club have been exposed; United have been shown to be an ordinary club, just like any other," he says.

Swales stresses that he is not knocking United — merely making a realistic appraisal of the new possibilities for City which have been opened up by the disenchantment over the George Best affair, the sacking of Frank O'Farrell, and the appointment of Tommy Docherty as United's third manager in as many years.

"United have received a tremendous amount of publicity, as they have always seemed to do, and we have apparently been hidden in the shadow of Old Trafford. Docherty has arrived amid a fanfare of trumpets and taken the eye with his swift, big-money signings. But, in spite of all the publicity for United, I think it's been a good thing for Manchester City.

"The directors of both clubs are friendly with each other, but we're under no illusions about one thing: each club wants to be recognised as the No. 1. Now, I believe we are competing against just another football club, and not against a legend. And if they're just another team, we can whack them.

"United have been seen to have made mistakes, and therefore they are not members of a magic circle. Sir Matt Busby, the biggest personality in football during the past 25 years, has seen certain sections turn against him—unjustifiably, let me say. If that can happen, it is just as fair to assume that supporters can turn away from

the club; and it is up to us to turn them our way.

"Manchester City have had a reputation for behind-the-scenes activity which hasn't done them any good in recent years. But it has now been proved that such things happen at most clubs. And we are striving to build a new image for ourselves. We have already started by inviting schoolboys to watch games at Maine Road, and we have become much more closely involved with local schools.

"Youngsters of today don't remember past glories or tragedies . . . they're concerned with the present."

Manchester United have topped the 45,000 average for Old Trafford matches this season, leaving City still trailing. Swales admits that the £200,000 signing of Rodney Marsh was designed for two things—to improve the team, and attract the fans.

"There's no doubt now that Marsh is recognised as a player of great ability; as for adding to the gates, we might have discovered that they were going down, if he hadn't arrived. I'm sure he brings people to Maine Road.

"And one thing people forget, when they compare City's gates with those of United—we may have lagged behind them, but we are still probably in the top half-dozen or so for attendances all over the country.

"Manchester United have made their moves, but they still have to convince people that they can stay in the First Division. And that's going to be a fight in itself. It all boils down in the end to winning matches, and the important thing is that we simply don't accept that we shall always play second fiddle. Indeed, I'm convinced that we won't."

While United have had their outsize headaches, City have been concerned with one aspect of their image—the fact that only goalkeeper Joe Corrigan,

PETER SWALES

of the first team, has not had his name jotted down in the referee's notebook.

Wyn Davies was sent off away back in August, while still a City player; Francis Lee and Mike Summerbee received marching orders in December—Lee at Bramall Lane, Summerbee in a testimonial game at Loftus Road. Colin Bell, booked four times in League games, has served a two-match suspension, and so has Willie Donachie, while Lee has had a three-match ban.

Tony Book, Tony Towers, Tommy Booth and Summerbee were within one caution of an automatic two-game suspension, before the New Year had been forgotten. And all these happenings have been discussed at board level.

Swales says: "In the early part of the season, our players appeared to be timid, if anything—there didn't seem to be a tremendous amount of effort coming from the team. Now the workrate and enthusiasm of the side has shown a marked improvement."

City, striving to win new friends and influence people, are trying hard to put their own house in order and create a new image. And, in the process, they are serving notice on their greatest rivals.

CITY'S NUMBER ONE

THE PROFILES

28 – FRANK HIGGS

Frank Higgs had found success in Northern Ireland winning the Irish Cup and in 1931 he joined Barnsley from Linfield, after previously having a spell with Chelsea. In June 1932 he joined City as the Blues looked to strengthen their squad. On the face of it the Club had a variety of 'keepers at this time, but it has to be remembered that Langford had not been brought in to be City's first choice and so the Club management clearly felt a replacement for Barber was still needed. As a result both Higgs and Jim Nicholls arrived during the 1932 close season with Higgs being the first to get his chance in the first team.

On 3rd September 1932 the big day arrived and Higgs replaced Langford for a Maine Road game with Middlesbrough. It was the Blues third game of the season and City had won one (home) and lost one (away). It was important home fans saw another victory. Sadly, despite two goals from Bobby Marshall the Blues were defeated 3-2. It's fair to say that fans were not impressed.

Higgs never got his first team chance again and after conceding 32 goals in 15 reserve matches he moved on at the season's end. Spells at Aldershot, Walsall, Carlisle, Southend and Barrow followed. He passed away at the age of 41 in 1948.

Appearances: League: 1

29 – JIM NICHOLLS

With his debut coming a week before his 24th birthday, Jim Nicholls knew the reaction Higgs' debut had generated and so he must have been a little apprehensive to say the least when he appeared for the Blues in the 2-1 defeat at Everton on 17th September 1932. Clearly, the fact the game was away from home had meant Nicholls' role was not analysed by fans as much as it would at home, and so the real test came in the next game. On his birthday Nicholls performed well as City defeated Blackpool 5-1 at Maine Road, but after a 12 consecutive appearances he lost his place when Langford returned to full fitness.

Two further appearances followed that season, and then after performing well in the annual public practice match Nicholls was selected as 'keeper for the opening game of the 1933-34 season. Unfortunately, a 3-2 defeat meant Langford returned for the next game and Nicholls next opportunity on 23rd December ended in a 8-0 defeat! He was never given the chance to impress again and youngster Frank Swift quickly eclipsed him as City's second choice and then first choice.

On 14th May 1934 Nicholls joined Brentford and later had a spell with Port Vale.

Appearances: League: 16

30 – FRANK SWIFT

Frank Swift became one of the most famous goalkeepers in European history and a major star for City and for England. He was born in Blackpool on 26 December 1913, the second son of five children. From his earliest memories, he was always obsessed with the game of football, playing at every opportunity with his brothers, including Fred who became first team goalkeeper for a variety of clubs, most notably Blackpool, Oldham Athletic and Bolton Wanderers.

On leaving school Swift went to work for the Blackpool Gasworks as a coke-keeper and each Saturday he kept goal for his employers' football team. As his confidence grew he took the unusual step of writing to prominent Lancashire Combination side Fleetwood. In August 1931 they tested him in a trial match containing a mix of first team and reserve players, and after a good performance Harold Colley, secretary of

Fleetwood, signed Swift. The goalkeeper was named in the Fleetwood reserve side for the opening West Lancashire League game of the 1931-32 season. Sadly, nerves got the better of Swift and he pulled out of the match shortly before kick off. Despite this setback Colley and the Fleetwood committee recognised Swift's potential and persuaded him to make his debut in the Fleetwood Reserve side against Blackburn Rovers 'A' team on 23rd September 1931. By the end of the season Swift was established as the regular Reserve goalkeeper and at the start of the 1932-33 season it was widely acknowledged that he was on the verge of replacing first team 'keeper Phil Barraclough, father of actor Roy Barraclough. He was also drawing attention from several League clubs.

On 8th October 1932, 17 year old Swift was given a trial by the Blues and on 16th November 1932 he became registered as a City player. No transfer fee was paid as Swift

Frank Swift

was not a contracted Fleetwood player, however City secretary Wilf Wild made a donation of 10 guineas to the Fylde club in recognition of their role in his development on 23rd March 1934.

Swift's progression at City was rapid. In February 1933 he first appeared for the reserves, and on Christmas Day 1933 he made his first team debut against Derby County. The game resulted in a 4-1 defeat but was still an improvement on City's previous match when the Blues lost 8-0. Swift kept his place, and with injury to Langford limiting competition, the young 'keeper managed to retain his place for the rest of the season. In fact he didn't miss a single League or Cup game until 17th September 1938 (a 6-1 defeat by Millwall).

The 1933-34 season brought much attention Swift's way as he helped City to FA Cup glory. The Blues beat Portsmouth 2-1 however the emotion of the game took its toll on the twenty year old goalkeeper. As referee Stanley Rous blew the final whistle Swift fainted. Immediately, the press found an appropriately sensational story to sell the following day's newspapers and Swift – at

the time the youngest goalkeeper to appear in the FA Cup final - became a household name. Twelve months earlier he had paid 2s 6d to watch City face Everton in the 1933 final. The transformation from spectator to cup winning hero touched the nation.

Enormous crowds watched most of City's cup games during 1934 with both the Maine Road (84,569) and Hillsborough, Sheffield (72,841) attendance records being set, but these crowds brought tragedy and Swift, with his close position to the packed terraces, witnessed many injuries and in later life he commented on the sight of a dead supporter being carried out at Hillsborough. Possibly because of that experience he remained passionate about conditions for supporters.

Swift's career continued to progress, however during the summer months football took a back seat as he and his brothers operated a sailing boat providing trips along the Blackpool coast. It was while performing this activity that he met his future wife, Doris Potter. Swift was married on 27 July 1935 in Blackpool. That year he appeared in a trial match for 'The Rest' against the England side.

Wembley celebrations 1934 with Frank Swift on the far right.

In 1936-37 he was a key presence as City won the League Championship for the first time, and two years later he was on the verge of an England cap when war broke out, causing all League football to be cancelled. A decision was taken to keep morale boosting internationals going and, on 18th November 1939, Swift made his international debut against Wales at Wrexham, although officially wartime internationals were not recognised as full internationals by the FA. Inevitably, opportunities were few and far between during the following years – only two internationals were played in 1940 – however Swift did manage a total of 14 wartime and victory international appearances.

Post-war he made 19 full international appearances, keeping 9 clean sheets, including two games as captain, making Swift the first goalkeeper to captain England in the twentieth century. His first match as captain was against Italy in Turin, May 1948, and he guided England to a significant 4-0 victory. At the final whistle, Swift was carried shoulder high by his team mates after a tremendous performance and in later years Tom Finney and Tommy Lawton, amongst others, claimed this as Swift's greatest game.

After representing Great Britain in 1947, Swift made his final international appearance on 9th April 1949 against Scotland at Wembley. Much to the annoyance of City and the regret of supporters, he had chosen to retire while at the top of his game, and on 27th April 1947 he appeared in what was supposed to be his final home game – a surprise 3-0 defeat by Arsenal. Supporters invaded the pitch as Swift was chaired off the field by team mates. Similar scenes were observed eleven days later at his final match in Huddersfield and Swift was feted with a celebratory procession back over the moors to Manchester.

Fate determined however that Swift was to play again. Alec Thurlow, his replacement became ill with Tuberculosis, and Swift

Frank Swift receiving post match treatment in the Maine Road dressing room.

was persuaded to fill the void, although he stipulated he would only keep goal until City found a replacement. He went on to make four appearances with his last match being a goalless game at home to Everton in September 1949.

6ft 2 inch Swift could have played both domestic and international football for a further couple of seasons at least, however his desire to retire increased his reputation. His former teammate at City Matt Busby tried tempting him out of retirement to play for Manchester United, while City stubbornly retained his registration until 1951 – he would only have been 37 at that time.

In retirement Swift became a representative for the confectionary firm Smallman's and developed a career as a sporting columnist for the *News of the World*. His opinion on issues such as World Cup football, refereeing, European competition, and all the other main issues of the 1950s entertained readers. By 1957 he was assigned to cover Manchester United's European campaigns and he took the opportunity to call for the authorities to subsidise supporter travel abroad. He was very much a supporters' man.

It was while fulfilling this role that Swift was killed on 6th February 1958. He was flying with United back from their February 1958 match in Belgrade when their plane crashed while trying to take off at Munich. In fact it was the sight of Swift – a man very popular on the continent and well known as England's former 'keeper - which made Professor Frank Kessel of the medical team aware that the victims were members of an English football team.

Swift, who by this stage was also President of the Manchester City Supporters' Club, was sorely missed. The Sports Editor of the *News of the World* wrote a touching obituary. He revealed how the newspaper had received calls, letters, and telegrams from thousands of people around the world expressing their sorrow. These calls came from ordinary supporters and from significant international figures, even Senor Bernabeau, the President of Real Madrid, called. Swift's humour, courage, and

Ooch! Swift saves a terrific shot at Maine-road.

FRANK SWIFT

Every Saturday
Special Articles by
Manchester City's
International Skipper

•

Tom Markland on all City's matches
and full reports of all the big games

•

EVENING CHRONICLE
FOOTBALL EDITION

general humility had touched everyone in the game.

Swift possessed the common touch, always known for his great rapport with the public. He was recognised more as a showman than a daring style of goalkeeper, nevertheless he was a tremendously gifted goalkeeper who found League and Cup success before the age of 24, and appeared in 373 peacetime League and FA Cup fixtures for City, and a total of 33 full and wartime internationals for England. Both his retirement and his death were premature.

In 1977 a street close to Manchester City's Maine Road ground was named in his honour.

Appearances: League: 338 FAC: 35

31 – JACK ROBINSON

From the moment Frank Swift made his debut it was almost impossible for any other 'keeper to displace the 'Big Fella'. In fact the first opportunity for any 'keeper to make

their mark didn't come until 17th September 1938 when 20 year old Jack Robinson was the lucky one, although it's unlikely he felt fortunate at the end of the match as City were defeated 6-1 by Millwall – the Blues biggest defeat since the game before Swift's debut over four years earlier!

Despite the disappointment of that game Robinson remained a Blue for several seasons and appeared in 62 wartime games for City. Post war he managed to return to the first team once more – this time the Blues drew 2-2 at Bury on 18th September 1946. Inevitably, Swift returned for the next game and with other 'keepers such as Alec Thurlow on City's books at this time, opportunities for 28 year old Robinson ended.

He moved to Bury in November 1946 and went on to play for Southend in 1947. Sadly a shoulder injury cut short his career there and he returned to the north-west. He died in Accrington in April 1993.

Appearances: League: 2

32 – ALEC THURLOW

Of all the goalkeepers to have appeared in the League Alec Thurlow's story is perhaps the saddest. However, his career did not start that way. 24 year old Thurlow joined the Blues from Huddersfield Town on 26th September 1946 and two days later he made his debut as City drew a goalless game with Tottenham at White Hart Lane. The circumstances behind Thurlow's transfer are not exactly clear, however it is known that the Blues needed to find a 'keeper for the Spurs game as regular choice Frank Swift had been selected to play for England against Northern Ireland that day in Belfast. In those days international matches were often played on League dates and clubs had no choice but to release their best players.

Thurlow was not a first team player at Huddersfield but it is clear that his transfer to Maine Road came as a direct result of Swift's England selection. At City Thurlow knew he stood little chance of ever replacing Swift, however the opportunity to be understudy to the greatest 'keeper in Europe, as Swift was perceived as, was one no 'keeper could turn down.

Thurlow's next appearance came in the goalless Manchester derby of September 1947 – the first post war derby – and then in October he helped the Blues defeat Stoke 3-0. Both of these selections came as a result of Swift's appearances for England.

After several further appearances, Thurlow was anticipated to be Swift's replacement when the England star announced his retirement. However, Thurlow was now suffering with Tuberculosis and in 1950 he was forced into retirement. After major surgery, in which seven ribs were removed, it was hoped Thurlow would regain a level of fitness that would allow him to enjoy as normal a life as possible. However, a collapsed lung, followed by a serious relapse brought real concern. Sadly, at the age of 34 he passed away in a sanatorium.

It was a sad end for a wonderful Club servant.

Appearances: League: 21

33 – KEN OXFORD

Another one appearance wonder, Ken Oxford joined City as an amateur from Ardwick Lads Club in May 1946, turning professional on Bonfire Night 1947. The following April with Thurlow unfit and Swift unavailable Oxford's debut came against Arsenal at Maine Road. The game ended goalless and 18 year old Oxford had performed well, but with Swift available for the final home game of the season Oxford returned to reserve team action.

The following December the 19 year old moved to Derby County – had he stayed at Maine Road his chance to become City's number one would have come though he could not possibly have known that at the time. A spell in Derby's reserve side was followed by a similar role at Chesterfield, before a move to Norwich gave Oxford his chance to shine in the League once more. After 128 games in East Anglia he re-joined Derby for a fee of £34,000 and became a regular first teamer.

In later life, after a time as caretaker manager at Boston United, he became a security guard and in 1993 he suffered a heart attack and died. It was said that injuries sustained during a robbery attempt that he tried to foil played a part.

Appearances: League: 1

OBSCURE HISTORY

Wherever you walk in Manchester there are places that have a City connection. Some of these are obvious – Albert Square and the numerous homecoming parades, particularly the three that took place there between April 1969 and May 1970 – but the majority are not.

So, in a bid to identify some of our more obscure locations the Big Book Of City has trawled through the archives and walked the streets of Manchester to identify a couple of buildings that played their part in at least one moment of the Club's history.

The first 'obscure' building is the Monsoon store on the corner of King Street and Police Street in the city centre.

Looking at the building today it's hard to tell that it has ever played any part in the history of our Club, yet it has. So what part did it play?

Of course we know it's hard to guess. It's the sort of thing you either know or you don't and, in truth, it really is a bit of an obscure fact. The answer appears on the next page, but before you take a look please have a guess. To help here are four possible answers and, in the spirit of all multiple choice questions, when in doubt pick the most bizarre.

So, what part did this building play in City's history? Was it:

A During the 1920s the sportswear shop run by City star Billy Meredith.

B The headquarters of Alec Watson & Co, the sportswear company that made City's shirts for the 1926 FA Cup final.

C The home of Goodalls, furnishers, who made all the seating for Maine Road in 1923.

D Edwardia, the shop run by Mike Summerbee, in partnership with George Best, during 1968.

Take a guess and then turn over the page to see if you were right.

OBSCURE HISTORY – THE ANSWER

Well, the answer to our first 'obscure' building question and the part it played in City's history is:

The Monsoon store on the corner of King Street and Police Street in the city centre was (C) The home of Goodalls, furnishers, who made all the seating for Maine Road in 1923.

GOODALLS

Furnishers and Decorators
KING ST., MANCHESTER

Phone : 2500 City.   Telegrams : Allgood, Manchester

GOODALLS MAKE A SPECIALITY OF TIP-UP SEATING
AND THE WHOLE OF THE SEATING ON THE MAN-
CHESTER CITY FOOTBALL GROUND WAS SUPPLIED
BY THEM

The Football Season Daily Reminder
November

1st November 2003

Robbie Fowler & Paulo Wanchope both scored as City won 2-0 at Southampton and moved into fifth place.

2nd November 1929

Matt Busby made his debut as a replacement for Tommy Johnson in the 3-1 defeat of Middlesbrough. Johnson returned to the side for the next match and Busby didn't reappear in the side until January 1930.

3rd November 1937

League champions City defeated FA Cup holders Sunderland 2-0 in the Charity Shield at Maine Road. In those days the Charity Shield was staged at the ground of the Champions. City scorers were Alec Herd and Peter Doherty.

4th November 1995

A Nicky Summerbee goal gave City victory over Bolton Wanderers at Maine Road. This was City's first win of the season and was the start of Alan Ball's best spell as manager – he was awarded the Manager of the Month award.

5th November 1938

Former United man Eric Westwood and ex-Spurs star Bert Sproston both made their debuts against Sproston's former club on this day. City won the fixture 2-0 before a crowd of 47,998 with goals from Doherty and Milsom.

6th November 1920

City won 1-0 at Huddersfield, but later that night several thousand people attended City's Hyde Road ground in shock as the Club's Main Stand was engulfed by fire (below).

7th November 1987

The Blues beat Huddersfield Town 10-1. Paul Stewart, Tony Adcock, and David White each scored a hat-trick while the goal spree was started by Neil McNab. Even the Huddersfield goal was scored by former Blue Andy May. Exactly five years later White was amongst the scorers as City defeated League Champions Leeds United 4-0. The goalscoring rout that day was started by Mike Sheron (below).

8th November 1919

Blackburn Rovers were defeated 8-2 at Hyde Road. Seven days later City beat Blackburn again. This time it was 4-1 at Ewood.

9th November 2002

Cult hero Shaun Goater netted twice (the second of which was his 100th League goal) as

NOTE — Attention is drawn to the provisions of Regulation 21

BARCLAYS LEAGUE

SEASON 1987-88

Second Division

DATE OF MATCH ......7ᵗʰ November...... 198?

HOME CLUB ...Manchester City... VISITING CLUB ...Huddersfield Town...

RESULT: Home Club ......10...... Goals; Visiting Club ......1...... Goals

Total No. of Matches Played ...17... Won ...7... Lost ...5... Drawn ...5...

Total Goals For ...39... Goals Against ...25... Points ...26...

Signed .... Secretary of ...Manchester City... Club

TEAM

NOTE. — PLEASE COMPLETE IN BLOCK LETTERS

		SURNAME	FORENAME(S)
GOALKEEPER		NIXON	ERIC
	2	GIDMAN	JOHN
	3	HINCHCLIFFE	ANDY
	4	CLEMENTS	KENNY
	5	LAKE	PAUL
	6	REDMOND	STEVE
	7	WHITE	DAVID
	8	STEWART	PAUL
	9	ADCOCK	TONY
	10	McNAB	NEIL
	11	SIMPSON	PAUL
NOMINATED SUBSTITUTES		BRIGHTWELL	IAN
		SCOTT	IAN

*If a non contract player mark so JONES, A (non contract) or Associated Schoolboy, JONES, A (Associated Schoolboy)

...LAKE... was substitute for ...BRIGHTWELL...

...ADCOCK... was substitute for ...SCOTT...

Advertised Time of Kick-off ......3.0PM...... Actual Time of Kick-off ......3.0PM......

Manchester United were defeated 3-1 in the last derby match ever played at Maine Road.

10th November 1956

The great Don Revie (right) left the Blues for Sunderland. Revie had been in and out of favour with manager Les McDowall for over a year, but fans recognised his qualities.

11th November 1970

Defender Colin Barrett turned professional.

12th November 1966

A solitary goal from Mike Summerbee gave City victory over Stoke City at Maine Road. Defender George Heslop performed well that day but injury forced him to miss the next game.

13th November 1880

The first reported game played by St. Mark's Church side took place in Gorton and ended in a 2-1 defeat by the Baptist Church from Macclesfield. Both sides fielded 12 players and the first St. Mark's goalscorer was James Collinge. By the summer of 1894 St. Mark's had evolved into Manchester City.

14th November 1959

City's record appearance holder Alan Oakes (below) made the first of 564 League appearances on this day. The game ended in a 1-1 draw with Chelsea.

15th November 1990

Peter Reid was officially appointed manager.

16th November 1973

Future City forward Adie Mike was born in Manchester.

17th November 1915

Former City forward Frank Hesham was killed in action in Northern France. The

locally born player was on City's books for five years during the late 1890s.

18th November 2006

Two goals from Corradi (12th & 32nd mins) and Barton (45th min) helped City to a 3-1 victory over Fulham.

19th November 1966

Colin Bell's goal against a strong Everton side was enough to see the Blues win a controversial League game (above and right) at Maine Road before 39,572. Everton were disappointed when they had a goal disallowed but City deserved the points.

20th November 2004

Goals from Wright-Phillips, Sibierski & Bosvelt gave City a 3-1 victory at Portsmouth.

21st November 1960

Portsmouth became the first side ever to beat City in the League Cup. The round three tie ended 2-0 before a Fratton Park crowd of 10,386.

22nd November 1969

City and Arsenal drew 1-1 at Highbury. The goals were scored by Ian Bowyer (City) and Terry Neill (penalty for Arsenal).

23rd November 1957

Goalkeeper Steve Fleet made his debut in a 4-3 defeat by Wolves.

24th November 2007

Petrov (11 mins) and Ireland gave City a 2-1 victory over Reading. Ireland's goal came in the last minute of the game.

25th November 1989

Brian Gayle played his last League match for City. The game ended in a 1-1 draw (Clive Allen scored) and Chairman Peter Swales decided the time was right to dismiss manager Mel Machin. Machin, who had guided the side to promotion the previous May, was dismissed that weekend and not replaced until 8th December.

26th November 1949

Former German paratrooper Bert Trautmann played his first Maine Road League game on this day. Birmingham were defeated 4-0 with a brace each from Andy Black and Roy Clarke. Trautmann's debut had come a week earlier at Bolton. The attendance was around 2,000 more than the previous home game, despite a campaign to 'boycott Blues if German plays'.

27th November 1996

Two penalties from Kinkladze helped the Blues defeat West Bromwich Albion 3-2. Rosler netted the other City goal. This was the first victory of caretaker manager Phil Neal's reign at City.

28th November 1936

The League game with Brentford was abandoned after 40 minutes with the score at 0-0. The replay ended 2-1 to the eventual champions City.

29th November 1980

John Bond signing Gerry Gow netted twice as City defeated Crystal Palace 3-2.

30th November 2002

The last appearance by Bolton Wanderers at Maine Road ended 2-0 to City with Howey and Berkovic scoring.

Manchester Evening News

37,449   MONDAY, NOVEMBER 27, 1989   2

EXCLUSIVE Blues boss says: I had to act

Sack for Machin!

By Peter Gardner

MANAGER Mel Machin has been sacked by Manchester City.

He has lost his job just six months after taking the Maine Road club back to the First Division. But the Blues' dramatic dive back into relegation trouble forced chairman Peter Swales to take

CITY IN EUROPE

1976-77

Competition: UEFA Cup

Reason For Qualification:
Reigning League Cup holders

Manager: Tony Book

Round 1 Leg 1
Attendance: 36,955

City 1-0 Juventus

City Goalscorer: Kidd
City: Corrigan; Docherty, Donachie, Doyle, Watson, Conway, Barnes (Power), Kidd, Royle, Hartford, Tueart

England manager and former Blue Don Revie was watching from the Main Stand. Brian Kidd netted the only goal of the game shortly before half time and his first for the club, but with Juventus having such a European pedigree over the years, it was recognised that this lead would be advantageous but not decisive.

City manager Tony Book had made it clear that he had hoped for a two goal lead, but he was still hopeful of glory: "I am extremely confident. I do not promise victory in the second leg. Nor do I foresee defeat. The vital thing is going to be the first goal scored - the team that gets it could easily carry off the title."

During the 1990s Dennis Tueart explained that he felt City's failure was simply as a result of European inexperience: "Against Juventus we didn't do too badly in the first game, but we only got the one goal. I think that was because we were a little inexperienced compared to the likes of Liverpool. They had a European head on. They knew how to play in Europe. We

U.E.F.A. CUP - First round - First leg

MANCHESTER **CITY**

v

JUVENTUS
TORINO

Match Mag
15p

Wednesday, September 15th, 1976

didn't. We still went out with all the flair and the creative things that we had in the English League. We just didn't have the ability to play European style at that time. We weren't ready.

"We'd only just come together within 18 months and then we were in Europe. Probably from Tony Book's view as well, he was a little inexperienced as far as Europe was concerned. There wasn't any major change in tactics. We only got the one goal lead which Juventus were happy with. It would have been nice to have been drawn away first - see what we could do there - and then bring them back here. The goal was just before half-time, which is a great time to score, but we couldn't break them down in the second half. They just got behind the ball."

Dennis Tueart is ready to take advantage as renowned 'keeper Dino Zoff punches clear at Maine Road.

29th September 1976
Round 1 Leg 2
Attendance: 55,000

Juventus 2-0 City

City: Corrigan; Docherty, Donachie, Doyle, Watson, Booth, Keegan (Lester), Kidd, Royle, Hartford, Tueart

Many English sides would have struggled in Turin, but the hope had been to win 2-0 at home. Had the Blues managed that then anything could have happened in the second leg. As it was the 1-0 lead was not enough and Juventus knew exactly how to teach City a European lesson. Dennis Tueart, in the late 1990s, remembered: "They kicked ten bells out of us, unbelievable! Tommy Booth was

defending a corner and the ball came over. Tommy went up to head clear, and this guy came up behind him. I think it was Tardelli, the Italian international, and he came up with six studs in the middle of Tommy's back. Straight through the middle of his back. Tommy went flying... and the referee didn't do anything! He just played on, unbelievable! And that's where we were very inexperienced. Very, very poor in that European tie. No real steel, no European steel."

The defeat could have seriously affected City's motivation but Book, with Chief Coach Bill Taylor, managed to ensure everyone connected with the club realised how strong a side Juventus were. Defeat was no disgrace.

CITY'S NUMBER ONE
THE PROFILES

34 - RONNIE POWELL

Apprentice electrician Ronnie Powell joined City as an amateur in May 1948 from his home town side Knighton Town. He registered professionally for the Club the following November and, following the health concerns of Thurlow and Swift's desire to retire, Powell was in the right place to stake his claim for the goalkeeper's shirt when he made his debut on 24th August 1949 against Portsmouth. That game ended in a 1-1 draw but Powell's next match was a 3-1 defeat at Charlton, and Swift was persuaded to don the 'keeper's shirt once again. It was clearly not something he wanted to do and after three successive matches Swift reminded the Club of his intention to retire and urged them to give 19 year old Powell his chance again.

With Swift's support Powell returned to action and kept goal for ten consecutive games. Five of those ended in defeat and the Blues decided to take a gamble on another 'keeper, Bert Trautmann.

Powell remained as understudy until June 1952 when he moved on to Chesterfield (with Dennis Westcott for a combined fee of around £2,250). Powell made over 500 appearances for Chesterfield over the following thirteen years.

Appearances: League: 12 FAC: 1

35 - BERT TRAUTMANN

Bert Trautmann remains not only one of City's greatest 'keepers, he is also one of football's most important figures. He is one of the Football League's 100 greatest legends; one of City's most popular players - he received more votes than any other player in the City Hall of Fame when I created the awards in 2004; and he is one of sport's greatest ambassadors. He is also the main reason why my father became a Blue, and therefore is the reason I'm a City fan. Thousands of others have him to thank for their City roots.

Trautmann's upbringing and early life has to be considered in the context of the country he grew up in. Germany during the late twenties and thirties was at times a desperate place to be. The country was on its knees following the First World War and the early years of the depression. It was an environment in which the far right policies of Adolf Hitler flourished.

As a youngster Trautmann, already a keen sports enthusiast, became a member of the Hitler Youth. It wasn't as a result of strong political beliefs; he was simply following the route expected. During the war he joined the Luftwaffe and served in Poland and Russia. As a paratrooper he was captured by the Russians and by the French Resistance, escaping on both occasions, and won five medals for bravery including the Iron Cross (first class).

Trautmann saw the full horrors of war. It was a nightmare existence, although Trautmann has always been quick to point out it was no worse than the situation millions of others were in: "There was tragedy and there was humour, as there was on every battle front."

In 1945 he was captured by the Americans but somehow managed to walk free. Then the British caught him and eventually he was taken to a camp in Ashton-In-Makerfield. It was at this camp that he began to play in goal for the first time during football matches.

Trautmann was officially released from captivity in February 1948 but elected to stay in Britain as he saw no immediate prospects in Germany. Agricultural work and bomb disposal activities followed, and whenever possible he was playing football for St. Helen's Town.

As the 1949 season commenced several League clubs were showing interest in him. By that time City had hastened their search for a replacement to Frank Swift and the Club's management were ready to take a gamble on Trautmann. It is often overlooked that City's desperation to find a replacement for Swift caused the side to controversially select the former Prisoner of war.

City signed Trautmann in November 1949 but the move was not popular. For at least a month prior to the transfer newspapers were publishing letters from fans threatening to boycott the club. City had a large Jewish support and many believed the arrival of a former German paratrooper was one step too far. The national media soon

caught on to the story and considerable negative publicity was generated. The Club could have pulled out at any point, however Chairman Bob Smith answered critics by saying: "People can boycott or not as they like. I am very glad we have signed Trautmann. From what I have heard of him he is not a good goalkeeper, he is a superb goalkeeper. We had to get him in quickly or other teams would have taken him from under our noses." It was a very brave decision.

The players, including Captain Eric Westwood – a Normandy veteran, soon made Trautmann feel welcome. That all helped and then came Trautmann's debut on 19th November 1949 against Bolton. The Blues lost 3-0 but the 'keeper had impressed. Trautmann remembers this period as one of transition: "It was the first time I actually saw people protesting against me. But within a month, a lot of those same people who'd been against me were having a go at anyone having a go at me! It changed very quickly. When I signed for City the 'papers were full of discriminating headlines along the lines of 'If City sign a Nazi, what next?'. And then people realised I'd been digging unexploded bombs in their country. They started to see me as a person with a mother and father. It was all about the human touch."

Trautmann quickly established himself as a worthy successor to Frank Swift, and the former England captain went to great lengths to stress the quality of the German. City fans adopted Trautmann as one of their own and the 'keeper became more important to the Blues after every game. One game in particular, away at Fulham in January 1950, saw Trautmann in outstanding form. This was a landmark game for the 'keeper as at the start of the match his appearance had not been welcome. Trautmann: "I had been getting a good press in the north-west by this time, but Jack Friar, who was to become my father-in-law, pointed out that my first game in London would really test me because of the papers and publicity down there. He said

I wasn't just playing against Fulham, I was playing against London. I needed to make a good impression to get the national press on my side, and he told me he expected we could lose 7-0 or 8-0!"

As the players entered the Craven Cottage pitch shouts of 'Kraut' and 'Nazi' rang out. Trautmann received tremendous abuse and clearly a lesser player would have buckled under the pressure, but the 'keeper seemed to see the venom as a challenge, and he started to appear more confident and more determined than he had in any earlier City match. In the end the Blues lost 1-0, but the score would have been much worse had it not been for Trautmann: "I was at the Thames End of the ground and was the last player to come off. Both teams stood at the dressing room entrance and applauded. A very emotional moment. In London, at that time, that was a testimony. I was lucky in later years to win the FA Cup; win the player of the year, and play for the Football League. But Fulham was my greatest moment."

The attention the player was now receiving was all positive, and the German media were beginning to show interest. This led to attention from German League sides, including Schalke '04 who made an offer of £1,000 for the player. City rejected the bid, but for a while Trautmann became keen to return to Germany.

In 1955 Trautmann became the first German to play in a FA Cup final: "Today, I don't think the occasion means that much anymore in terms of the community spirit

and everyone singing 'Abide With Me' and so on. When I went there I enjoyed the whole thing – the build up... the media attention... everything. I have never known nerves like I had that day. Even when we went back a year later, they were still bad."

At Wembley in '56 Trautmann helped City defeat Birmingham City. It was a memorable game but for many the significant aspect of the day concerns Trautmann. Trautmann: "It was only years later I could piece together what happened that day. I have watched film of the match and you can see me coming out to intercept the ball. I was in the air and neither me nor Murphy, the Birmingham player, could stop. He tried to get over me, lifted his leg but caught me in the neck with his right leg. It was accidental. After that I was gone. Everything was grey until the final minute. I made a couple of saves but don't remember anything until our centre-half, Dave Ewing, collided into me. The pain was intense and I really didn't know what I had done. I was only aware of this pain – like an extreme toothache in my neck."

"On Sunday morning I was taken to hospital in London where they took X-rays and told me it was nothing. But I could not move my head. If I wanted to turn I had to move my whole body. I knew something was wrong."

Incredibly Trautmann played his part in City's homecoming and he made an impromptu speech at the Town Hall while the crowd chanted his name. Trautmann: "I must have looked like death. We had the homecoming in a packed Albert Square and I had to speak. At the reception I remember Frank Swift slapping me with his enormous hands – it felt like I had been split right down the middle with an axe!"

Unhappy with his medical treatment, Trautmann arranged to see an expert the Tuesday after the final. That's when the true extent of the injury became apparent. The Doctor told Trautmann he had broken his neck.

A few weeks after the final further tragedy struck when Trautmann's son was killed in a

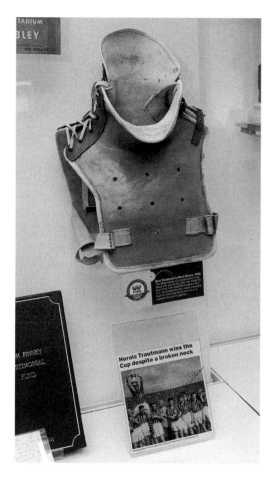

18 months before I was fit enough but, even today, my neck is still painful and restricted, especially in cold weather."

Trautmann continued to play for City until 1964 when he was awarded a testimonial. By that time he had eclipsed Eric Brook's first team appearance record for the Blues and inevitably fans were desperate to give him a great testimonial. The official crowd was approximately 48,000, however the actual attendance was at least 60,000 as Maine Road was packed to the rafters with thousands locked outside.

During the latter part of his time at City, Trautmann was viewed by the English authorities as the greatest goalkeeper playing in England, and in October 1960 he was chosen to captain the Football League's representative side for a match with the Irish League. This was a major honour at the time and compensated, to some degree, for the fact that he had not been picked to play for his national side. The reason he never appeared has been debated many times over the years. The most likely reason is that the German authorities had simply chosen not to pick him because he was playing outside of his home nation. Had he joined Schalke in the early fifties he would probably have been a regular for his national side.

Despite this, it's fair to say Europe's leading footballing figures recognised his greatness, especially in 1956 when he was awarded the Football Writers' Player of the Year award. This is not only significant because Trautmann was the first overseas player to receive the award but also because it was awarded to him in the days leading up to the 1956 final. Therefore his heroics that day played no part in the decision.

After leaving the Blues, spells at Stockport County and Wellington Town followed as player-manager, plus various spells working with the German FA. He had a significant role assisting Third World countries with the development of sport. Stints in Burma, Tanzania, Liberia, and Pakistan presented him with many obstacles but, as with his

road accident. Life was tough, immediately after Wembley, but Trautmann tried to be positive: "There was nothing I could do but lie there and do a lot of thinking. And never did I think that I would not play football again."

Then in December – only seven months after the injury – he returned to League action. His return came on 15th December 1956 – the first City League match filmed by the BBC at Maine Road. Trautmann: "It was very difficult coming back. I came back too quickly really. I would stand there with the forwards coming at me, saying 'Come on, have a go. Let me show you I'm still good enough'. But it never happened like that. I reckoned I was finished. I told McDowall so, but he told me I was wrong. I told him I had cost City at least six points but he said 'think of the number of points you've saved us over the years'. I think it took me about playing career, Trautmann was determined to succeed. These activities prove beyond doubt the importance of Trautmann to sport. As a player he had achieved so much. As a man he achieved more. Born in a country at a time when prejudice and bigotry was the norm, Trautmann's experience in England helped him develop as a man. His role as a sporting ambassador helped to break down barriers, remove prejudice, and encourage people from all walks of life and backgrounds to work and play together. He was later awarded the OBE for his contribution to Anglo-German relations. Often sportsmen receive awards simply because of success on the pitch,

Trautmann's accolade is not solely for activities on the pitch (if it was he would have received it over forty years ago), it is for the example he has set throughout his adult life.

Trautmann is a true sporting legend and a great ambassador. He is also, arguably, the greatest European goalkeeper of all time.

During 2008 writer and actor Bill Cronshaw wrote and starred in "I'll Be Bert" - a stage play focusing on how the 'keeper had affected a young boy's life.

Appearances: League: 508 FAC: 33 League Cup: 4

Bert makes a speech in a crowded Maine Road tunnel after his testimonial.

47,000 fans say 'Auf Wiedersehen'

THEY gave him a standing ovation when he came out. The band struck up For He's A Jolly Good Fellow, and every time he touched the ball cheers echoed around Maine Road. This was Bert Trautmann's night, and Manchester did him proud.

It was as though everyone in the crowd wanted to thank him personally for the pleasure he has given them, for with two minutes' play still left, the fans decided they wanted Bert, not football.

They swarmed on to the field in their thousands and Trautmann's green jersey was lost in a sea of well-wishers. The rest of the players hared for the dressing-rooms but pandemonium reigned as police raced to rescue Trautmann from his predicament, writes MIKE ELLIS.

ATKINSON FOR ENGLAND

PART ONE

An Excerpt from "Atkinson For England"
By Gary James & Mark Brown

In 2001 Mark Brown and Gary James
wrote a novel about a plumber who
became the England football manager.
The book was called "Atkinson For
England" and contained many, many
City references. The following excerpt
focuses on one section of the story
which sees the two main characters,
Reg Atkinson and Norman Whaddon,
arrive at the City-themed Kippax
Hotel.

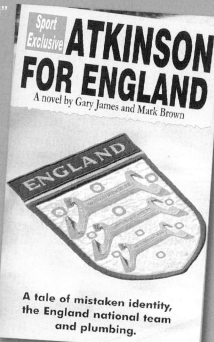

Sport Exclusive **ATKINSON FOR ENGLAND**
A novel by Gary James and Mark Brown

A tale of mistaken identity, the England national team and plumbing.

As background it's worth knowing
that the story takes place around the
time of old Wembley's last season,
and that Reg is a plumber who
has applied to install the undersoil
heating at the new Wembley. He is also a
Sunday league football manager for a team called The Forest Inn,
Nottingham. The FA were still based at Lancaster Gate and England
are without a manager during a crucial period in which they will face
Germany for a place in the World Cup finals.

This excerpt comes from Chapter Three, "The Kippax Hotel". Reg,
supported by his Septuagenarian colleague Norman, has arrived in
London in preparation for his interview at the FA .

ATKINSON FOR ENGLAND

During the ride on the tube, Norman stayed silent. He was content to let Reg usher him everywhere, knowing that Reg had done this sort of thing countless times before. It was easier than he had imagined - train journeys to Norman meant interminable lengths of time waiting at stations followed by a long journey standing up in a smoke filled carriage. Blissfully unaware of the non-smoking prevalence these days on public transport, Norman found the tube a more pleasant experience than he had expected.

"This is us," nudged Reg as the tube began slowing into Marble Arch tube station. The two men stood up and manoeuvred their baggage to the doors of the carriage. When the tube train stopped and the doors opened, they jumped out. Reg ushered Norman over to a quiet wall.

"Right," he said, "let's have a look at this map they've sent us."

He removed the fax sent by the FA from the side pocket of his travel bag. He turned it around in his hand until it was the right way up and studied it closely.

"Looks like about five or ten minutes walk to the FA and then it's only about hundred yards after for the hotel," Reg announced. He looked at his watch - two fifteen.

"Do you want to check in first and then get a sarny?" he asked.

"Aye," Norman replied, "could do with getting shut of these bags."

They made their way out of the station and Reg headed towards Lancaster Gate. The map was absolutely spot on, he thought. As they approached the FA Headquarters, Reg pointed it out to Norman.

"That's where we're going tomorrow."

"Oh," said Norman, "looks nice."

It looked quite impressive, Reg thought. He had never actually seen it before - he'd seen pictures of it of course, but never in reality.

They carried on past the building and were soon in front of the Kippax Hotel.

"This it?" asked Norman.

"Seems to be," said Reg, "come on."

They climbed the four steps to the revolving doors and stopped. Above their heads was a sign that said "MAINE ENTRANCE".

"Bit odd," Reg remarked.

"Schoolboy error," announced Norman, "you'd have thought they'd have taken more care with the spelling."

Reg led the way through the revolving doors and entered the hotel. Norman followed and they both stood in the foyer gazing at their surroundings. Away from the main street, the silence was deafening.

The Kippax Hotel was at first glance a rather bizarre building. In a previous existence it had been called the Elsinore Hotel. It's current owner, Dave Bayley was a totally obsessed Manchester City supporter who had travelled from Droylsden, Manchester to London at the grand old age of seventeen for the 1981 FA Cup Final to watch his beloved City play Tottenham Hotspur. He had never returned home.

Dave had stayed in the Elsinore back then, originally for a couple of nights, but with the first game ending in a draw - thanks to the efforts of Tommy Hutchison who rewrote the history books by scoring for each team - Dave prolonged his stay to take in the replay. Unfortunately for Dave, and for City, Spurs won the replay 3-2 in one of the better Cup replays of recent times. Dave had been so heartbroken he broke down and wept in front of the old hotel owner, Max Novotny.

Max had seen this sort of behaviour many times and was used to it, but Dave seemed to strike a chord deep within him. He came to a decision - he offered Dave a job in the hotel, nothing special, just cleaning, portering, odd jobs, that sort of thing. Dave said yes - this could be his penance: he could serve out a personal sentence in London, not leaving until City returned triumphant in a Wembley Final. In 1986, he almost achieved his dream, but City were beaten in a Full Members Cup Final by Chelsea. Dave's mother had not been too happy - Dave was the youngest of three and was the only one to be still living at home. She had travelled down to London in an effort to persuade him to go home, but to no avail. She had returned to Droylsden alone.

In 1992, Max Novotny died. In his last will and testament, he had left the hotel to Dave. Having no family to speak of, the old man had left everything to his 'surrogate' son. Dave was astonished - obviously he had grown to love the old man and he knew Max had treated him kindly over the years, but this was completely unexpected. Dave then spent the next year trying to run the hotel as Max had, but found it difficult to meet the overheads.

In early 1994, Dave made a decision: in order to save the hotel, some changes were required. Firstly, the name changed to the Kippax Hotel - a tribute to Manchester City's main terracing. Secondly, all the rooms were given names instead of numbers - the names were of cult City players of yesteryear and gave a personal aspect to each room. Thirdly, advertising was extended from the usual tourist trade to football programmes and fanzines.

Business boomed fleetingly as the novelty value put the newly named hotel on the map. Supporters came from all over the country to see their teams play in the capital and enjoyed the experience of staying at a speciality hotel. Not all recognised the depth of Dave's devotion, but that didn't matter at the time - it was different. But attitudes change, novelties wear off and Dave was left with a number of faithful guests and the occasional visit by the Manchester City Supporters Club. The best weekend by far in recent times had been the May 1999 Second Division Play-off Final when City had prevailed against Gillingham. Dave's self imposed exile may have ended if he had not been the owner of the Kippax Hotel.

Reg and Norman moved slowly through the foyer, taking in the atmosphere of the hotel. On each side of them, photographs of footballers in mostly white England shirts adorned the walls in glass covered frames. Some were head and shoulders shots, but most were on their haunches with the ball between their feet, one hand resting on the ball. Reg recognised a few - Trevor Francis, Mike Channon, Francis Lee for definite, a yellow shirted Joe Corrigan - but could not put names to faces for most of them. Sunlight glinted from the pictures allowing dust motes to ride on reflected sunbeams cutting through the lobby. The footballers watched their every step until Reg and Norman reached the reception desk. Norman noticed a bell on the desk marked "Colin". He rang it.

Within seconds, Dave Bayley appeared.

"Afternoon gents," he said cheerily, "can I help you?"

"Party of two," said Reg, "Atkinson."

"Oh," said Dave, surprised, "and you are Mr...?"

"Atkinson," repeated Reg. He had thought his original statement had been clear enough.

"Oh," said Dave again, frowning momentarily, "I'm sorry, when the FA sent the details...oh never mind, I must have got my wires crossed."

Dave reached under the desk and pulled out two registration cards.

"Could you fill these in please?" he asked. As Reg and Norman patted their pockets ineffectually, searching for pens which they knew were not there, Dave reached below the desk again. His hand emerged with two pens.

"Thanks," said Reg, looking at the pen. Instead of the usual hotel name, it had "LEE WON" inscribed upon it.

"Those are my Franny Lee pens," Dave Bayley said by way of explanation, "Lee Won Pen - that was his nickname, scored a lot of penalties for City."

Reg acknowledged the explanation, although he wasn't entirely clear what Dave was talking about, and began to fill in the registration card. After name and address, the questions became unusual. Reg frowned, confused.

"Oh sorry," Dave said, "I forgot to tell you - this is a hotel which pays homage to football, well Manchester City anyway. The questions are designed to assess your allegiances and preferences."

"I see," said Reg, not seeing.

"I mean," Dave continued, "If you were an Arsenal fan for example, I wouldn't put you on the same floor as a Spurs fan."

"Oh," said Reg, "right."

"It also helps to determine the level of service you get off me," said Dave.

"Why?" said Norman innocently, still examining the pen.

"Well, if you're from Watford, say, and you put your favourite team as Man United, then you will probably not get good quality service because you have jumped on a bandwagon."

"Do you not like Man United then?" asked Norman.

"Bloody media circus they are. Forgotten their fan base in search of profit. Oh yes,"

Dave was now on his favourite subject. He continued his diatribe while Reg and Norman filled in their registration cards.

Reg filled in his place of birth and favourite team as Preston. Norman completed the necessary sections as Nottingham and Nottingham Forest, his team since childhood. Dave was still at full throttle - he had left the subject of Manchester United and was now berating Luton Town, a team that had once caused Manchester City's relegation in the 1980's.

"Oh good," he said as he examined Reg and Norman's cards, "if you'd have put Luton down, I would have chased you across reception!" He laughed. Reg and Norman returned a polite but nervous chuckle. Dave gathered the cards together and filed them away. He gave them the pens back.

"Souvenirs of your stay," he said, "right gents, I'll show you to your rooms."

******

The Kippax Hotel had been chosen primarily for its proximity to Lancaster Gate, but a massive benefit was that it was usually empty. It was viewed by the FA as the best possible place for the prospective new manager to be hidden until the interview and subsequent press conference.

Reg and Norman were unaware of the FA's motives. They thought they had wandered into Fawlty Towers, such was the initial impact of Dave Bayley. Dave was taking the opportunity of explaining the layout of the hotel as he escorted Reg and Norman to their rooms. He had already given them a brief history of his own - how he originated from Manchester and the reason he was the owner of the hotel.

"Everything has been named after Manchester City Players or key moments in the club's history," he said grandly, "for example, did you notice the bell at reception?"

"Yes," said Reg, "Colin wasn't it?"

"That's right," said Dave pleased, "Colin Bell - and the reception or lobby is called the Maine Entrance, as in Maine Road."

"Ah, so that's why it's Maine with an 'e'," said Norman, suddenly clicking.

"Indeed," said Dave, pleased that Norman had made the connection.

"I like the footballer pictures in the lobby," said Reg, "you can sense the atmosphere as soon as you walk in."

"Oh good, do you like it?" asked Dave, "that's a collection of City players who have played for England since I started supporting them. Only trouble is that I've not had any new ones for a while."

Reg and Norman, despite their first impressions were starting to warm to Dave. His love for City was passionate and he had obviously taken every step to make sure everything within the hotel had substance, a personality. The hotel's heart beat with the same fervour as Dave's own.

As Dave led them into the lift, Reg noticed that each floor had a name too, from the Alan Ball Basement, to the Mercer Floor at the top.

Norman stared at the floor names too.

"Mercer?" he enquired to no-one in particular.

"Oh yes, Joe Mercer," replied Dave, "best times in the club's history were when Joe was at the helm. We were always top when he was there, that's why I've called the top floor after him."

Norman snorted. Dave looked hurt - before he could respond, Reg interjected.

"Take no notice," he said to Dave smiling, "Norman once played football for Joe Mercer at Sheffield Utd."

"You're kidding," said Dave in awe.

"Aye," Reg continued, "three whole weeks wasn't it Norm?"

Norman grunted and muttered something unintelligible under its breath.

"Mercer sold him...to Notts County. Norman had the cheek to ask him for a pay rise, didn't you Norm?"

"Blimey," Dave whispered. This was the first time that anybody had stayed in the hotel who had actually played under Joe Mercer. Three weeks only did not matter in the slightest - Norman had just achieved hero status.

The lift stopped at the third floor - Division One. The men heard a 'ding' before the lift doors swung open.

"I must admit that when the FA made the booking, I thought you were someone else," said Dave as he helped Reg and Norman get their bags out of the lift.

"Did you?" said Reg.

"Yeah, with all this business about the England manager vacancy, I thought you were Big Ron," Dave continued, "FA said R. Atkinson and I just assumed..."

"Never assume," barked Norman, never missing an opportunity for his favourite adage.

Reg had no idea why the FA would even consider putting an important candidate for the England job in this hotel, but saw no reason to question it. This was about the standard he would expect for someone like himself.

"Nope," he said, "I'm a plumber. I've come down to hopefully sort out the tender for the undersoil heating at the new Wembley. Norman's my right hand man."

"I see," said Dave in realisation, "of course, everything's happening at once isn't it?"

Reg nodded in agreement.

"Here we are," Dave said, stopping outside a door with 'The Royle Suite' engraved on a brass plate on the door, "I've given you two of the best rooms."

Dave opened the door and led Reg and Norman into what was an absolutely massive room. 'Royle Suite' was about right, Reg thought, good enough for the Queen of England this. Every wall was covered with memorabilia covering Joe Royle's reign at Manchester City as manager, and even his playing days in the Seventies.

"This room has just been renovated," Dave said proudly, "it used to be the Allison Suite, after the best coach we've had, but I decided to rename it. Bit more pizzazz, eh? The Royle Suite?"

Reg and Norman nodded in agreement - it certainly was an impressive room.

"This is yours Mr Atkinson," said Dave, breaking the silence. "Your room is next door Mr Whaddon. Will you follow me please."

Norman followed meekly. Reg went too, he was fascinated. He wanted to see

Norman's room - if it was anything like this it had to be special.

The next door had a similar brass plate. Engraved on this was simply '10-1'.

"I thought you'd got rid of the room numbers," said Norman.

"I have," said Dave, "that's not a number, that's a score - ten one against Huddersfield, biggest win in modern history for us. The Huddersfield goal was actually scored by an ex-City player."

"Was it?" said Norman.

"Yeah, Andy May," smiled Dave, "got the biggest cheer of the game it did. Made it 9-1 and brought Huddersfield back into it."

Dave laughed at his small joke, opened the door and stepped inside. Reg and Norman followed him in. In size, the room was similar, but the decoration was so much different. Memorabilia again covered the walls, but most significant were the giant inflatable bananas suspended from the ceiling.

"What do you think?" asked Dave, nervously.

"Brilliant," said Reg - he had never seen anything like it in his life.

"Well it's certainly different," said Norman.

Dave, missing the irony, carried on enthusiastically, "it's called the 'Ten One Suite' but it's actually a homage to City during the period 1987 to 1989 - the Machin era."

Dave was not wrong - both Norman and Reg surveyed the room. They spotted photographs of various players from that era; team and action pictures; newspaper cuttings. One full wall was decorated entirely in Manchester Evening News sports pages covering City games. Reg went for a closer look.

"My mum used to send me copies of the Evening News from Manchester," Dave explained, "but they started piling up. So I thought, why don't I do something like this? People tell me they spend hours reading bits and pieces from it. Bit different to anaglypta, eh?"

Reg agreed. He was currently engrossed in a large section covering City's victory over neighbours Manchester United by five goals to one. Norman could not take his eyes off two large pictures: one of Imre Varadi which seemed to stare back at him, and one of John Gidman. Frightening, he thought - Varadi looked sinister, but the more he looked at Gidman, the worse he felt. As he moved to check out another wall, he looked at the Gidman picture again - he was sure the eyes were following him around the room.

"Well I'll leave you chaps to settle in," said Dave, "call me if you need anything. There's a guide beside your bed telling you how everything works and the telly's operated by the remote on the bedside table."

"Thanks," said Reg and Norman in unison as Dave left them in the 'Ten One Suite'.

The second part of the excerpt appears on page 196.

CITY'S NUMBER ONE

THE PROFILES

36 – DEREK WILLIAMS

The opportunity for 17 year old Derek Williams to appear in City's first team came when a hand injury to Bert Trautmann made his selection impossible, while Trautmann's understudy Ronnie Powell was already travelling with the Reserves to Blackburn. Williams, after only three reserve outings, was given his First Division debut against Blackpool on 9th February 1951. Interestingly, this was the first time Trautmann had missed a City League game.

A Maine Road crowd of 47,528 witnessed a good performance by the youngster as City played out a goalless draw. Blackpool hardly troubled Williams but the 'keeper was said to have appeared confident with good positional sense.

Inevitably, Trautmann returned to action for the next game and the regular 'keeper did not miss another League game until the end of December 1954. By that time Williams had turned down an ultimatum by the Blues which basically said sign professionally and give up on your education or else. Williams chose to continue his education and had spells with Mold Alexander, his home town team, and as an amateur with Wrexham. In September 1956 he joined Oldham Athletic and during the 1956-57 season he made 30 first team appearances for the Latics.

Described by Oldham journalists as a 'well-built' and 'brave' goalkeeper, Williams was progressing well when fate played its hand. Williams, as with most men of his age, had to have a spell of National Service and in February 1957 his role as first choice for Latics was brought to an end as he was called up. Despite his many qualities, he was never to appear in the Football League again, although Oldham retained his registration until 30th June 1959.

Appearances: League: 1

37 – JOHN SAVAGE

City paid Halifax Town £3,500 to sign John Savage on 17th November 1953 and it is clear that from the moment he arrived the 23 year old stood little chance of shifting Bert Trautmann out of the number one shirt. Nevertheless, being understudy to Trautmann was in itself an education.

Savage's first chance to appear in the first team came on 27th December 1954 at Newcastle United – two days earlier Trautmann had been injured against the same side. The Blues had won the first game 3-1 but at Newcastle it was a different story as City lost 2-0. Clearly the cold statistics would suggest that the goalkeeping change may have played its part, however it has to be stressed that the Christmas period often threw up contrasting results against the same side in consecutive games. For example, four years later the Blues lost 6-1 to Birmingham on Boxing Day and the following day won 4-1 against the same side. Trautmann appeared in both those games.

Despite his debut day defeat, Savage kept his place for the following fixture, but as soon as he was fit Trautmann returned to the first team. A couple of further appearances followed towards the tail end of the 1955-56 season (both defeats), and then Trautmann suffered his horrific injury in the FA Cup final. When the 1956-57 season opened Savage missed the opportunity of replacing Trautmann initially as City had signed George Thompson that summer, but the new 'keeper broke his leg in only his second game. Savage's chance came again.

The Bromley born 'keeper was given an extended run – appearing in 19 consecutive League games – before Trautmann returned to action. Sadly, the Blues had only won seven games and drawn a further 3 of

Savage's games and it has often been claimed that the City management rushed Trautmann back to try and avert a potential relegation crisis.

For Savage a further seven League appearances followed in 1957-58 before the 'keeper was sold to Walsall for £1,650 in January 1958. He made 51 League appearances for the Midlands' club.

In later life Savage became a builder and moved to Blackpool.

Appearances: League: 30

38 – GEORGE THOMPSON

George Thompson was a month short of his 30th birthday when he made his City debut on 18th August 1956. That debut came because Bert Trautmann had suffered his horrific neck injury in the 1956 FA Cup final and Thompson, an experienced 'keeper, was signed in July knowing that he was to be City's first choice until Trautmann returned to fitness.

Prior to City, Thompson had made 140 League appearances for Preston and had also enjoyed spells at Chesterfield and Scunthorpe. He was recognised as a reliable 'keeper and the Blues paid £7,500 for his services.

His debut game saw the Blues suffer a 5-1 defeat (Revie scored a consolation penalty!) at an extremely strong Wolves. Thompson's second game ended in a 2-2 draw, however the 'keeper broke his leg during the match. This blow caused Thompson to spend many months trying to regain his fitness and, inevitably, by the time he returned to action Trautmann was back in the first team himself.

Thompson suffered a further blow when he broke his collar bone during his spell in the Reserves.

Almost a year after arriving Thompson moved to Carlisle for a fee of £1,000. It turned out to be a good move as the 'keeper went on to make over 200 first team appearances for the club before retirement.

Appearances: League: 2

39 – STEVE FLEET

He only made six first team appearances in total for City but it is fair to say that Steve Fleet was one of Manchester City's greatest servants. He joined the Club as an amateur in 1953 and remained with the Blues for ten years as a player. Spells at Wrexham, Stockport and Altrincham followed, as did coaching overseas, before Fleet returned to City in 1973. Fleet played a significant role on the Maine Road coaching staff and was instrumental in City's Central League success of 1977-78. He later managed the Platt Lane complex for the Club.

As a goalkeeper Fleet had impressed as a youth with Salford Boys and he joined as an amateur with City in 1953, turning professional after his National Service ended. His debut came in November 1957 when the Blues lost an amazing game by the odd goal in seven.

Inevitably, Trautmann returned and Fleet's chances were few and far between. He ended his City playing career after a handful of first team games (including a League Cup quarter-final appearance), but went on to make 79 League appearances for Wrexham and 36 for Stockport.

Appearances: League: 5 League Cup: 1

The Steve Fleet Interview

In April 2004 Steve Fleet was interviewed by Gary James. He talked about his fifty year plus involvement with City. This included the following questions and answers.

You made your debut against Wolves in 1957 (opposite), can you remember much about that day?

I actually heard I was making my debut from the *Manchester Evening News*. I woke up to find a newspaper reporter and photographer on my doorstep, and they told me I was actually going to play. City had told me to report for training pre match but hadn't said anything about being in the team.

The game was a thriller and ended 4-3 to Wolves, how do you think you played?

I was fairly happy with my performance. I remember it was a bit of a foggy day and also that Wolves were powerful – they won the League that season and were one of the great sides of the period. Afterwards I saw the reports and they were full of praise. In addition Frank Swift wrote a very complimentary piece in his newspaper column and said I had a great future ahead of me, while Bert Trautmann told reporters I was the best young 'keeper he had ever seen. All of that praise made me feel terrific of course, but I also knew I was only filling in until Bert was ready to return. He was an outstanding 'keeper and there was no way any other 'keeper would replace him if he was fit.

Left to right: Steve Fleet, Bert Trautmann and Roy Dixon.

Did you feel despondent knowing you had little chance of replacing him on a regular basis?

No, not at all. I suppose I felt I had to serve out my apprenticeship first of all. There were other good 'keepers at City, including Roy Dixon – the father of the famous Arsenal player (and City fan!) Lee Dixon – but I was sure my day would come. I was also delighted to be second choice to Bert.

Did he coach you or help in any other way?

Bert helped in every way. He was a great role model and taught me so much about life as well as football. He was like an older brother to me and I was fortunate to be taken under Bert's wing. He insisted I presented myself well – clean shoes, wear a tie etc. – at all times. I listened and followed his lead both on and off the pitch.

My father needed a car to go south on holiday once and Bert offered to let Dad use it. For a fortnight my Dad had his car and when it came time to give it back, Bert refused any payment of any kind. He was terrific to be with and he remains a great man. There are few men in football or in life like Bert. Even today every former player looks at Bert Trautmann in awe – he is a true great and there are very few around.

As I was 14 years younger than him I thought I was being groomed as his natural successor. It didn't quite work out like that, but Bert tried to ensure I was given some opportunities. I only managed to play 5 League games and 1 League Cup match during my City career but Bert ensured I'd play in some of those. I only found out recently but Bert deliberately pulled out of a couple of games simply so that I could get the opportunity. City would try and make him play every game, no matter how fit he was – and he often played when not fully fit because everyone demanded it – but for those games he made sure I got my chance.

What was training like at City when you first started to make it into the first team?

We'd train in the mornings, but nothing in the afternoon. We'd finish at lunch and I'd then go over to United's training ground, The Cliff, to meet my best friend Eddie Colman. All the United youngsters would still be training hard for Bert Whalley – I think that was the big difference at the time.

As a young boy I was brought up in Ordsall and played for Salford Boys with Eddie and they used to take us to watch United. Sadly, Eddie later died in the Munich disaster and I was a pallbearer at his funeral – no one can underestimate how the disaster affected all Mancunians.

At one point as a youngster I got the chance to go to Maine Road to watch City. I loved the colour of City's shirts – a beautiful colour – and I also knew that City's ground was better than Old Trafford - it definitely was.

One of your League appearances was

against United in 1961, do you remember much about that?

It was highly controversial! City were the better side in the opening minutes and United's key danger was Alex Dawson but every time he challenged I had the better of him. Every time he jumped for the ball I would jump higher and catch it. There were no problems. Then it all changed. We both went up and his only chance of beating me was to punch the ball with his fist! He did that and amazingly the referee gave United the goal. I could not believe it, and afterwards Dawson admitted what he had done – I still have the newspaper cutting! – but it was too late, and United went on to win the match.

When Bert's City career neared its end did you feel your time had arrived?

Unfortunately not. I made a big mistake waiting all those years because, despite the promise and the positive coverage at the start of my career, I had stagnated to some extent in the reserves. It was great being number two to Bert, but I now realise I should have moved on earlier. I would never advise a young boy to wait to fill anybody's shoes now. You do need first team football if you want to develop. I never achieved my full potential.

I was frustrated when Harry Dowd's opportunities came but, fortunately, Ken Barnes was now the manager at Wrexham and he asked me to go there. I was at last a true first team footballer.

A couple of years later Bert was manager at Stockport County and he asked me to go there. We won promotion and I started to do a bit of coaching – I coached Ken Mulhearn who became City's keeper.

Is that when you started moving into coaching?

In 1969 I moved to Altrincham as a player and started coaching there, then a year later I moved back to Stockport as Chief Coach. In 1973 I got the chance to come back to City and work with the Youth team. It was then that we tried to create a Busby style youth dynasty at Maine Road. We figured that if we could find good lads, coach them correctly, and give them the right opportunities we'd be able to keep the Club progressing.

During the 1970s with Harry Godwin, Ken Barnes, and all the other members of City's backroom staff, you helped bring City success during a golden period for youth football at City. How did it compare to your own playing career?

I loved playing of course, but I believe my biggest contribution to football came after my own playing days were over. The development of the Youth set up during this time saw Ken Barnes, myself and the others give the Club much more than the occasional victory. Some of our players were the backbone of the League side in the seventies and eighties. It was a highly productive time for youth at City with two FA Youth Cup finals (1979 & 1980) and the Club's first Central League title.

Clive Wilson was a very skilful player, but I suppose I was most pleased for Kenny Clements. Initially nobody rated him and he had to go on the groundstaff. We kept throwing him into practice matches and eventually Ian McFarlane recognised his ability and his career blossomed.

Gary Owen was the most enthusiastic player I ever had, while Alex Williams was another nice young man who developed well.

Once John Bond arrived as manager, the youth emphasis changed and you found yourself moving on. How do you view the period that followed?

It was a great period for me personally because I went coaching in Iceland and gained a great deal of experience but also developed further as a person. I was in charge of Akranes – Arni Arason's team before City – and then IB Vestmann in 1982. At Vestmann we managed to get into Europe two years running.

I returned to England in 1984 and worked for

Ron Saunders at Birmingham – I know Ron has his City critics but I always got on well with him, and was delighted when he gave me the opportunity he did. At Birmingham I coached Tony Coton and, of course, David Seaman was also there then.

You eventually returned to City as Sports Development Officer and later managed the Platt Lane Complex. Was this another period of personal development for you?

Definitely. Every period of life teaches you something and I found that the experience away from City helped me, but I also found I gained a great deal at Platt Lane. As a player I think I always knew that I wasn't destined to be a great player, but I always tried to do things in a 'great way'. I wanted to ensure my approach was right and I think my spells coaching at Maine Road and Platt Lane were my major contribution to this Club.

I still watch City of course, and I also love the involvement with the Former Players' Association. I enjoy helping people and I do love attending functions and so on. Most of all though retirement allows me to look back and consider how my life has progressed so far. Like everybody else I've suffered some major tragedies and problems over the years and, at times, these were extremely hard to face, however I now look back and realise that all of this has helped shape my life and personality.

I am a great believer in fate and I do think that everything happens for a reason, so I'm not one to feel bitter. I've enjoyed my footballing life, and am delighted with every aspect of it. I particularly loved coaching City's youngsters, but I have to say that I am happier today than I have ever been.

CITY IN EUROPE

1977-78

Competition: UEFA Cup

Reason For Qualification:
Runners-up in the League (one point behind
champions Liverpool)

Manager: Tony Book

14th September 1977
Round 1 Leg 1
Attendance: 33,695

City 2-2 Widzew Lodz

City Goalscorers: Barnes, Channon
City: Corrigan; Clements, Donachie, Owen,
Watson, Booth, Barnes, Channon, Kidd,
Hartford, Keegan (Royle)

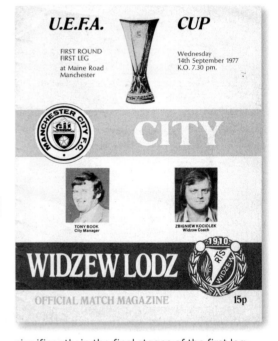

This was City's first meeting with Polish
opposition in the UEFA Cup and it was also
Widzew's first season in European competition.
Prior to the match manager Tony Book –
captain when City beat Gornik in 1970 – told
the media he wanted a three goal lead to take
into the second leg. For most of the match
it looked as if the Blues would have a decent
cushion as they led 2-0 with only ten minutes
remaining.

City seemed in total control. The goals had
come from Peter Barnes and Mike Channon,
and it looked as if the Blues were already well
on their way to the next round. City fans sat
in the Platt Lane Stand laughed and joked
with a small band of Widzew followers who
had found seats at the back of the stand
and, despite the scoreline, had been singing
throughout the game.

Unfortunately, the atmosphere changed

significantly in the final stages of the first leg.
Dennis Tueart, a spectator on the night due to
hamstring problems, later admitted: "We were
2-0 up with ten minutes to go and then Boniek
scored from a penalty and a free kick. At 2-0
with ten or fifteen minutes to go we were
cruising... justifiably 2-0 up. Then the free kick.
He scored direct from it and then got a penalty
when one of their guys dived. Suddenly it's
2-2."

Polish international Boniek's goals changed
everything. A fan from the North Stand ran
on the pitch and attacked the Widzew scorer
and the game also saw the sending off of Willie
Donachie.

UEFA fined the Blues £400. A nineteen year
old supporter – whose name and address

details appeared in the match programme - was found guilty of using threatening, abusive and insulting behaviour, and was fined £100. The club named and shamed him and also banned him from Maine Road, but City were also instructed to erect fencing behind both goals (fencing already existed in front of the Kippax terracing). Initially, the club in consultation with the police and local authority erected the fencing for only high profile fixtures, but as time went by the fences became a permanent barrier between the players and the fans.

When the supporter was found guilty City were keen to publicise the event, hoping it would act as a deterrent. Bernard Halford said at the time: "We trust that our supporters will take notice of this case, what it has resulted in for the individual and the club, and realise that at all times it has got to be important to uphold the very good name which Manchester City have got.

"Believe me, we are totally aware of the great effort made by the fans to support City and we are delighted with the numbers who turn up on the Kippax and follow the team away from home. But we have to make every effort to reduce trouble, provocation and make the ground a place where any person is proud to come. I have been asked to implore the City fans to cut out the abusive language. It is doing no good for the club and is often at the root of troubles by its very provocative nature. We can do without it and if the fans responsible feel anything for the club they claim so strongly to support, then they will listen to this appeal."

When I interviewed Peter Swales in 1994 he

Opening goalscorer Peter Barnes (on ground) watches anxiously as the ball heads goalwards.

admitted that this was not a particular issue at City: "Putting the fences up was a national thing. City were no worse than many, many grounds in the country, but it was the age. It was the hooligan age which finished up with us being out of Europe for several seasons. I think we were forced to put the fences up at Maine Road when somebody came on to the pitch when we played Widzew Lodz in the first leg of a UEFA match. But you know that was the age."

28th September 1977
Round 1 Leg 2
Attendance: 40,000

Widzew Lodz 0-0 City

(City lost on away-goals rule)
City: Corrigan; Doyle (Clements), Power, Owen, Watson, Booth, Barnes, Kidd, Royle, Hartford, Tueart

The return leg was always going to be difficult after City surrendered a two goal lead in the first. Dennis Tueart felt this was a miserable European game for the Blues: "It was an afternoon kick off and the pitch was awful, rock hard. It was just one of those games. Nil-nil and they were happy because they were through. It was that European knowledge that let us down. All we needed to say was 'let's not be silly'. 1-0 in a lot of instances like that is enough. We missed a couple of chances and it ended nil-nil. Out again, another bit of inexperience showing through."

Widzew went through on the away goals rule. Joe Royle felt he was made the scapegoat: "This is one European game that I was probably never forgiven for. I wasn't even due

to be playing in the game, although I was in the squad, because Mike Channon had signed. The day before the game Channon pulled out with an hamstring, and I was told I was playing. So I was going to be thrown into it really. I wasn't due to be anywhere near ready.

"In the game I chased the ball down, challenged the goalkeeper, and the ball dropped. Whilst I was waiting for it to drop and then take it into the empty net, I lost it. I should have volleyed it first time. I was always blamed for that. It was City's way. The fact that we'd lost a 2-0 lead at home was the real reason we went out, but I know what they used to say.

"The players used to joke about it - Asa would say to me, 'what's it like to cost the club a quarter of a million pounds?' It was immaterial really. I knew I was on my way out of the club anyway. I knew that when Mike Channon was signed. I was probably the first of that great side to go."

City went out of the competition on the away goals rule. Tony Book was bitterly disappointed: "It was galling to go out at the first stage against a team that, on our normal form, we should have taken apart. We called the tune for the majority of the match, but we did not break them down. We could point to bad luck, losing striker Mike Channon with injury on the day before the match in Poland; then losing skipper Mike Doyle with an ankle injury in the first half. But we should never have put ourselves in a position where we needed to win in the away leg."

Widzew faced ultimate UEFA Cup winners PSV Eindhoven in the next round.

The Football Season Daily Reminder
December

1st December 1970

1969 FA Cup winning 'keeper Harry Dowd joined Oldham Athletic.

2nd December 1929

Goalkeeper Ronnie Powell was born in Knighton. Powell was one of a number of 'keepers on City's book around the time of Frank Swift's retirement and the early years of Bert Trautmann's career.

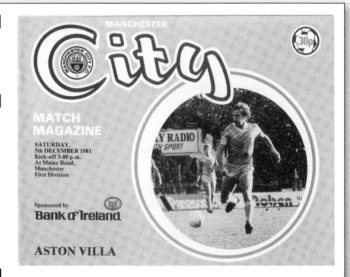

MANCHESTER City
MATCH MAGAZINE
SATURDAY, 5th DECEMBER 1981
Kick-off 3·00 p.m.
At Maine Road,
Manchester
First Division
Sponsored by
Bank of Ireland
ASTON VILLA

3rd December 1951

John Burridge was born. 43 years and 147 days later he appeared for City's first team and became the oldest player to appear in the Premier League.

4th December 2005

Goals from Andy Cole (2), Trevor Sinclair, Joey Barton and Darius Vassell helped Stuart Pearce's City to a 5-2 victory at Charlton Athletic.

5th December 1981

A crowd of 32,487 witnessed a Dennis Tueart goal to give City victory over Aston Villa at Maine Road. Tommy Caton had returned to the side that day following injury against Swansea two weeks earlier.

6th December 2004

Bradley Wright-Phillips marked his first League appearance with an 80th minute goal against Middlesbrough.

7th December 1957 °

Ken Barnes netted three penalties as City defeated Everton 6-2 at Maine Road. The other goals came from McAdams (2) and Hayes.

8th December 1993

Brian Horton's Blues defeated Everton 1-0 with a goal from Carl Griffiths.

9th December 1967

A famous meeting between City and Tottenham ended 4-1 to the Blues. This Maine Road match became known as the 'Ballet on Ice' and convinced *Match Of The Day* viewers of City's Championship credentials.

10th December 1932

Two goals from Fred Tilson and one from Sam Cowan gave the Blues a

THINGS YCU NEVER SEE

The cause of all the excitement at Maine Road this afternoon. One of the staff blows up the ball in preparation for the City v. Portsmouth match.

Blues to Wembley for the inaugural Full Members' Cup Final. City's scorers at Maine Road were David Phillips and Jim Melrose before a crowd of 10,180.

12th December 1970

A hat-trick from Francis Lee, together with a goal from Mike Doyle, gave City a comfortable 4-1 victory over United before an Old Trafford crowd of 52,636. That victory meant City had won five and only dropped four points in eight consecutive League derby meetings with the Reds.

13th December 1986

Imre Varadi scored twice as West Ham were defeated 3-1. David White scored the other City goal.

14th December 1989

Former Everton defender Alan Harper joined his old boss Howard Kendall at Maine Road.

15th December 1956

The first City League game at Maine Road filmed by the BBC ended in a 3-2 victory by Wolves. The match was noteworthy for the fact it was also Bert Trautmann's first League game back after his devastating injury in the 1956 FAC final.

Division One 3-1 victory over Portsmouth at Maine Road. A crowd of 22,312 watched this match. Pre-match one newspaper focused on the 'cause of all the excitement' – the ball being pumped up.

11th December 1985

A 2-0 victory (3-2 on aggregate) by Billy McNeill's City over Brian Horton's Hull sent the

17th December 2005

Birmingham City suffered a 4-1 Premiership defeat

before 41,343 at the City Of Manchester Stadium.

18th December 2004

Joey Barton scored in the 52nd minute to give City a 1-0 win at Bolton.

19th December 1994

German Maurizio Gaudino started his loan spell from Eintracht Frankfurt at Maine Road.

20th December 1924

Future City captain Sam Cowan made his debut in the 2-2 draw with Birmingham City.

21st December 1939

City midfielder Roy Cheetham was born.

22nd December 1993

Midfielder David Carlyle Rocastle joined City from Leeds United.

23rd December 1942

Future City player and manager John Benson was born at Arbroath on this day.

24th December 1959

Kilmarnock paid City £6,388 for the services of Andy Kerr.

25th December 1896

City played their first competitive Christmas Day fixture. The game, staged within sight of where the City Of Manchester Stadium now stands, was a derby match with Newton Heath (United). It was played at Bank Street, Clayton (behind the Velodrome and earmarked for development as a BMX track in 2009).

26th December 1989

Clive Allen scored the only goal of the win over Norwich. This was Howard Kendall's first home match as City manager. Ian Bishop's first spell as a City player came to an end in this game. Together with Trevor Morley he was viewed as surplus to requirements by the new manager. The transfer was not a popular one and fans vented their feelings throughout the 1-0 victory over Norwich.

27th December 1938

City defeated Tranmere 5-2 before 43,894 in Division Two. The previous

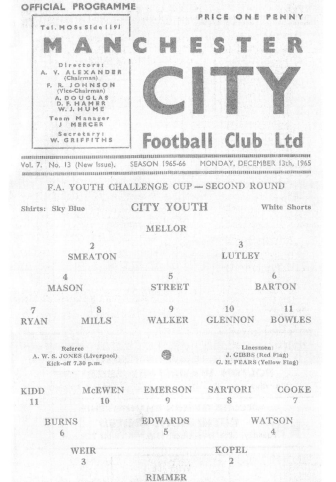

OFFICIAL PROGRAMME

PRICE ONE PENNY

Tel. MOSs Side 1191

Directors:
A. V. ALEXANDER (Chairman)
F. R. JOHNSON (Vice-Chairman)
A. DOUGLAS
D. F. HAMER
W. J. HUME
Team Manager
J. MERCER
Secretary:
W. GRIFFITHS

MANCHESTER CITY Football Club Ltd

Vol. 7. No. 13 (New Issue).   SEASON 1965-66   MONDAY, DECEMBER 13th, 1965

F.A. YOUTH CHALLENGE CUP — SECOND ROUND

Shirts: Sky Blue   CITY YOUTH   White Shorts

MELLOR

2 SMEATON   3 LUTLEY

4 MASON   5 STREET   6 BARTON

7 RYAN   8 MILLS   9 WALKER   10 GLENNON   11 BOWLES

Referee
A. W. S. JONES (Liverpool)
Kick-off 7.30 p.m.

Linesmen:
J. GIBBS (Red Flag)
G. H. PEARS (Yellow Flag)

KIDD 11   McEWEN 10   EMERSON 9   SARTORI 8   COOKE 7

BURNS 6   EDWARDS 5   WATSON 4

WEIR 3   KOPEL 2

RIMMER

Shirts: Red   MANCHESTER U. YOUTH   White Shorts

The teams are subject to alteration

day City had annihilated the same side 9-3 at Prenton Park.

28th December 1992

A goal from Niall Quinn ensured a 1-1 draw at Anfield for Peter Reid's City. Immediately after scoring Quinn, along with David White and Ricky Holden, was mobbed by jubilant fans behind the goal (below).

29th December 2001

A Paulo Wanchope hat trick helped City to a 5-1 victory over Burnley. The game, watched by a capacity 34,350, came during the Division One Championship winning season.

30th December 1996

Frank Clark became City manager.

31st December 2005

The last game of 2005 ended in a goalless draw at Middlesbrough for Stuart Pearce's side.

CITY'S NUMBER ONE

THE PROFILES

40 – HARRY DOWD

Harry Dowd joined the Blues as an amateur in 1958 before turning professional in 1960. He managed to achieve what no other 'keeper had achieved and replaced the great Bert Trautmann as City's number one and, apart from occasional spells out of the side, he remained first choice for most of his time at Maine Road.

During the 1965-66 season Dowd appeared in 38 of the 42 League games and was a strong defensive presence as City powered their way to the Second Division title and he was City's first choice as the Blues started their Division One campaign in 1966-67.

He was replaced for part of the 1966-67 season by Alan Ogley, and then he lost his place to Ken Mulhearn in September 1967. This meant Dowd only managed seven appearances during the 1967-8 Championship season, however he did find his way back into the side after Mulhearn was dropped following the defeat by Fenerbahce in the European Cup. He kept his place for most of the season and played in each of City's seven FA cup ties of the season, including the 1969 final.

Prior to the 1969 FA Cup final Malcolm Allison described him as: "completely fearless. Completely unaffected by nerves."

Dowd did seem unaffected by the hyperbole and pressure placed around the Club during this period and as a result his performances were steady. After victory at Wembley in 1969 he went on loan to Stoke, then joined Oldham in December 1970.

Earlier in his career he had managed to get on

the scoresheet during a game with Bury on 8th February 1964. He had broken his finger and was moved to centre-forward while Matt Gray went in nets, and managed to score City's equaliser from a rebound – Derek Kevan had hit the bar. Incidentally, this was the game in which Colin Bell made his League debut for Bury and had scored the opening goal.

Today, when supporters talk fondly of the late 1960s the name of Harry Dowd is remembered affectionately. Joe Corrigan went on to become by far the more successful 'keeper, however Corrigan is perceived more as a 1970s/early 80s 'keeper while Dowd is firmly viewed as City's number one during the great Mercer-Allison years even though the goalkeeping honours were ultimately shared between Mulhearn, Corrigan, Dowd and Ogley.

After City Dowd made 121 League appearances for Oldham, including 20 appearances during their 1973-74 Division Three Championship winning season.

Appearances: League: 181 (1 goal) FAC: 22 League Cup: 16

41 – ALAN OGLEY

It was accepted that Bert Trautmann could not go on for ever, even though all fans and City staff dreaded the day his career would come to an end, and so from the start of the 1960s the City management were pro-actively looking for potential replacements. The Blues still remembered the pain the Club had gone through at the time of Frank Swift's retirement and, although Harry Dowd and Steve Fleet were on the Club's books, it was felt more cover was needed. City could not afford to be reactive this time.

Alan Ogley, a former England Boys player, signed in July 1963 and with Dowd becoming City's first team regular that season Ogley became the Blues'

Central League 'keeper. Trautmann was still with the Club but, when Dowd broke his finger against Bury in February 1964, Ogley was promoted to the first team.

His debut was a 4-3 thriller at Charlton – another debutant Ronnie Frost scored while Derek Kevan scored for both City and Charlton! – and by the end of the season he had appeared in seven League games.

During the frustrating 1964-65 season, Ogley appeared in exactly half the League games with his longest run of consecutive games coming between October and December 1964 – ten games.

The following summer Joe Mercer arrived as manager and Harry Dowd was given the new manager's support. Ogley was clearly the second choice 'keeper and managed only four League appearances as the Blues won the Second Division title – only one of his four games ended in defeat however.

The situation changed significantly in Division One the following season and, although Dowd started the season as first choice, Ogley had a run of 17 consecutive League games from December through to April. He also started the 1967-68 season as first choice but after one two games – a draw and a 3-2 defeat – he was replaced by Dowd.

In September 1967 Ogley was transferred to Stockport as part of the negotiations that ultimately brought Ken Mulhearn to Maine Road. It was a good move for both men and Ogley went on to appear in 240 League games for County. A move to Darlington came in 1975 and Ogley made 80 League appearances there.

Appearances: League: 51 FAC: 5 League Cup: 1

42 – KEN MULHEARN

Ken Mulhearn was a month short of his 22nd birthday when he arrived at City on 21st September 1967 from Stockport County. Earlier he had been on Everton's books but the Merseyside club were blessed with several talented 'keepers and so the young

Ken Mulhearn behind Tony Book (above) at the League Championship trophy presentation in 1968 and (below) with Joe Corrigan.

Mulhearn appeared as an outfield player at times for Everton's youngsters.

At County Mulhearn impressed, and City were so keen to sign him that they initially offered £12,000 plus Alan Ogley and Chris Jones. Nine days after signing Mulhearn made his debut against Manchester United – Dowd had dislocated a finger forcing the unexpected promotion of Mulhearn.

It is now part of City folklore that Mulhearn was locked in a cupboard by Malcolm Allison pre-match. Mulhearn: "I turned up ridiculously early – it must have been an hour and a half before any of the other players. Malcolm Allison took one look at me and locked me in the medical room! He obviously saw how white faced I was. I must have been the most nervous person

ever to appear at a football ground, so he just locked me up out of the way until the rest of the team reported and were getting changed. There were something like 63,000 at the game, and not many days earlier I'd been playing for Stockport in front of a few thousand. The noise and the atmosphere were unbelievable, the first time I'd sampled anything like it."

Despite suffering a 2-1 defeat, Mulhearn retained his place for the rest of the Championship winning season. He thoroughly deserved his medal.

The following season Mulhearn appeared in the opening eleven League games and seemed destined to remain City's first choice when fate played its hand. The Blues lost their first European Cup tie 2-1 on aggregate and Malcolm Allison was highly critical of Mulhearn. The 'keeper was dropped and, apart from an appearance in the ECWC second round second leg against Lierse in November 1969, he never had a chance to impress in the first team again. Nevertheless, Mulhearn remains the only 'keeper to have played in the European Cup while with City.

In March 1971 he joined Shrewsbury Town where he made 370 League appearances and then in August 1980 he signed for Crewe. In retirement he became a licensee and later emigrated to the States.

Appearances: League: 50 FAC: 5 League Cup: 3 Euro: 3

43 – JOE CORRIGAN

Four years after Joe Corrigan joined City as an amateur he was the Blues' number one as they won the European Cup Winners' Cup in Vienna. The 21 year old was also goalkeeper for the League Cup success that season, however that success perhaps disguises the fact that it was actually several years before Corrigan was recognised as a truly great goalkeeper. Despite strong support from Malcolm Allison in the late 1960s, Corrigan was not seen by all as a long term goalkeeping solution.

Once Allison left the Blues in March 1973, it was clear moves would be made to find a replacement and in October 1973 – six months after Allison had left Maine Road - the Blues signed expensive Scottish 'keeper Keith MacRae. Corrigan's City career appeared over, however he fought hard to get back into the side.

Inevitably, 6ft 4.5 inch Corrigan managed to return to the side and the mid to late seventies saw his career quickly develop. In 1976 he gained international honours when he played in the 3-2 defeat of Italy, and he went on to play nine games for England. He was on the losing side only once (1981 V Scotland), and was only kept out of the side at other times because of the strength of competition. As well as Corrigan, England were blessed with quality 'keepers such as Ray Clemence and Peter Shilton, while Phil Parkes was also another contender for the number one shirt. Had Corrigan been a player in the years that followed the creation of the Premier League, instead of the Seventies & Eighties, it is clear he would have been England's number one on a regular basis.

Corrigan was a true City hero and seemed typical of the type of committed, hard-working player the supporters wanted. The fans loved him and his regular appearances at supporter events and at Junior Blues meetings – he was a significant figure behind the development of the organisation – made him a well loved and popular player.

Throughout the late 70s and early 80s as City strove to find success both at home and in Europe Corrigan was probably the most consistent of all the squad and, as with Trautmann before him, many games were won simply because of the 'keeper's determined performances.

In 1981, when City played in the 100th FA Cup final, Corrigan was voted man of the final. It was an award he thoroughly deserved.

He remained with the Blues until March 1983 when he moved to Seattle Sounders. He later had spells with Brighton, Norwich and Stoke, and also became goalkeeping coach at Liverpool (where he was presented with an official UEFA Cup winner's medal for his role as goalkeeping coach), Stockport and a variety of other clubs.

Corrigan is unquestionably one of England's greatest post-war 'keepers, and will always remain a true Blue hero. In 2004 he became the first player to be inducted into the Manchester City Hall of Fame, and then during 2005-06 the City magazine held a poll to find the Club's greatest 'keeper. Inevitably, the age of the magazine's readers had a bearing but it is significant that Corrigan won the poll. In historical terms the names of Swift and Trautmann may always be ahead of him, however in terms of heroes from the modern era, Corrigan is clearly a major figure. By the end of 2009 he remained the most decorated City 'keeper with medals for winning the ECWC and two League Cups plus a finalist's medals for the FA Cup. He had also made more European appearances with City than any other player.

Appearances: League: 476 FAC: 37 League Cup: 52 Euro: 27

The Joe Corrigan Interview

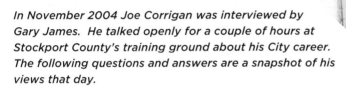

In November 2004 Joe Corrigan was interviewed by Gary James. He talked openly for a couple of hours at Stockport County's training ground about his City career. The following questions and answers are a snapshot of his views that day.

Let's start with your school days. I believe you went to a rugby playing school?

I went to Sale Grammar School and there was no football at all. I played rugby union for the school and for Cheshire, and I guess that helped my ball control, catching ability etc. Despite this, I always wanted to be a 'keeper and I played football at any opportunity really. When I started as an apprentice at AEI in Trafford Park the chance came to play for the works side and I played at centre-half. I had no choice about that – I wanted to play 'keeper. I guess my size made me a defender.

Then one day I had to go in nets at half time and I suppose I must have looked all right because I was encouraged to go for a trial. Both City and United were contacted, and a reply came from Maine Road within a fortnight. After the trial Harry Godwin, City's Chief Scout, asked me to sign and I joined a youth set up that included Tommy Booth and Ray Hatton – Boxer Ricky Hatton's dad.

United offered me a trial as well, but once City showed the interest they did I turned them down. I wanted to be loyal and City had faith in me. That mattered a great deal.

You mentioned you'd always wanted to be a 'keeper, who were your early heroes?

There were two – Harry Gregg and Bert Trautmann. I was fortunate enough to go on loan to Shrewsbury when Gregg was there and he taught me so much. He really helped. Trautmann of course was a phenomenal 'keeper and a wonderful man. Being a City legend he was the type of 'keeper I aspired to. He offered me good advice as well.

I remember one day after West Ham had beaten us 5-1 – it was Jimmy Greaves' debut (21/3/70) – I felt awful. It was my first proper season and I felt I'd ruined my chance. This was the game when my clearance went straight to Ronnie Boyce and he sent it straight back over my head. When something like that happens, being a goalkeeper is the loneliest job in the world.

Anyway, I was told that Bert was at the game. He took me to one side and told me not to worry about that result or that goal. He pointed out that these things can happen to any 'keeper and that he'd had some awful individual moments. I felt much better after that and, I guess, because he had said it, it meant more than if the manager or anyone else had said it. Bert had been one of football's greatest 'keepers and so he knew more than most about how I was feeling. Mind you, it didn't stop the BBC showing the goal whenever they had the opportunity!

One of my strongest early City memories is of you watching Bert play in Johnny Hart's testimonial in 1974. How did that feel?

Bert was such a great player that I thought it'd be good to crouch on the touchline and just watch. Even at that age – he must have been 51 - he was fit and agile and someone you could learn from. The only problem was that I had to tell him he was coming off! I went over to him and a bloke in the stand shouted, "leave him in nets, he's still better than you!"

Thinking about your early City days, you made a couple of League Cup appearances in 1967/8 and then 1969/70 saw you make your League debut. You made 34 League appearances and also played in the ECWC Cup run. Did winning the ECWC make you feel as if you'd 'made it' as a player?

Never! I never felt that. Even when I was playing for England I didn't take anything for granted. Playing in the ECWC final was awesome. It was a terribly wet night and the crowd was low, but that didn't detract from the importance at all. To play in such a great side and at that level is a tremendous feeling but you have to keep your feet on the ground. I'm glad I did, because it wasn't long before it looked as if my City career was over.

You remained first choice for most of the period up to the signing of Keith MacRae in October 1973, did his arrival feel like the end for you?

Definitely! They paid an incredible amount – I think it was a world record fee for a 'keeper – so you know that he has to be first choice. You don't pay that and leave him in the reserves. Plus he was a great 'keeper. No question.

I was on my way out and this was a very difficult time. The Club was also going through a few managerial changes, so it wasn't easy. Then in 1975 Keith was injured shortly before the transfer deadline. I thought I'd get back in, but I bought the *Evening News* and saw photos and names of

a whole host of 'keepers that the Club were supposed to be interested in. It seemed to me at the time that anybody but Corrigan would do. This was a tormenting time. I couldn't bear it. Every night it was the same.

Fortunately for me transfer day came and went and no one was bought. I don't know if time ran out or what, but I know I was relieved.

You got back into the side and retained your place when MacRae was fit. What was the turning point?

I'd been working hard when I was in the Reserves. I'd tried to develop and I was determined not to lose whatever opportunity came my way. Having said that, we had mixed results and I was worried. Then we played at Wolves and they were all over us. I remember Dougan and Richards

both came up for a cross and I was whacked. The ball ended up in the net and I felt awful. Then the ref blew for a foul on me and from that moment on the luck was on my side. I truly believe that a lot of football is about luck and opportunity and that day everything switched to my favour. We beat Chelsea and Burnley in the weeks that followed and I only missed 1 League game in the following 5 seasons.

You became a major hero over those seasons, how do you think the fans treated you throughout your City career?

There were two definite spells. The early years when received a lot of criticism – I accept that because if you pay your money you are entitled to say what you think, but it was difficult to take at times. Then there were the later years when I had matured and developed, and the fans gave me incredible support. I loved going to events like the Junior Blues and meeting real fans. I think we had it drummed into us when we first arrived at the Club by Joe Mercer that supporters are the most important people – they pay your wages and you must never forget that! Once the Junior Blues were created it was stressed that these children would in the future pay your wages. They

are not simply here for a party, they are here because you are an important part of their lives. Every player should always make the effort.

I had it drummed into me by Mercer that you should visit hospitals and kids' homes and the like. It's all great PR for the Club and the player. Actually, when I was playing in the States at Seattle a local policeman was shot. I was appalled and told the team I was going to see him in hospital. They all thought I was out of my mind. "Why do it? What is he to you?" I went to see him, invited him to a game, and he loved it, but I was stunned to find that I made the news. The headlines read "Do Gooder Joe Corrigan" – they made out I was a saint, but all I was doing was the PR that was the norm at City.

Thinking of fans, Helen Turner (the lady with the bell) must hold special memories for you?

She always sat behind me in the North Stand and before every game she would give me a sprig of heather for good luck. At away games she wasn't always near me, so sometimes it was difficult for her to get the heather to me. If I hadn't received it by kick off time I'd be worried. Partly I'd wonder if she was all right, but I also used to worry about my luck. If ever we lost and I'd not seen Helen I'd believe that was the reason. She's a marvellous, devoted fan, and I know she's done a tremendous amount of work for good causes (Helen passed away in 2005, after this interview).

Your career spanned several managerial reigns, is there one manager who stands out as the best for you?

Because the goalkeeper's role is so specialised, I gained most from other goalies such as Trautmann and Gregg, but Joe Mercer was the greatest City manager of all time. He was such a warm, nice man. He knew how to tell you off as well, of course, but his enthusiasm and love of football was clear. Malcolm Allison, as coach, was tremendous. He was doing stuff in 1969 that coaches are only just introducing now and often they claim it's a new idea! He tried to make sure the 'keepers received their own coaching and specialist time, and when Tony Book became manager he tried to ensure this developed further. Coaches Bill Taylor and Ian McFarlane worked hard with me and

I used to come in on the morning of a game to do additional training. The view was that I would get used to the actual conditions of the day and this definitely worked.

If we were playing away I'd train in the hotel grounds, or in a park. On the morning of the 1981 FA Cup final I was training in a public park.

Thinking of the 1981 final, one of my key memories is of you immediately going over to Tommy Hutchison when he scored the own goal. You lifted him up, patted him on the back and whispered something to him. What encouragement did you give?

My view was that we still had a few minutes left. We'd still been on top for most of the game. We could still win. I also knew that what had happened to him could have happened to any one of us. So I just told him to "get up, get on with it. It's only 1-1 and we are still going to win!" He was devastated to be fair, but we did almost win it in the dying minutes. Personally, I believe the game should have been played to a conclusion on that night. The FA Cup is all about the Saturday and I know we would have won had it gone to a conclusion. I

never liked facing penalties – I think I only saved two – but that night we'd have won. No question. The Saturday was our day, after that it all switched.

Tottenham had no travelling to do; their fans could buy tickets from either Spurs or directly from Wembley's allocation; and our fans were simply outnumbered in the replay even though we were by far a better supported team.

Despite our eventual defeat, you were made 'man of the final' for your performance. That must have felt like a great achievement.

Obviously, it does mean a lot to me, but I'd rather have won the final. After the second match I was presented with it by the Spurs manager Keith Burkenshaw. I remember thanking him and then saying something like "Good luck in Europe next season" and at that very moment it hit home to me what had happened. I suddenly realised that we'd lost and that we wouldn't be playing in Europe. I was devastated. It was an awful feeling. I missed out in another way because the game went to a replay. England were playing Brazil at Wembley on the Wednesday after the final and, although there was nothing official, I understand I was due to play, but the replay (played the following night) meant I couldn't play.

You played during many great seasons, what were your own highlights?

There were two great sides – the one I joined in the 60s that had already achieved so much and the mid to late 70s. Both sides were tremendous and the players really knew how to entertain. Colin Bell was a truly great player and I'm certain he would have gone on to captain England had it not been for that horrific injury. Losing him was the biggest blow this club has had to face. He bridged the two great sides and had he been fully fit he would have helped that late 70s side achieve the League title. People often forget how good that late 70s side was – Dave Watson, Dennis Tueart, Joe Royle, Willie Donachie and the rest.

The John Bond transformation was great as well. Steve Mackenzie's goal in the 81 replay has to be one of the greatest Cup Final goals of all time. The problem with that replay was that Hutchison and Gow had given so much in the first game that they must have been drained for the second match. They still did well, but they didn't have enough time to recover in between games. Kevin Reeves was injured early on and that was a major blow – he is one of City's most underrated players. Reeves was a very, very good player.

Let's talk about England. You were unfortunate to play when there were so many great English 'keepers. Do you ever wish you'd played at another time?

No. I enjoyed playing when I did. It was good that there were so many great 'keepers around because that pushed you more. Sadly, for me it meant I'd have to try and reach a level above Shilton, Clemence, Parkes, and Rimmer. If I'd been an outfield player, it may have been easier because with a goalie there is only one place to fill. When I did play for England it meant more than anything else – in football playing for the national side is the highest honour you can have. One of my favourite performances was when I played against Brazil – the best team in the world at the time by a long way

– and we managed a 1-1 draw. I was under pressure the whole time and remember a couple of saves I am particularly proud of.

Did you enjoy being under pressure more than trouble free games?

Sometimes 'trouble-free' games are the worst because you have to be more alert. It would be easy to sit back and focus on other things, but then if you're tested you could fail. I remember one game I had no saves to make at all, but I came off the pitch totally drained. Everyone said 'what's up with you, you've done nothing?' I would much have preferred to be under pressure for 90 minutes.

Eventually you left City. First for Seattle Sounders and later for Brighton, why did you move on?

I think I should have left a little earlier. I love City but it got to the stage where I knew I wasn't really wanted here. The fans were marvellous; the players were great; but maybe it wasn't really my time any more. I was approached by Spurs, shortly after the Cup Final, and then Liverpool after we'd beat them 3-1 (Boxing Day 1981) but both moves were blocked, so that made it clear someone still wanted me, but then when Seattle made their approach in 1983 I was told I could go. Something had changed.

At Seattle I had a great time and the pressures were completely different. It was a wonderful time. Sadly, City were relegated while I was away and I felt awful. It really hit me. I know I wouldn't have changed things – Alex Williams did an excellent job – but I felt the same pain I would have felt had I been here. I worried about the fans. Funnily enough when I was in the States I played a game at New York and I wasn't happy with our performance and tactics and I shouted a bit of abuse at the bench. My own

supporters started booing me and telling me I shouldn't swear at a football match – in my early days at City I was given abuse for being too quiet! It was all so different.

You eventually moved into coaching – something you still do today. Presumably, you enjoy putting something back in to the game.

That day when Bert Trautmann came to offer advice and reassure me in 1969 meant so much to me that I guess I've always felt I should do the same. Bert and the other 'keepers taught me more than other coaches could because they had been there. They had experience what I was experiencing, and I feel that I need to do the same. I've coached all over the UK and, at one point, I was flying to Scotland, driving to Yorkshire and the north-east the next day... every day I was on the road. Then I had ten very enjoyable years at Liverpool, and now there's Stockport and Chester as well. It's great to put something back.

Finally, you were one of the inaugural entrants into City's Hall Of Fame. You received the 3rd highest number of votes after Trautmann and then Bell. How does it feel to still be remembered by fans in this way?

The Hall of Fame is such a wonderful honour. On the night I had no idea. I was interviewed by TV and thought I was making up the numbers but then I was the first one up. I was choked, truly choked, and couldn't get the right words into my head. Can I take this opportunity to pass on my thoughts to Norah Mercer – Joe Mercer was a fantastic man and he made such a big impression on me when I was first starting out. Also, I'd like to thank all the players who have worked with me, and of course the supporters. I was deeply touched by the award.

GOLDEN GOALS

Georgiou Kinkladze

1996 v Southampton

One of the best goals of the modern era saw the brilliant Georgiou Kinkladze at his best. Kinkladze was a major star – some would say City's biggest during the mid 1990s – and livened up many dull days for City fans. This goal was obviously popular with Maine Road regulars but, thanks to television and the game's appearance on Match of the Day, many neutrals recognised the quality of this Golden Goal.

The idea of this 'GOLDEN GOALS' feature is to remember a significant or spectacular goal from yesteryear. The *Big Book Of City's* hope is that modern day supporters will learn more about some of these goals. If you would like to nominate a goal for possible use in a future 'Big Book' then email: **city@manchesterfootball.org** with details of game, goalscorer and date.

Match Stats

Date: 16th March 1996
Score: City 2-1 Southampton
Venue: Maine Road
Scorers: Georgiou Kinkladze (32 & 37 mins), Tisdale (64 mins)
Attendance: 29,550

City Team: Immel, Summerbee, Frontzeck (Hiley), Curle, Symons, Brightwell, Clough, Lomas (Quinn), Rosler, Flitcroft, Kinkladze

Pre-Match

This was City's 31st League game of the season with only seven games remaining. The Blues, under manager Alan Ball, were struggling. A disastrous opening to the season had seen City gather one point from the opening nine matches and supporters were highly critical of Alan Ball, who had replaced Brian Horton during the close season.

November had seen some promise – so much so that Alan Ball was named Manager of the Month – but by March it was clear the Blues needed to grind out a few decent results to avoid relegation. Two sides, QPR and Bolton, were enduring a much worse season and seemed certainties for the drop but City were one of seven other sides fighting to avoid that third relegation space.

Immediately prior to this meeting with Southampton City had managed three draws in four games and there was some optimism that with the skills of Kinkladze and the commitment and quality of players like Uwe Rosler and Niall Quinn safety could be assured. Quinn however had been injured and did not seem to fit with Alan Ball's plans as much as supporters hoped.

The Game

Pre-match Alan Ball described this game as the most important since his arrival at City, and there is no doubt that it was vital the Blues managed a victory over fellow strugglers Southampton if they were to stand any hope of avoiding relegation. Unfortunately, the opening five minutes

or so saw a jittery City performance. Fortunately, Southampton were unable to take advantage and after about ten minutes the Blues had settled.

In the 14th minute, Kinkladze made a brilliant shot from well outside the area which had Southampton 'keeper Dave Beasant totally beaten. Sadly, the powerful shot hit the crossbar just as the majority of fans thought it a certain goal. A minute later Kinkladze set German Michael Frontzeck clear on the left, but the move failed.

City were clearly in control and Beasant made a good save from a Nicky Summerbee effort, while Nigel Clough was also performing well. A goal seemed inevitable, but it wasn't until the 32nd minute that the first one came. Nicky Summerbee sent an accurate ball towards Clough. The former Forest star's follow up shot was far too strong for Beasant and the ball rebounded out. Kinkladze picked it up and sent it straight into an empty net. The goal was later described by journalist Dave Hadfield as: "not the most spectacular goal he will score for City, but one of the most significant."

Five minutes later our featured goal came. Hadfield: "Kinkladze's second goal was both significant and stunning. Taking the ball 30 yards out with no obvious avenues open, he beat Simon Charlton and shimmied around three other baffled Southampton defenders to chip past Beasant."

It sounds simple, but the goal was absolute class. Jon Champion, reporting for the BBC's Match of the Day, declared: "That's mesmeric, that's sublime... that is Georgiou Kinkladze!"

When I set up the Manchester City Experience (museum & stadium tour) in 2003, this goal was the first I selected to be included in a commentary box interactive which allowed visitors to add their own commentary. The idea was that Champion's commentary would be played, alongside footage of the goal, and then visitors could record their version of the commentary before having it played back. Without doubt, despite other significant goals being available, this goal became the most popular goal within the attraction.

Inevitably, Kinkladze continued to impress throughout the rest of the game that day. So much so that Hadfield claimed: "There were times when the Georgian's high level of skill seemed to be contagious, especially when Ian Brightwell's flick to Frontzeck launched a mesmerising attack."

City being City, Southampton were allowed to come back into the game a little and in the 64th minute they scored with only their second chance of the game. Substitute Gordon Watson ran half the length of the field before sending a pass to Paul Tisdale, who then lifted the ball over Eike Immel.

A worrying final twenty minutes or so followed, but City did have a couple of chances. Then in the final minute Southampton's Matthew Robinson netted, but the flag had been raised for offside just before the ball crossed the line. Nevertheless Southampton's Watson wasn't too impressed. So much so that the referee sent him off for arguing.

The game ended in a much needed City win, but the talking point was without doubt the second Kinkladze goal.

Man Of The Match

Inevitably, Kinkladze was acclaimed as the star. As well as the goals, he also contributed with his usual brand of mesmerising skill.

Post Match

The victory placed City five points above Southampton and, more importantly, meant that survival was totally within City's hands. Sadly, a 4-2 defeat at West Ham followed, then a 1-1 draw against bottom club Bolton, and a 3-2 disappointing defeat at home to United meant that all the good work of the Southampton game had been wiped away.

Another defeat at Wimbledon (3-0) on 8th April made the situation bleak, and then 1-0 victories over Sheffield Wednesday and Aston Villa gave the Blues hope for their final match of the season – a home game with Liverpool.

Despite the best efforts of several City players – and even the Liverpool star Ian Rush seemed keen to help the Blues as much as he could (there were rumours he would be joining City if the Blues stayed up) – a 2-2 draw meant City were relegated on goal difference.

Alan Ball later claimed: "Had we escaped it would have been like getting out of Alcatraz." The truth however is that the Kinkladze goal should have inspired the Blues, but ultimately no matter how great the goal or how talented the player, the season became one of struggle.

Elsewhere

City were relegated alongside QPR and Bolton, while United won the League and FA Cup double. Aston Villa won the League Cup. Euro '96 was staged in England with some games, involving Germany, played at Old Trafford. Bert Trautmann acted as Germany's ambassador.

Manchester was rocked by a terrorist bomb that obliterated parts of the Arndale centre, Marks & Spencer's store and other parts of the city centre. Several hundred people were injured in the attack.

CITY TIMELINE

The purpose of *The Big Book Of City* is to provide features on City's history rather than a detailed history of the Blues. However, it's important to understand the development of the Club through time and so over the following pages *The Big Book Of City* provides snapshot material on the Club's history.

1865

■ The building of St. Mark's Church (below), Clowes Street, West Gorton was finished in this year. The church was consecrated by the Bishop of Manchester on 30th November and a few days later Irishman the Rev. Arthur Connell (right) was inducted.

1875

■ The sporting life of St. Mark's became apparent. Newspaper reports show that St. Mark's (West Gorton) Cricket Club played games in the summer of 1875. The earliest known reported game was against The Crown, Newton Heath (played 12th June 1875). Today Manchester United claim their formation (as Newton Heath) year as 1878 when they first started playing sport, but there is no evidence they played football before 1880, so should City claim 1875 as their formation?

1879

■ Rev Arthur Connell's eldest daughter, Anna, suggested forming Working Men's Meetings. She was concerned with violence, including a form of gang warfare known as Scuttling, and domestic issues in the Gorton area and wanted to build community spirit. William Beastow worked hard to help the meetings succeed.

1880

■ St. Mark's (West Gorton) Football Club is known to have played football. The first reported game (though there could have been earlier matches) took place on 13th November

1880 on waste ground near the church, and their opponents were the Baptist Church from Macclesfield (a 2-1 defeat). It is believed the idea of a football team came from William Beastow with support from Thomas Goodbehere, and many of the first players had been members of the St. Mark's Cricket team at either a youth or adult level. The first known goalscorer was James Collinge.

1881

■ After a slight name change 1881 saw West Gorton (St. Mark's) face Newton Heath (LYR) for the first time in November. Newton Heath later reformed as Manchester United.

1882

■ The first home derby match with Newton Heath ended 2-1 to West Gorton on 4th March 1882.

1883

■ West Gorton is believed to have merged with another Gorton based side. According to research by Paul Toovey that side was Belle Vue Rangers.

1884

■ The side reformed as Gorton AFC and the first known kit of black shirts, with a white Maltese Cross, and white shorts was given to the side by founder William Henry Beastow.

1885

■ According to information recorded in the 1930s Gorton ended their first season with the following playing record: Played 16, Won 7, Drawn 2, Lost 7, Goals For 31, Against 21. Match reports and other statistical information available today has failed to identify all games, but evidence exists for the following statistics: Played 11, Won 4, Drawn 2, Lost 5, Goals For 16, Against 14.

1886

■ After their first season at the Bull's Head ground in Reddish, Gorton made a profit of £1 16s 1d at the end of the 1885-86 season.

1887

■ After seven seasons of moves and name changes the club renamed itself Ardwick AFC and took on a more professional outlook. They also identified a permanent home in Ardwick between Hyde Road and Bennett Street. The club's first professional was existing player Jack Hodgetts who was paid 5 shillings per week. To keep the other players happy, the leading first team players were paid a similar amount as travelling expenses. Ardwick's kit was described as royal blue and white stripes. This is the first recorded use of blue by the side.

1888

■ The Ashton Charity Cup game between Ardwick and Hyde ended 8-1 to Ardwick, however the game was ordered to be replayed at Hyde because of the poor condition of the Hyde Road pitch. The replay ended 3-1 to Ardwick but the side were knocked out by Lower Hurst in the semi-final.

ARDWICK v. HYDE.—(Ardwick District Charity Cup, second round).—At Ardwick. Hyde kicked off. Ardwick scored first from the toe of Drinkwater, and from the kick off they took it down and scored again. Then Parker scored for Ardwick, and all the first half Ardwick pressed. On change of ends, with wind in their favour, it was thought that Hyde would press, but it was not so. Parker, Hodgetts, and Callagan scored, and from Manning, at half back, Callagan scored. Then Hyde scored one. McKenzie afterwards scored the eighth for Ardwick, the result being :—
ARDWICK .... 8 goals.
HYDE .... 1 "

1889

■ During the 1888-89 season attendances rocketed as gate money increased from £47 in 1887-88 to £213 the season after. Ardwick played Newton Heath at Belle Vue in a floodlit charity match to raise money for the Hyde Colliery disaster fund. Lawrence Furniss became Club secretary.

1890

■ On 4th October Ardwick defeat Liverpool Stanley 12-0 at Hyde Road in the club's first F.A. Cup match, while another Merseyside club Everton made its first visit to Hyde Road for a friendly. Everton won 3-0 but this was seen as a landmark moment in the growth of the Blues. During this year Ardwick were photographed wearing what appears to be sky blue and white halved shirts. It's not known if this was the Club's regular colours.

1891

■ Ardwick won the Manchester Cup for the first time. They defeated Newton Heath 1-0, with a seventh minute goal from influential captain David Weir. They also reached the final of the Lancashire Junior Cup (losing to Blackpool) and applied to join the Football League, as did Newton Heath. Both Manchester sides were rejected (Ardwick received 4 votes, Newton Heath none) in favour of Stoke and Darwen. Ardwick joined the Football Alliance – an unofficial second division of the League.

1892

■ Ardwick finished seventh out of 12 clubs in the Alliance and won the Manchester Cup for the second year running by defeating powerful League side Bolton 4-1. The Football League was extended with City choosing to apply to join the Second Division. The Blues were accepted.

The defeat of Bolton Wanderers by Ardwick in the Manchester Cup competition probably surprised no one more than Ardwick people themselves. Certainly the eleven have done one or two fine performances during the season, but nothing to lead their most sanguine supporter to believe them capable of defeating such a team as the Wanderers. However, they did so, and, what is more, did it by playing better football than their opponents. This is the second time David Weir's men have won the cup, and the victory will do much to enhance the reputation of the team.

1893

■ Ardwick defeated Bootle 7-0 at Hyde Road on the first day of the new season to put the Club top of the very first Second Division table. Manchester's biggest crowd pullers ended their first League season fifth out of 12. Joshua Parlby replaced Lawrence Furniss as secretary-manager in the summer.

1894

■ After a dismal second League season (they finished 13th out of 15 in Division Two) and financial problems (the players had been forced to resort to fare dodging on trains to get to away games!) the club collapsed. In April Manchester City F.C. was formed by the bulk of the Ardwick committee. They wanted to create a club for all Mancunians to support and that kind of ambition was significant in enabling the reformed club take Ardwick's place in the League. Billy Meredith made his debut against Newcastle on 27th October.

1895

■ The Blues finished ninth in Division Two in their first season as Manchester City. City didn't bother to enter the F.A. Cup in 1894/5 and withdrew from their October 1895 qualifying round game with Oswaldtwistle. Sam Ormerod became secretary-manager in Summer 1895.

1896

▦ The Blues finished second in Division Two, but failed to gain promotion via the Test Matches (similar to play-offs). The Club upset fans by raising admission prices for the first Test Match home game, and supporters boycotted as a result. The lack of atmosphere had a negative impact on the game.

Meredith takes a corner

1897

▦ Defeated 6-0 by Preston in First Round of F.A. Cup in January, the Blues ended the season sixth in Division Two.

1898

▦ City reached the second round of the Cup but were defeated 1-0 at Bolton. They also narrowly missed out on the final year of the Test Matches, finishing 3rd.

1899

▦ City (below) became Second Division champions for the first time and, alongside second placed Glossop North End, became the first side to gain automatic promotion. The Blues lost 3-2 to Small Heath in the first round of the Cup.

■ Billy Meredith (left) became the first City player to score more than 20 League goals in a season. He actually netted 29 from 33 appearances.

■ The First Division One game ended in a 4-3 defeat at Blackburn, while the first Hyde Road Division One match ended 4-0 to the Blues.

1900

■ The first League game of the century was a no score draw at Derby County. The Blues finished their first season in Division One seventh out of 18. They lost 3-0 to Aston Villa in a first round Cup replay.

■ In September 1900 future Prime Minister (and City patron) Arthur Balfour attended Hyde Road.

1901

■ The Blues were defeated in the first round of the Cup (West Bromwich Albion won 1-0) and finished eleventh in Division One.

1902

■ City managed to reach the second round of the Cup (losing to Forest 2-0!), but League form suffered. City were relegated for the first time. Former Celtic player (and founding member of the Glasgow club) Tom Maley became the club's secretary-manager during the close season.

■ Welsh international and key City defender Di Jones gashed his knee in the annual public practice match in August, within a week he was dead. The wound had turned septic.

1903

■ Top scorer was Billy Gillespie with 30 goals – the first time any player scored 30 League goals for the Blues – as City became champions of Division Two for the second time.

1904

■ City (below) won the F.A. Cup beating Bolton 1-0 via a Billy Meredith first half goal at Crystal Palace. The Blues also narrowly missed out on the League & Cup double,

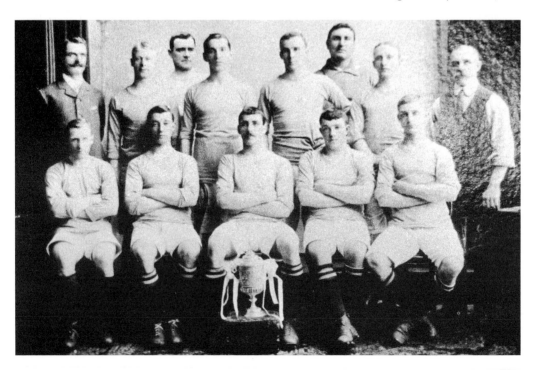

finishing second to Sheffield Wednesday. This was Manchester's highest League position at the time.

1905

■ The Blues finished third (2 points behind champions Newcastle). Aston Villa's Alec Leake accused Billy Meredith of attempting to bribe him to throw the Villa-City match on 29/4/05. Leake also threw dirt at City's Sandy Turnbull who retaliated by sticking 2 fingers up to the Villa man. Turnbull was later dragged into the Villa dressing room and thrown out with cuts and bruises a few minutes later. Inevitably, a full-scale enquiry was ordered, but City were punished, not Villa.

1906

■ City ended the season fifth. The findings of the investigations following the 1905 Villa match resulted in the F.A. identifying financial irregularities at the club. 17 players, including virtually all the first team squad,

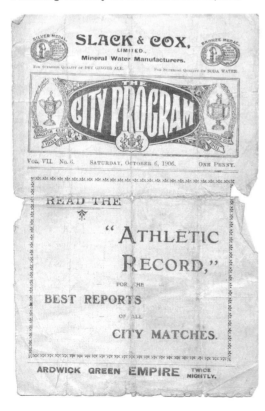

were banned and fined; Directors Allison and Davies were suspended for 7 months; and manager Tom Maley and chairman W. Forrest were banned from English football sine die.

■ When new manager Harry Newbould joined City in July he had only 11 players available. The club was virtually dead. Despite the problems, City won the first Division One Manchester derby 3-0 at Hyde Rd on 1/12/06.

1907

■ Billy Meredith, Herbert Burgess, Sandy Turnbull, and Jimmy Bannister - the key City players forced out of Hyde Road - were transferred to United in December 1906. Most Blues were happy at the time as it was seen as a good way to ensure the players remained in Manchester.

City sawing Chelsea's wooden leg off.

1908

■ City finished third with 'keeper Walter Smith becoming the first City man to be an ever-present in all 44 League and Cup matches.

1909

■ Newbould's City were relegated on goal average. The Blues should have survived but Bradford City, the favourites for the drop, stunned football by defeating a strong Manchester United side 1-0.

1910

■ City became Second Division champions for the third time since 1899. Their record was impressive for the period - 23 victories, 8 draws, and only 7 defeats. Star man was George Dorsett who was top scorer with 13 goals. His brother Joe joined City in August 1910.

■ Major ground improvements at Hyde Road resulted in 3 multi-span roofs being erected. This allowed the Blues to boast they provided cover for over 35,000, and had all 4 sides of the ground covered. The directors were quick to point out that Old Trafford, opened in February 1910, only provided cover for about a quarter of City's figure.

1911

■ Goalkeeper Jim Goodchild signed in December. He stayed with City until August 1927 and was a firm favourite with the fans.

1912

■ United manager Ernest Mangnall (below) – the man responsible for bringing the Reds their first successes and for the move to Old Trafford - announced he was leaving the Reds for the Blues. His final game in charge was the Old Trafford derby, played after he

announced he was leaving. City won 1-0 and the *Umpire* newspaper summed it up nicely: "United speeded their manager rejoicing with 2 points to his new club."

1913

■ City finished sixth, but the biggest story came in the FA Cup when the Hyde Road tie with Sunderland was abandoned after 58 minutes due to crowd control difficulties. Many people were crushed. The official crowd was 41,709 but an estimate of 50,000 seems more believable, particularly as many ticket holders were locked out. Manager Ernest Mangnall was held responsible for the organisation of the day, with the *Daily Dispatch* claiming that he should always 'ensure mounted police are available to control the huge crowds that watch the City club'.

1914

■ City finished thirteenth. War broke out shortly into the 1914-15 season but the decision was taken to continue with the League programme. The Blues encouraged their players to join the armed forces and fight in the Great War. In addition, players and officials agreed to give 5% of their wages to the Prince of Wales' Fund.

1915

■ The Blues ended the 1914-15 season fifth, only three points behind champions Everton.

1916

■ Billy Meredith returned to City as a guest player, making his second debut in the 11/3/16 1-1 draw with Liverpool. A week later he scored his first Blue goal since 1905 as City drew 1-1 at Everton.

■ City won the Lancashire Section of the wartime Football League – which comprised of all the Lancastrian teams of the period plus Stoke - and the Subsidiary Tournament (southern section) which followed.

1917

■ City finished fourth in the Lancashire section and third in the subsidiary tournament.

■ In May Sandy Turnbull, FA Cup winner in 1904, was killed while serving with the Manchester regiment in the trenches. His death is recorded on the monument at Arras.

1918

■ After four seasons of regional wartime football Eli Fletcher had made most wartime appearances for the Blues (133), closely followed by Jim Goodchild (130). United's Billy Meredith had appeared 107 times for City. Top scorer – by a margin of 50 goals – was Horace Barnes with 73 goals from 73 games.

1919

■ City were champions of the wartime regional Subsidiary Tournament, which finished on 26th April 1919.

1920

■ King George V visited Hyde Road (below) for City's 2-1 defeat of Liverpool. It was the first time a reigning monarch had attended a provincial football match. His son, the Duke of York (who also became King), attended a game at Maine Road in 1933, while his granddaughter (Queen Elizabeth II) attended the City Of Manchester Stadium in 2002 for the Commonwealth Games.

1921

■ City finished second to Burnley in Division One and hit the headlines when they brought to an end Burnley's record breaking 30 game unbeaten run. Tommy Browell became City's leading goalscorer for a season with 31 goals from 42 appearances.

1922

■ Plans to build a stadium capable of holding 120,000 at a site near Moss Side were announced. The 16½ acre site, adjacent to a relatively minor street called

CASKET CIGARETTES.

F.B. MAX WOOSNAM

Maine Road, cost £5,500. The builders Robert McAlpine worked with architect Charles Swain to design and build a stadium in two phases. The first phase opened in 1923. The second phase was never completed.

▨ Manager Ernest Mangnall was said to be chiefly responsible for the plan.

1923

▨ Horace Barnes scored the first goal at Maine Road after approximately 68 minutes of the first League match. Sheffield United were defeated 2-1 before a crowd of 58,159.

1924

▨ Billy Meredith returned to City, making his third Blue debut in the F.A. Cup third round at Brighton. The Blues won 5-1 with Meredith claiming one of the goals – one that journalists claimed was fumbled in by the goalkeeper - as his own.

▨ The next round proved the worth of Maine Road with a crowd of 76,166 paying £4,909 to see Meredith & Co. take on Cardiff. The game ended goal-less, but City won the replay, giving Meredith his first City semi-final appearance since 1904. Sadly, a 2-0 defeat by Newcastle ended the possibility of 49 year old Meredith making a fairytale appearance at the two year old Wembley Stadium.

▨ In May the City directors refused to renew Ernest Mangnall's contract. Former Oldham Athletic and Liverpool manager David Ashworth replaced Mangnall in July 1924.

1925

▨ David Ashworth led the Blues to tenth place in 1924/5. Unusually for the period Ashworth had insisted on a 'get-out' clause in his contract with Oldham which allowed him to leave if 'a better post' came along.

1926

▨ City defeated United 6-1 at Old Trafford to record the highest derby victory of all time. In March they beat them again, this time it was 3-0 at Bramall Lane in the F.A. Cup semi-final. Unfortunately Bolton beat the Blues 1-0 in the final at Wembley, and then a week later City were relegated. Ashworth had resigned in November 1925, and

Chairman Albert Alexander took control of team affairs until the last few days of the season. Peter Hodge (left) became the new manager on 26th April 1926 and expected to avoid relegation but sadly this was a typically City season!

1927

▨ City missed promotion by the narrowest goal average margin of all time – City's average was 1.7705; promoted Portsmouth's

was 1.7755. Another goal would have been enough.

1928

■ City won the Second Division championship watched by an average crowd of approximately 37,300. This was the largest average in the entire Football League and the Blues were recognised as one of the game's giants.

1929

■ Tommy Johnson scored 38 goals in 39 League games and remains City's highest goalscorer in a League season.

1930

■ Against the wishes of the supporters, hero Tommy Johnson (left) was sold to Everton for £6,000. City fans boycotted as a result – the average attendance dropped from almost 33,400 in 1929-30 to around 26,800 in 1930-31. During his career he had broken all City's goalscoring records.

1931

■ City finished eighth after a season when the goals seemed to dry up. Brook was top scorer with 16 goals – the worst seasonal highest since 1914.

1932

■ Wilf Wild became manager on 14th March 1932 and went on to be City's longest serving (in terms of years) manager.

1933

■ Everton, with former Maine Road hero Tommy Johnson, defeated City 3-0 in the 1933 Cup final. Both sides wore numbers for the first time (Everton were 1-11, City were 12-22). City wore red shirts.

1934

■ In the FA Cup semi-final City defeated Aston Villa 6-1 (below) – a semi-final goalscoring record. Fred Tilson netted four.

In April City defeated Portsmouth 2-1 to lift the F.A. Cup. Fred Tilson was the star man again as he scored both City's goals.

1935

A Maine Road crowd of 79,491 watched the crunch match with eventual champions Arsenal on 23/2/35. The game ended 1-1 before a crowd that was the League's highest at the time. A couple of months later City finished fourth.

1936

Peter Doherty, proclaimed as the greatest Irish player of all time by other leading Irish stars, including Danny Blanchflower, arrived at Maine Road for £10,000. He made his debut in a 3-1 defeat by Preston and later proved to be one of City's greatest acquisitions.

1937

The Blues won their first League Championship (below). One of the best results of the 1936-7 season was the 2-0 victory over perennial challengers Arsenal

on 10/4/37. A crowd of 76,000 – some 13,000 more than the Manchester derby – enjoyed goals from Toseland and Doherty.

The following August a Manchester Liners ship was named 'Manchester City' in honour of City's success. The Blues also had a train named after them.

1938

Despite reaching the sixth round of the F.A. Cup, League champions City became the first side to win the League one year and be relegated the next.

1939

City ended the 1938-39 season in fifth place in Division Two. Three games into the following season the campaign was abandoned due to the outbreak of war.

1940

Football was restructured for the duration of the war, with regional leagues set up. With many players joining the forces, a system that allowed guest players to appear was introduced.

1941

The Blues finished third in the North Regional League.

1942

The wartime regional leagues became extremely complicated with clubs being allowed to pick how many games they wanted to play post-Christmas, so long as they featured in 18 or more. City only managed 17 in the post-Christmas league as a result of Blackpool withdrawing from a couple of fixtures. This meant that the Blues were not placed despite gathering 19 points from 17 fixtures.

1943

In July, former Blue Irishman Mick Hamill died in tragic and mysterious circumstances.

His body was found in a river amid rumours that he was actively involved in the Irish republican movement.

1944

A hat trick from Les McDowall helped the Blues defeat United 4-1 in the April home derby match.

1945

Despite the end of war in Europe, the Football League could not be resurrected in time for the 1945-46 season. The final season of regional football saw the Blues finish tenth in the Football League North.

1946

The F.A. Cup was resurrected with games played on a two-legged basis. In the fourth round first leg the Blues beat Bradford Park Avenue 3-1, then lost 8-2 at Maine Road in the return – City's record home defeat.

1947

■ City won the Second Division title by four points under manager Sam Cowan, but the season didn't end for City until 14th June – the latest finish the Blues have ever known. Cowan had been appointed on 2nd December 1946 but issues with the City directors connected with his travel arrangements (he lived near Brighton) meant he was dismissed in June 1947, shortly after promotion. He was replaced by Jock Thomson.

1948

■ City's average attendance was 42,725 – the highest average the Club had known at the time and this remained City's highest until 2003-04.

1949

■ Frank Swift retired at the end of the 1948-9 season with thousands of fans journeying to the last game of the season at Huddersfield to say their farewells. Swift joined the official supporters club's main coach for the journey back across the Pennines. Unfortunately Swift's replacement, Alec Thurlow, was taken seriously ill with tuberculosis (he died in 1956 at the age of 34). Eventually, Swift agreed to fill in until the Blues found a suitable replacement.

■ In November former German Prisoner of War Bernhard Trautmann made his debut despite protests from some supporters.

1950

■ City were relegated in 21st place. Manager Jock Thomson had moved on in February and the following summer former player Les McDowall replaced him.

1951

■ Bert Trautmann was City's only ever present as the Blues achieved promotion in second place.

1952

■ City struggled during the final half of their first season back in Division One and they ended the season fifteenth.

1953

■ The Blues avoided relegation by a mere point. In October City beat Hearts 6-3 in the first floodlit match at Maine Road. The estimated cost of using the lights per game was a mere £3.

1954

■ Les McDowall's tactical brain started to see possibilities with a new style of play, later dubbed the Revie Plan, the style basically revolved around a deep lying centre forward. Johnny Williamson had been the deep lying centre forward when the Plan was first tried in the Reserves, while Ken Barnes was acclaimed by many as being the man who actually made the Plan succeed.

1955

■ The Blues finished seventh and reached the Cup Final but injury to Jimmy Meadows meant City were down to ten men for a significant period of the match. Newcastle won the game 3-1, while Don Revie was the Football Writers' player of the year.

1956

■ The Blues finished fourth in Division One. This was followed with a second consecutive trip to Wembley. This time City defeated Birmingham City 3-1 with goals from Joe Hayes, Jack Dyson, and Bobby Johnstone. For the second year running a City man was names the Football Writers' player of the year. This time it was goalkeeper Bert Trautmann.

1957

■ Old FA Cup foes Newcastle defeated City 5-4 in an amazing third round Cup replay at Maine Rd. The Blues led 3-0 within 30

minutes, but in the second half Newcastle fought back and levelled with only five minutes left. In extra time City made it 4-3, but Len White scored twice for the Geordies.

1958

City finished the season fifth in Division One. The 1957-58 season was noteworthy as it saw City concede 100 goals and score 104.

1959

A 3-1 victory over Leicester City, in front of 46,936, on the final day of the 1958-59 season preserved City's Division One status and sent Joe Mercer's Aston Villa into Division Two.

1960

Denis Law marked his City debut with a goal at Leeds United on 19/3/60. A month later Colin Barlow scored a late winner against Preston to ensure the Blues avoided relegation. They ultimately ended the season three points above relegated Leeds.

1961

Kilmarnock star Bobby Kennedy signed for the Blues on 20th July 1961. He made his debut on 19th August and went on to score nine goals in 251 (plus 3 as substitute) appearances during his City career.

1962

After finishing the 1961-62 season twelfth, it was hoped the following season would show an improvement. Unfortunately, the opening day of the 1962-3 season brought a 8-1 thrashing at Wolves. Even City's goal was scored by Showell, a Wolves player.

1963

A 1-1 draw in a heated and highly controversial Manchester derby helped relegate the Blues. Former Blue Denis Law scored a debatable penalty. At the time this was perceived as the most controversial derby of all time.

1964

A sixth place finish in Division Two during the first season of George Poyser's spell as manager, was not greeted particularly well by fans.

1965

■ Poyser was dismissed at Easter during a particularly poor season. City ultimately finished eleventh in Division Two. Rumours that Bill Shankly or Peter Doherty would replace him were ended when Joe Mercer arrived as the club's new manager in July. He soon appointed a highly talented coach called Malcolm Allison.

1966

■ City won the Second Division title.

1967

■ After a fifteenth placed finish in 1966-67 the Blues were not perceived as a real threat in the title race. However, on 9th October Francis Lee signed from Bolton with Joe Mercer telling him he was to be the final piece in City's jigsaw. Prior to Lee, the Blues had only gathered 11 points from 11 games – they would gain a further 47 points from 31 games with him.

1968

■ The League Championship was won in style with Neil Young top scorer on 19 from 40 games. Francis Lee scored 16 from 31 matches.

1969

▧ Tony Book was voted joint Football Writers' player of the year with Derby's Dave Mackay, and then helped City win the FA Cup against Leicester. Neil Young netted the only goal of the final.

1970

▧ According to legend, City became the first English side to win a domestic and European trophy in the same season. Over the years much has been said about this achievement and followers of Leeds United will claim that they achieved this feat in 1968, however when Leeds won the League Cup during the 1967-68 season not every League side competed in the competition. In addition their European success came at the start of the 1968-69 season, meaning that their two major trophies in 1968 occurred over two seasons. However, it has to be stressed that Leeds won the League in 1968-69 and so the Yorkshiremen did win a European trophy and an English trophy in one season. Winning the League Cup and European Cup Winners' Cup within a two month period proved City's position as one of football's greatest clubs, however.

1971

▧ City reached the semi-final of the ECWC, losing to Chelsea. On 7th October 1971 Malcolm Allison became Team Manager with Joe Mercer taking on a role as General Manager.

1972

▧ Despite leading the table after their final game of the season, the Blues ended the season fourth – one point behind champions Derby County. General Manager Joe Mercer moved to Coventry in the summer feeling he had no real position at the club. In August Malcolm Allison won his first trophy as a manager – the Charity Shield – when City defeated Aston Villa 1-0 at Villa Park.

1973

▧ On 30th March Manager Malcolm Allison left claiming he could no longer motivate the players. Former player John Hart was his successor.

▧ On Friday 5th October 'peacemaker' Peter Swales became Chairman. On 24th November Ron Saunders became Swales' first managerial appointment.

1974

▧ City were defeated 2-1 in the League Cup Final by Wolves. Despite this Wembley appearances, the following Easter Peter Swales sacked Ron Saunders. Tony Book became City's fourth manager in 13 months on 12th April.

1975

▧ The Blues finished fifth in Division One. Colin Bell received a devastating injury in the following season's fourth round League Cup tie with United. City won the game 4-0 but Bell would never again return to full fitness.

1976

Young PFA player of the year Peter Barnes and 'King of the Geordies' Dennis Tueart both scored as City won the League Cup (below). The Blues beat Newcastle 2-1 but it could have been more - Joe Royle, who had scored in every round leading up to the final, had an effort disallowed.

1977

City missed the title by a point, finishing a creditable second to Liverpool.

1978

The Blues ended 1977-8 in fourth place.

1979

In January Malcolm Allison returned to City as 'coaching overlord' to Tony Book. City also reached the quarter finals of the UEFA Cup.

On 9th September Steve Daley became the most expensive footballer in Britain when City paid £1,450,277 to Wolves.

1980

Malcolm Allison and Tony Book were dismissed in October. Shortly afterwards Peter Swales appointed former West Ham player John Bond. His assistant was former Blue John Benson.

1981

The Blues reached the final of the 100th F.A. Cup and the semi-final of the League Cup. Tommy Hutchison scored for both sides in the FA Cup final and in the replay Kevin Reeves scored a penalty, while Steve Mackenzie netted an incredible goal, but it wasn't enough. A Ricky Villa inspired Tottenham won 3-2.

1982

Work started on City's ambitious £6 million redevelopment of Maine Road. The idea was to build a replica of the North Stand at the Platt Lane end, and to replace both the Kippax and Main Stand roofs with white barrel-style affairs. In the end only the Main Stand roof was replaced, and even then it wasn't completed - the 36 private boxes planned to be suspended from the roof were never erected. After Maine Road's demolition in 2004 the white barrel-style roof was dismantled and sections used on a farm to house pigs.

1983

After John Bond's resignation John Benson became City manager on fifth February 1983. The following May David Pleat jigged across Maine Road to his captain Brian Horton as his Luton side relegated City to Division Two. In June former Celtic star Billy McNeill became manager.

1984

City finished their first season in Division Two since the 1960s fourth.

1985

David Phillips (2), Andy May, Paul Simpson, and Jim Melrose scored in the 5-1 thrashing of Charlton to guarantee promotion on the last day of the season. Promotion was vital as City's debts were reported to be £4 million with interest costing £1,000 a day.

Following disasters at Heysel and Bradford, City were ordered to make the 9,702 capacity Platt Lane Stand away fans only for the start of the 1985-6 season.

1986

■ The Blues won the F.A. Youth Cup, beating Manchester United in a two legged final. City's side included future stars Steve Redmond, Paul Moulden, Andy Hinchcliffe, David White, Ian Brightwell and Paul Lake.

■ City lost the inaugural Full Members' Cup final 5-4 to Chelsea at Wembley. Chelsea treated this as a major success at the time. The attendance was 68,000.

■ Billy McNeill left to manage Aston Villa and Jimmy Frizzell became the City manager from 21st September.

1987

■ City were relegated to Division Two. Mel Machin arrived in May 1987 as Team Manager while Jimmy Frizzell became General Manager.

■ On 7th November Huddersfield were beaten 10-1 in City's largest League victory at Maine Road. David White, Tony Adcock, and Paul Stewart each netted a hat trick, but the opening goal was scored by Neil McNab.

1988

■ City finished ninth in Division Two, but reached the quarter-final of both major cup competitions.

1989

■ Mel Machin's side achieved promotion in a tense 1-1 draw at Bradford (below). Trevor Morley was the goal scoring hero.

■ On 23rd September, City beat United 5-1 in the 111th Manchester League derby match.

Two months later Peter Swales sacked Mel Machin and after Joe Royle turned the club down, he appointed Howard Kendall on 8th December. Shortly afterwards Kendall sold cult-figure Ian Bishop to West Ham.

1990

■ Howard Kendall purchased Niall Quinn.

■ Former manager Joe Mercer died in August on his 76th birthday.

■ Kendall resigned in November to return to his 'first love' Everton. Fans' choice Peter Reid was appointed in his place.

1991

■ Reid guided City to fifth place in Division One. The final game of the 1990-91 season saw City relegate Sunderland. Future Sunderland Chairman Niall Quinn scored twice in the 3-2 victory.

1992

■ Reid's City finished fifth in Division One for the second season running.

■ City drew 1-1 with QPR in the first match of the new Premier League. This was also the first Monday night League match shown live on Sky TV.

1993

■ On 26th August, after only four games of the new season, manager Peter Reid was dismissed. The season was only 13 days old. Demonstrations against the Chairman followed. These intensified when supporters heard the news that former player Francis Lee was to mount a takeover bid.

■ Brian Horton was appointed following the match with Coventry on 27th August. He was the eleventh and last manager of Swales' chairmanship.

1994

■ In February after a long and difficult take-over Francis Lee finally became chairman. Horton's City finished sixteenth, and on the

30th April 1994 the terraced Kippax Stand witnessed its final match. It was a highly emotional day.

1995

■ After City ended the season 17th Brian Horton was dismissed despite producing a side that thrilled when on top form. Alan Ball became the next City manager but the season started with only two points from the opening eleven games. In November, however, the best spell of his City career saw him win the Manager of the Month award.

1996

■ Alan Ball's City were relegated out of the Premier League. After several depressing performances at the start of the following season Ball was dismissed. A managerial merry-go-round followed with Asa Hartford taking control (26/8 – 7/10); Steve Coppell formally appointed (7/10 – 8/11); Phil Neal filling in (8/11 – 29/12); before Frank Clark was appointed on 30th December.

1997

■ Clark guided City to fourteenth in Division One in 1996-97, but these were grim times for the Blues.

1998

■ Joe Royle replaced Frank Clark as manager. Royle was appointed on 18th February, leaving him with little time to avoid relegation. A gallant effort followed, but the Blues were relegated on 3rd May 1998 to the third tier of English football for the first time in their history. Further struggles followed with the turning point in City's fortunes coming on Boxing Day 1998 when Wiekens scored the only goal of City's victory at Wrexham.

1999

■ City achieved promotion via the play-offs but, City being City, the Blues were two goals down in the play-off final against Gillingham as the game drew to a close. Two remarkable injury time goals forced extra time, and then City gained promotion to Division One via a penalty shoot out. A crowd of 76,935 attended the match, though many had left only to return later.

■ Royle's City kept the momentum going in Division One and, by Christmas, promotion seemed possible.

2000

■ A thrilling final game of the 1999-2000 season saw Royle's City promoted back to the Premier League at Blackburn.

2001

■ Kevin Keegan was appointed manager during the 2001 close season after Joe Royle's side struggled in the Premier League. The side were relegated at the end of the 2000-01 season. The new season saw Keegan's City entertain.

2002

■ City achieved promotion as Champions of Division One and broke several records including the Club's record points total and most goals in a season (equalling the 1926-27 season).

2003

■ Manchester United were defeated 4-1 in Maine Road's last derby match. A highly emotional final season at the old ground was

followed by the premature death of player Marc Vivien-Foe (above).

◼ City moved to their new stadium in August 2003.

2004

◼ Keegan's City finished 16th in the Premier League. The first season at the new stadium had seen the Blues average attendance increase to 46,830. This was City's highest official average of all time.

2005

◼ Kevin Keegan resigned on 11th March 2005 and was replaced by former player Stuart Pearce. Initially, Pearce was appointed caretaker manager prior to City's match at Tottenham on 19th March, but was given the job officially on the 12th May, three days before the last match of the season. Of the nine games played under Pearce that season, only the opening game against Spurs ended in defeat. Victory against Middlesbrough on the last day would have brought a UEFA Cup place but City could only manage a draw.

2006

◼ The Blues finished fifteenth in the Premier League and reached the quarter-finals of the FA Cup. Sadly, despite a goal from Kiki Musampa, West Ham won 2-1. Earlier Micah Richards had made the headlines with a 94th minute equaliser against Aston Villa in the fifth round.

2007

◼ City were successful in their bid to host the UEFA Cup Final in 2008. Stuart Pearce left his position as manager, with Sven-Goran Eriksson appointed as his replacement. On 15th December the Blues established a 'top flight' record of nine straight home League wins at the start of the season.

2008

◼ City won the FA Youth Cup with a two legged victory over Chelsea, much to the delight of Academy boss Jim Cassell. The City Of Manchester Stadium staged the UEFA Cup final between Rangers & Zenit St. Petersberg.

◼ Sven-Goran Eriksson took City to ninth in the Premier League and qualification for the UEFA Cup (via the fair play league) but was still replaced in the summer. The new manager was Mark Hughes – the former Wales, Barcelona, Bayern Munich and Manchester United star.

◼ In an enthralling transfer deadline day City smashed the British transfer record when they signed Brazilian star Robinho. News of a takeover of the Club by the Abu Dhabi United group filtered through at the same time.

2009

◼ City reached the UEFA Cup quarter-finals. Shortly after the season ended a new sponsorship deal was announced with Etihad and a new kit deal with Umbro. By the end of August, new signing Emmanuel Adebayor had scored in the opening three League games of the 2009-10 season.

GOLDEN GOALS

Eric Brook

1934
v Stoke City

It has virtually slipped out of living memory but this goal is possibly the greatest ever scored at Maine Road. It is also the goal that was viewed by the largest paying audience of all time at the old stadium.

The goalscorer Eric Brook remains one of City's biggest stars and he was idolised by thousands of Mancunians throughout his career. This goal was obviously popular with Maine Road regulars at the time but it has to be stressed that it was also highly significant in the Blues quest to re-establish themselves as a major force.

The idea of this 'GOLDEN GOALS' feature is to remember a significant or spectacular goal from yesteryear. The Big Book Of City's hope is that modern day supporters will learn more about some of these goals. If you would like to nominate a goal for possible use in a future 'Big Book' then email: city@manchesterfootball. org with details of game, goalscorer and date.

Match Stats

Date: 3rd March 1934
Score: City 1-0 Stoke City
Scorers: Eric Brook (14 mins)
Venue: Maine Road
Attendance: 84,569
FA Cup Quarter-final

City Team: Swift, Barnett, Dale, Busby, Cowan, Bray, Toseland, Marshall, Tilson, Herd, Brook

Pre-Match

City had been developing as a good cup fighting side for several seasons. In 1932 the Blues narrowly lost out in the FA Cup semi-final (a last minute goal from Arsenal knocked the Blues out); in 1933 City had reached the FA Cup final; and here in 1934 the pressure was on for City to reach the FA Cup final again. Victories over Blackburn, Hull (after a replay), and Sheffield Wednesday (another replay) had encouraged Mancunians and significant crowds had watched each game – the away tie at Sheffield Wednesday remains Hillsborough's record crowd (72,841).

Stoke were an exciting, forward looking side who had gained promotion the previous

year as Second Division champions. Within their ranks they included several star men including exciting youngster Stanley Matthews. This was not going to be an easy tie for the Blues.

Fans of Stoke felt excited by this tie and were convinced they could win. Thousands travelled up from the Potteries and, together with the interest in Manchester, this meant this game was likely to see the greatest footballing crowd ever assembled in Manchester. The scene in the city centre was outlined in the *Manchester Guardian's* "In Manchester" diary column: "The distinction of having helped, even by the addition of a single unit, to make a record crowd at a cup-tie, excluding the final, is one that involves a great deal of discomfort and commends itself rather in retrospect than at the time.

"A good judge of numbers might have prophesised the record any time after noon on Saturday, when a drab tide of humanity pressed relentlessly down Oxford Road and Wilmslow Road and loaded cars and cabs and trams crawled in the same southerly direction. The discomfort began early, for there was no eating-house but was full to the doors at lunch-time, and waitresses ran

MARCH 4, 1934

THE ONLY WAY—CUP-TIE VERSION

ARTHUR THOMPSON, the "Sunday Dispatch" photographer, shows in this page of pictures the remarkable adaptability of the Cup-tie fan. These striking photographs were secured during his wanderings among—or behind—yesterday's record crowd of 84,569 at Maine-road, Manchester.

THE MATCH

"HIS WHITE SCARF made an excellent foot support."

distractedly from table to table, never quite catching up with the orders of the hungry visitors from the Potteries.

"The thousands who stayed to eat in the city were proved foolish when the ground was reached, for two hours before the game was due to begin masses of people were standing outside the turnstiles waiting to enter and climb on banks that from all appearances were packed so tightly that no fish in a tin seemed an adequate comparison. So, indeed, it proved after having penetrated, triumphant, but bruised, those narrow entrances. The elation born of having achieved the apparently impossible, by getting in at all, was short lived, for it soon became all too clear that one would see little or nothing of the game."

The Game

The official attendance that day was 84,569 - the largest ever crowd in the provinces and to this day the record for any club fixture. For the first time in Maine Road's history the gates were closed before the start of the game – a full twenty minutes before it was due to start. Thousands were locked out.

For much of the match supporters jostled for position, causing many to claim that the attendance was simply too large, but the City management claimed it could have been greater, despite being forced by the police to close the gates. Maine Road's capacity at this time was viewed as being around 88,000 as the stadium had undergone some improvements in 1931 – the corner between Platt Lane and the Main Stand had been re-profiled, roofed and extended. The huge crowd did bring a few problems and at one point a crush barrier collapsed causing a few injuries. The First Aid men were kept busy.

In the opening minutes City were under considerable pressure as Stoke attacked in force. Sale and Matthews were their two most attacking minded players at the commencement of play, and they caused Swift to take a gamble early on when they combined in one attack. Swift, who had

only made his debut the previous Christmas, was inexperienced and still finding his feet. He came out of his net to narrow the angle thinking that either Sale or Matthews would attempt to shoot. It was a mistake, for the two players clearly had opportunity to easily wrong foot the 'keeper. Fortunately, Matthews' own inexperience, and the sight of Swift coming towards him was enough to cause Matthews to miss kick.

A short while later Matthews tried again. *The Manchester Guardian* described the scene: "Another chance fell to Matthews and, after Swift had beaten away the ball it rolled the full width of the goal, not two feet from the line, with no one able to master this excitement sufficiently to be able to kick it one way or the other."

Apart from the occasional attack City were now dominating the match, causing the *Guardian* to claim: "the famous Liddle-Matthews wing was thoroughly mastered by Bray and Dale" and "Swift had hardly anything to do."

Off the pitch the size of the crowd continued to cause issues. Supporters were sitting on the touchline and goalkeeper Swift, in particular, was conscious of the large group of supporters sat around his goal. He tried to joke with them, however his thoughts must surely have been on the problems experienced at Hillsborough when a dead supporter was stretchered past the team in the tunnel as they prepared to take to the field in an earlier round.

The Manchester Guardian: "For some time the late-comers lived in hope that the police would permit them to climb over the barriers at a certain point and range themselves behind the goalposts. Lively exchanges of badinage gave place to angry shouts from the back as the police proved adamant, but as those who were at the front could see there was no reason why they should risk any sort of collision with the law, which was represented in considerable force. As last those to whom the game was invisible accepted the inevitable and stopped pushing."

THE WAY TO WEMBLEY
BROOK'S AMAZING SHOT BEAT STOKE

Eric Brook, out near the left touchline.

The Sunday Graphic reported, under the headline "Cup Fans Trapped in Amazing Crowd", of the problems faced: "Having got in, hundreds wandered about looking at a solid array of backs – spectators' not players' – and then tried to get out. But they were trapped, until a turnstile was opened to let them out. Some youths scaled a 12ft wall to get out. These unfortunate people did not even get a good look at the field, let alone the game. Ambulance men were kept busy and treated about 100 people for crushing and abrasions. Three were taken to Manchester Royal infirmary."

With the terraces packed it was difficult for some to know exactly what was happening on the pitch. Several ingenious solutions were found and some newspapers focused on this rather than the game. According to *The Guardian* one fan tried to help those squashed in behind him: "An anonymous person at the front out of the goodness of his heart began to describe the game for them. At first they took it as a joke and there were derisive cries of 'Square Four' and 'Square Six' in the manner of the announcer at a wireless running commentary. However, this unofficial commentator stuck to his self appointed task, and being something of an expert in the game, gradually won silence for his remarks. Thus it came about that several

hundred people who might have got really bad tempered and made trouble were satisfied with hearing about a game instead of seeing it. The only interruptions came when men who had fainted, and there were scores in this corner of the ground alone, were passed roughly but efficiently over the heads of the crowd to the grass, where the ambulance squads laid them abut and splashed water in their faces."

With the Blues in control it was inevitable that City would take the lead. It was this goal that became one of the most talked about goals in Maine Road's history.

After about fourteen minutes, Eric Brook received a wide pass well out on the Kippax wing and raced for the Platt Lane corner flag. He was only feet away from the hundreds of supporters who had managed to climb over the white perimeter wall and sit on the touchline. He then made what was described as 'a speculative lob' from the wing, which seemed to change direction in mid-flight. The Stoke 'keeper Roy John appeared to have it covered, jumped up and somehow missed it as it curled past the 'keeper and into the net.

Supporter Joe Carley, stood at the Platt Lane end, had a good view: "Brook scored the only goal of the match – a goal which will be talked about by Manchester and Stoke supporters for many years to come.

He received a wide pass well out on the wing and raced for the corner flag. That wily old veteran, Bob McGrory [Stoke], made no effort to overhaul the City winger, for he realised his speed was not what it was. Instead, he turned goalwards to intercept the winger's centre when it came across.

"Now I was on the terracing, midway between the corner flag and the post, and had a full view of Brook's high lobbing shot or centre, taken from a position only a yard or two from the flag. With the exception of Roy John, no other player was in the penalty area as the ball travelled and dipped near the far post. Stoke's goalkeeper watched it carefully, appeared to have it covered, and – as I thought – jumped to make sure the ball would go over the bar and land on the roof of the net. I heard a comparatively faint shout of 'goal' from the crowd at the rear of the posts, and then to my amazement saw a blushing, annoyed goalkeeper stoop to pick the ball out of the net!"

Another supporter, Fran Parker, saw enough of the goal to realise it was something special: "I saw Brooky on the wing and he kicked the ball and it seemed to twist. I don't know how, but it did, and when it went in I closed my eyes tight. It was a great feeling and I was so excited at seeing such an amazing goal!"

Afterwards some claimed the goal had not been an intentional shot but Fran Parker disagreed: "He was a great player. He played for England, and was one of our biggest stars. He knew what he was doing. From where I sat on the edge of the pitch it was as clear as day that he had shot at goal. He may have been on the touchline himself, but goalscorers like that look for openings all the time. Most players probably wouldn't have been able to score it, but Brooky was different."

In 2003 Denis Houlston described this goal as one of the highlights of his entire City-supporting life. Houlston was 17 at the time of the goal: "It was a lovely warm day and Eric Brook's winning goal came from the area I stood. I was always a third of the way along the terracing from the Platt Lane corner, and about twenty yards from the wall. I think Brook played in every position for the Club – he certainly went in nets once – and was a very good player. When the goal went in it was marvellous. Nirvana."

In the final minute Stoke came close to equalising, but the game ended 1-0 and Brook's goal was enough.

Gate receipts totalled: £5,426.

Man Of The Match

Eric Brook was the undisputed star.

Post Match

The victory put the Blues into the FA Cup semi final where they defeated Aston Villa 6-1 (a record for the semi-final). They went on to win the FA Cup against Portsmouth.

Brook's goal against Stoke proved to be highly significant but it remained a memorable goal to the thousands who saw it because of the player's quality and the speculative nature of it. A similar goal today by an England international in a major cup game would be heralded as one of the greatest ever (for a few years at least!).

Elsewhere

The 1930s was not a particularly great time in the business world. A worldwide depression had dominated, yet this game may have had a bearing on the general attitude of Manchester businessmen that week. The Manchester Stock Exchange reported surprisingly brisk business on both the Friday and Saturday morning in the build up to the match. Overall, the city was full of pride and vigour.

Obviously, City won the FA Cup. Arsenal were League champions. Italy won the second World Cup. This was played in Italy with the final, against Czechoslovakia, staged in Rome. It is worth noting that none of the home nations had any interest in taking part.

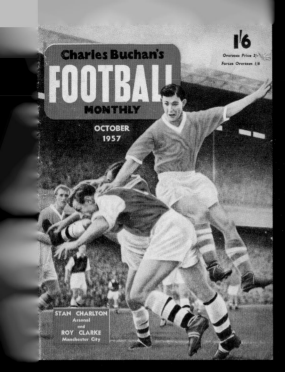

Charles Buchan's
FOOTBALL
MONTHLY

1'6
Overseas Price 2/-
Forces Overseas 1/6

OCTOBER
1957

STAN CHARLTON
Arsenal
and
ROY CLARKE
Manchester City

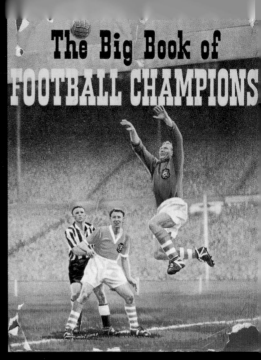

The Big Book of
FOOTBALL CHAMPIONS

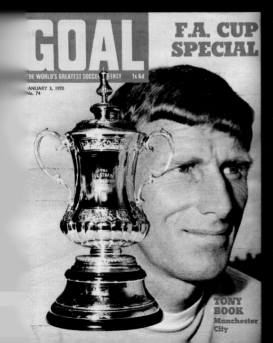

GOAL

F.A. CUP
SPECIAL

THE WORLD'S GREATEST SOCCER WEEKLY   1s 6d

JANUARY 3, 1970
No. 74

**TONY
BOOK**
Manchester
City

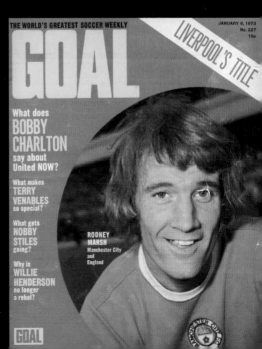

THE WORLD'S GREATEST SOCCER WEEKLY

GOAL

LIVERPOOL'S TITLE

JANUARY 6, 1973
No. 227
10p

What does
BOBBY
CHARLTON
say about
United NOW?

What makes
TERRY
VENABLES
so special?

What gets
NOBBY
STILES
going?

Why is
WILLIE
HENDERSON
no longer
a rebel?

RODNEY
MARSH
Manchester City
and
England

GOAL

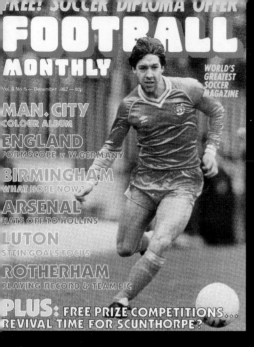

FREE! SOCCER DIPLOMA OFFER

FOOTBALL
MONTHLY

Vol. 9 No 5 — December 1982 — 80p

WORLD'S GREATEST SOCCER MAGAZINE

MAN. CITY
COLOUR ALBUM

ENGLAND
FORMSCOPE v W.GERMANY

BIRMINGHAM
WHAT HOPE NOW?

ARSENAL
HATS OFF TO HOLLINS

LUTON
STEIN GOALS FOCUS

ROTHERHAM
PLAYING RECORD & TEAM PIC

PLUS: FREE PRIZE COMPETITIONS...
REVIVAL TIME FOR SCUNTHORPE?

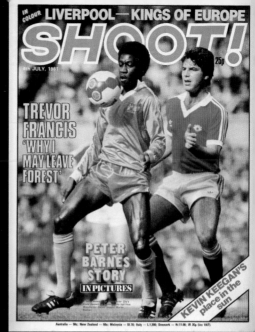

IN COLOUR **LIVERPOOL — KINGS OF EUROPE**

SHOOT!

4th JULY, 1981   25p

TREVOR FRANCIS
'WHY I MAY LEAVE FOREST'

PETER BARNES STORY
IN PICTURES

KEVIN KEEGAN'S place in the sun

Australia — 90c; New Zealand — 90c; Malaysia — $1.70; Italy — L.1,200; Denmark — Kr.11.00; (R.30p (inc VAT).

...and back page City

AL IS FIRST AGAIN

...yes, the first football publication with a full colour picture from the F.A. Cup Final. GOAL captures Tony Book's moment of triumph.

Classic City - Mike Summerbee & Francis Lee, March 1970 (Action Images)

Johnny Crossan leads City with goalkeeper Alan Ogley, January 1966 (Action Images)

City fans at Villa Park's Holte End for the 1981 FA Cup semi final victory over Bobby Robson's Ipswich Town (Action Images)

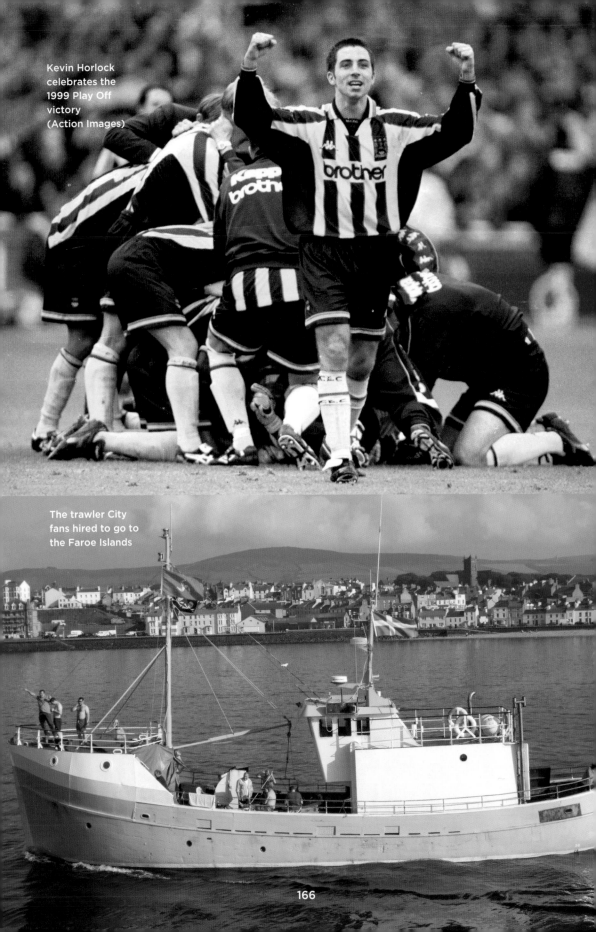

Kevin Horlock celebrates the 1999 Play Off victory (Action Images)

The trawler City fans hired to go to the Faroe Islands

Carlos Tevez in action during the 1-0 victory at Portsmouth, 30th August 2009 (Action Images)

Emmanuel Adebayor celebrates scoring against Wolves, 22nd August 2009 (Action Images)

OBSCURE HISTORY

As part of our bid to identify some of our more obscure locations, the *Big Book Of City* has trawled through the archives and walked the streets of Manchester to identify a couple of buildings that played their part in at least one moment of the Club's history.

The second 'obscure' building is Number One Aytoun Street. Currently apartments, this building has been significant at several times during the Club's history, however today we are after just one of these moments.

Looking at the building today it's clear this has been a significant Manchester landmark in the past, but even so it is still difficult to see what part it could have played in the history of our Club. So what part did it play?

As with our earlier 'Obscure History' teaser we know it's hard to guess and it really is an obscure fact. The answer appears on the next page, but before you take a look please have a go. To help here are four possible answers and, in the spirit of all multiple

choice questions, when in doubt have a guess.

So, what part did this building play in City's history? Was it:

A On 8th October 1905 City star Billy Meredith opened his first sportswear shop in this building.

B The Football League held its meeting here on 17th May 1892 that elected Ardwick AFC (City) as founder members of Division Two.

C 1930s Cup finalist Billy Dale was born on the fourth floor of this building on 17th February 1905.

D On 9th January 1905 the City players were presented with gold watches by supporters at a commemoration dinner held here to celebrate the 1904 FA Cup success

Take a guess and then turn over the page to see if you were right.

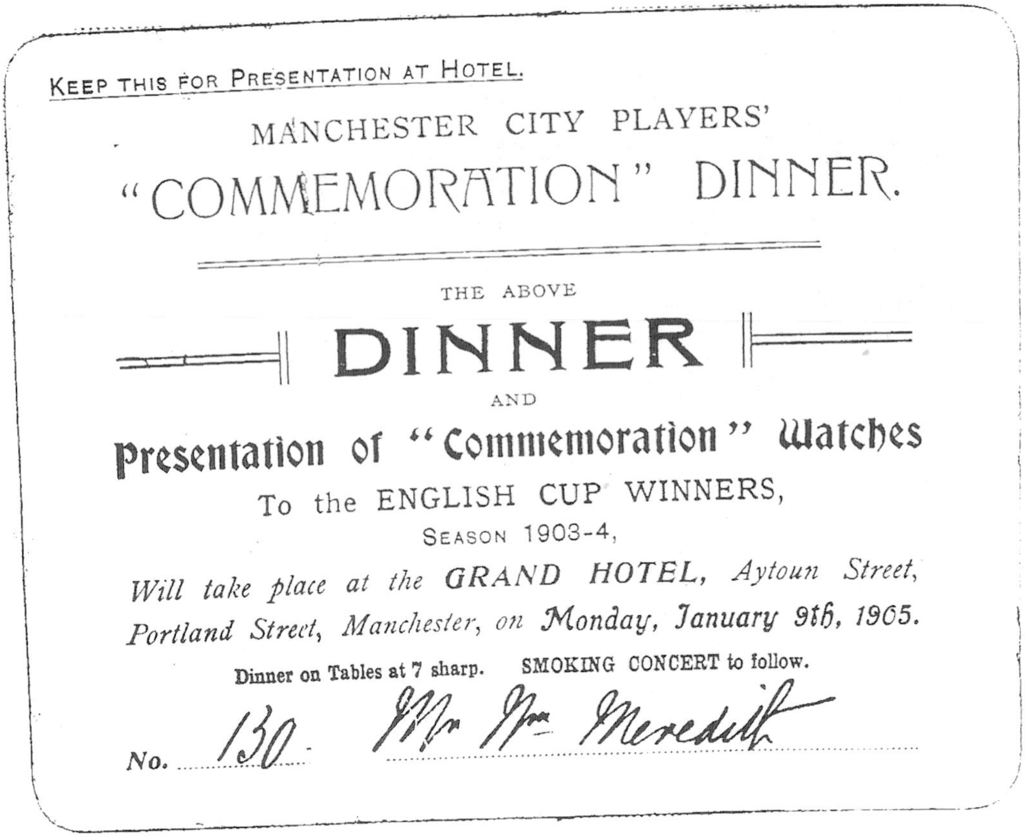

KEEP THIS FOR PRESENTATION AT HOTEL.

MANCHESTER CITY PLAYERS'

"COMMEMORATION" DINNER.

THE ABOVE

—| DINNER |—

AND

Presentation of "Commemoration" Watches

To the ENGLISH CUP WINNERS,

SEASON 1903-4,

Will take place at the GRAND HOTEL, Aytoun Street, Portland Street, Manchester, on Monday, January 9th, 1905.

Dinner on Tables at 7 sharp.   SMOKING CONCERT to follow.

No. 130.   Mr Wm Meredith

OBSCURE HISTORY – THE ANSWER

Well, the answer to our second 'obscure' building question and the part it played in City's history is:

Number One Aytoun Street was the place where (D) on 9th January 1905 the City players were presented with gold watches by supporters at a commemoration dinner held to celebrate the 1904 FA Cup success.

The building used to be the Grand Hotel and many of City's triumphs and end of season dinners were celebrated here. This was basically 'the' city centre hotel as far as the Club and its supporters were concerned.

We told you it was obscure!

Next time you're wandering along Aytoun Street take a look at this fairly quiet building and try to imagine what it was like 100 years ago when it was right at the heart of Manchester's night life and social scene.

If you would like to suggest other obscure locations for future editions of *The Big Book of City* then please email us. All locations will need to be backed up with hard evidence of the building's use. Please contact *The Big Book of City* by emailing: **city@ manchesterfootball.org**

CITY'S NUMBER ONE

THE PROFILES

44 - RON HEALEY

At the age of 18 Ron Healey made his first team debut at Ipswich Town on 26th February 1971 as replacement for an injured Joe Corrigan. The game ended in a 2-0 defeat and Corrigan was selected for the following game. Healey did return to first team action in March and made nine League appearances during 1970-71. He also appeared for the Blues in three ECWC games including appearances in the quarter-finals against Gornik and the second leg of the semi-final against Chelsea.

This was an amazing record for such a young player's first season but manager Joe Mercer was convinced Healey could be a great 'keeper. A loan period at Coventry followed before Healey returned to the City first team at the tail end of the 1971-72 season. Joe Mercer left the Blues that season and Malcolm Allison believed that Joe Corrigan was the better 'keeper and so Healey was very much the second choice. He did manage five League appearances during Allison's period in sole charge of the team. It's interesting to note that when Allison left City on 30th March 1970 Healey was immediately brought back into the first team. This could be coincidence, but Healey remained the first choice for the rest of the season (seven games) although Corrigan started 1973-74 as number one.

Loan spells at Preston and Cardiff followed later in the season before Healey signed for Cardiff on a permanent basis in May 1974. While there he helped Cardiff to promotion and the Welsh Cup and also became a Republic of Ireland international.

Appearances: League: 30 League Cup: 2 Euro: 4

The Ron Healey Interview

In December 2004 Gary James interviewed Eire international Ron Healey. In an interesting interview he talked of his time at City. Here's a selection of questions and answers from that interview.

At the beginning of your career who were the guys who gave you most encouragement and support?

Harry Dowd was perhaps the biggest influence in my first seasons at City. He had great patience and was always very supportive. I owe a lot to him and he was, in my eyes, a great 'keeper to learn from. Of course, Joe Mercer was very supportive as well. People always talk about the Mercer-Allison partnership and who did what, but for me Joe was superb. He seemed to enjoy talking to those of us in the youth team and reserves. Perhaps he thought we needed more support than the first teamers. Sometimes he'd take us for a walk around the pitch, arm on shoulder, talking about the game and his hopes. You never really knew how he'd do it, but if you started the walk feeling down, you'd end up back in front of the tunnel fully refreshed and ready to go. He just knew what to say and when to say it. A marvellous man. Malcolm was a great coach of course, but Joe was the calming influence. He knew how to lift you.

Ken Barnes was another key figure. I remember when my League career was just getting going he said to me: "enjoy it while you can because in this game it can all be over in five minutes." He's right of course. You have to savour every moment.

You made your first team debut at Ipswich on 26th February 1971, as a Blue that must have felt great?

It did, but it wasn't my first appearance in the first team. I had played at Ajax in a friendly a few months earlier but – how shall I put this – the journalist who followed us out there didn't notice that I was in nets, and he wrote his match report talking about how impressive Joe Corrigan was! So I had a great game and nobody at home knew it was me!

This must have been a wonderful period for you?

I couldn't believe how lucky I was to be playing for the team I loved at such an important time. I remember running out at Maine Road and feeling the excitement build up. You'd be in the dressing room sometimes and hear the noise from the Kippax. I used to sit there and think I was the luckiest man alive. If fate had gone another way I'd have been on the Kippax chanting for the team – I'd have loved doing that of course, but playing is incredible. I used to get in the tunnel ready and then I'd catch sight of the Kippax as I walked up the tunnel, and the adrenaline would build. I'd run out and the feeling was incredible.

Although I was born in Manchester, most of my family supported United, but I was different. I'd chosen City as my team because their fortunes seemed more like real life to me. One minute they'd reach the highest level possible, then they'd suffer a bad spell. That's life and it's important we all understand that. City's spent its entire existence like that, and that's why we are all so passionate about the club.

You played in the ECWC quarter-final 2nd leg and replay against Gornik, and the semi-final 2nd leg against Chelsea (28/4/71), do you remember much about those games?

Against Gornik Joe Corrigan had played in the first leg and we lost 2-0 away and I think he got injured, so my chance came. We won the 2nd leg 2-0 and the game went to a replay at Copenhagen. It was a great side to be in and, although I was a young 'keeper, I managed to get some praise. Then came Easter. I dislocated my finger in a match against Nottm Forest and missed the first leg of the semi-final with Chelsea. We lost 1-0 away, but still had a lot of hope for the second. I came back into the side then, sadly, I was at fault for the only goal – I diverted a free kick into the net! That one mistake mattered and I did feel a very heavy burden for some time.

You played in three Manchester derbies, did they mean more to you because you are a Mancunian?

They meant a lot to all the players – don't forget most of the side either came from the Manchester area or were with City from boyhood – but I do remember the feeling when we won my first game at Old Trafford. Funnily enough I was pretty nervous beforehand but Summerbee took me around meeting people before the match. Summerbee was a great motivator. He got me signing autographs and the like then he introduced me to Denis Law. Law made me feel really welcome – remember he was a United player at this point so he didn't have to do anything. He offered a bit of advice and encouragement.

Anyway, once he was on the pitch he was still chatting to me and being supportive, and that helped a great deal. Then late on United were given a corner and Denis knelt down next to me, tying his lace. Just as the kick was about to be taken he got up, moved away a little and then said "Ron, your lace is undone". I looked down and he was right. The ball came in and I was all over the place. I'm convinced Denis undid my lace!

Like many of the great names from the period, Denis was a great character and he did help me settle my nerves that day, but he also taught me to be alert at all times! We had the last laugh of course winning 3-1.

I remember him once 'phoning on a Friday night asking if we'd like to go round for a cup of tea – you don't turn down something like that. He used to talk to us about professionalism and, basically, about conduct. He'd explain the behavioural expectations people had and we'd all listen and learn.

Despite the early acclaim chances became limited for you and after several loan spells you moved to Cardiff City. Was this your choice?

As a Blue I would never want to leave, but it was clear I was not moving up the pecking order. We had Keith MacRae and Joe Corrigan and I know Joe felt he was on his way out, so inevitably I felt the same. The Cardiff loan came along and then it was made permanent. I was offered more money than I was earning at City and with a young family – I married at 17 – I couldn't jeopardise my future. I couldn't guarantee a future if I stayed at City, but Cardiff were planning to make me their first choice, big star signing. There was no choice at the end of the day. Although Rodney Marsh came up to me and said, "Ron, don't go to Wales... You'll never come back out!" He was almost right!

Cardiff was a great time for you. You made 216 League appearances; won the Welsh Cup; played in European competition again; and played internationals for the Republic of Ireland. It's a record any 'keeper would be proud of. How do you feel about that time?

Of course it was a great period and I enjoyed most of it. The fans loved this period and I got a lot out of it. However, from the age of 26 I struggled. I had pelvic problems and I was given lots of injections to keep me playing. I always wanted to play of course, but when I made my international appearances I was already at a stage where my body was seriously struggling.

Actually, one of my Eire games was against England at Wembley in 1980. Bryan Robson made his debut and Kevin Keegan chipped me! I had to turn down a few caps because I simply could not have made it on to a pitch. There were times after a game when I couldn't walk. My career ended at 30 – for a goalkeeper that's young – and I was replaced at Cardiff by Andy Dibble.

I still suffer today with serious hip problems and arthritis.

Once your career ended, was it difficult coping?

Very difficult. There was a void which couldn't be filled. Naturally, you have your family around you, but at 3pm on a Saturday you feel an enormous loss. Every Saturday was the same and you had to find a way of filling that time. It wasn't easy and I had some very, very bad days. Being a footballer, and especially a goalkeeper, is like being a tightrope walker without a net. The day you fall off the rope is the day your life ends in many ways.

So what did you do to fill your time?

As far as work is concerned, I worked in factories, clocking in, doing nights and the like. Now I know a lot of fans do that, but when you've gone from international football to that within a short period of time it's hard to take. A lot of players also find solace in the pubs and similar places. There's a gap and it has to be filled some how. Fortunately, I eventually got a permanent role at Styal Prison as OSG officer, and then Andy Dibble looked me up. Together with my son Scott, we set up a goalkeeping school. It's actually Scott who makes it a success. He puts in a tremendous amount of work and really gets everything organised. Of course it helps that he was a 'keeper himself, playing at York and at a good standard in non-League, and then with Dibble and myself we give a few examples of how to develop.

How important is the goalkeeping school to you personally?

It gave me a new lease of life. For ten to fifteen years after my career ended I had this black cloud hanging over me. It wouldn't move. I'd come out of the game unqualified for any 'normal' job and there were plenty of financial problems as a result. It was definitely the worse time of my life and in all honesty it felt as if my life was over. Now it's so different. My son does the majority of work, but for me it's great to be involved. Whenever I've been with the kids I've always left in a very positive frame of mind. They want to learn and we teach. The school tries to encourage kids in all aspects of life. My son will ask them how many times they've helped their mum or whatever, to try and get them to realise that you only get out of life what you put in.

Because we are not figures of authority in the way that teachers are, we sometimes get more out of the kids. They want to be great 'keepers and so they'll listen to us. We've also been very successful – we've placed 14 'keepers with clubs and have helped turn a few others off a destructive path.

Finally, how do you feel about City and its fans today?

I still love this club, and I do love the fans. I guess I was a fan who got lucky. I worked hard to make the grade of course, and I would like to thank all the fans and other Mancunians who helped along the way. The fans encouraged me at times when it was difficult and, for as long as I live, I will never forget that tremendous feeling of excitement generated by supporters at every game I played in. Manchester City's supporters are the best by a long, long way.

CITY IN EUROPE

1978-79

Competition: UEFA Cup

Reason For Qualification: Finished fifth (2nd placed Liverpool won European Cup, providing extra European place)

Manager: Tony Book

13th September 1978
Round 1 Leg 1
Attendance: 12,000

FC Twente 1-1 City

City Goalscorer: Watson
City: Corrigan; Clements, Power, Viljoen, Watson, Futcher, Channon, Owen, Palmer, Hartford, Barnes

Tony Book had spent £100,000 to sign Colin Viljoen from Ipswich Town only three hours before the deadline for registering players to appear in this UEFA Cup tie. The entire purchase was concluded within 12 hours of Book first approaching Ipswich and was seen as a major coup at the time. The midfielder had been on loan to QPR, but once he heard that City were interested he was desperate to move north: "When I was going to move it did seem that financial considerations would be my only priority. But while the finance has still been important, this transfer to City

has opened up a whole new world of prospect to share in success. When I heard they were interested in me I just had to come. It's a dream come true."

The Blues dominated the first half and captain Dave Watson scored in the 24th minute. According to journalist Peter Gardner the goal capped a perfect performance: "City's man of the match. He was a tower of strength throughout despite playing with a recently aggravated stomach injury. It was Watson who scored City's important goal, stealing forward on a blind side run to head in Asa Hartford's free-kick."

City were a bit more subdued as the second half progressed, however Roger Palmer came close to scoring when his 31st minute header

Barnes in full flow against Twente

Paul Power tries to make it 2-1 at Enschede

hit the crossbar. Sadly, Palmer found that his first taste of European football ended in disappointment. An injury sustained in this game forced him to miss City's League game at Chelsea and prevented him from playing for the England Under-21 side in Denmark. He was still missing by the time of the second leg match with Twente.

In the second half the Blues had to be more defensive minded as Twente searched for a goal. A strong, fighting character emerged that perhaps had been missing in every earlier UEFA Cup game. Joe Corrigan was superb, as was the rest of City's defence, but inevitably the home side found the net. Norwegian winger Hallvar Thoresen scored a 51st minute equaliser.

Afterwards most journalists praised Corrigan. Denis Lowe, the *Daily Telegraph*: "Corrigan, as consistent as ever, produced three notable saves in quick succession – from Thoresen, Otto and Van Ierssel."

Ronald Crowther, the *Daily Mail*: "The result might well have gone against City – and it might even have been a crushing one – but for the ever-dependable Joe Corrigan."

27th September 1978
Round 1 Leg 2
Attendance: 29,330

City 3-2 FC Twente

City Goalscorers: Wildschut (og), Kidd, Bell

City: Corrigan; Clements, Power, Viljoen (Bell), Watson, Futcher, Channon, Owen, Kidd, Hartford, Barnes

Despite being gifted an eighth minute own goal from World Cup defender Piet Wildschut, the Blues found this match to be an extremely tense, edge of the seat affair. A couple of strong City chances were missed in the first half and then Niels Overweg scored from a free kick to make the score 2-2 on aggregate with

both sides scoring an away goal. City knew they had to win this match outright and could not afford to concede another goal as that would swing the advantage Twente's way.

City's most experienced European campaigners – Brian Kidd and Colin Bell – proved to be the stars as the game progressed. Bell, making his first appearance of the season and coming on as a second half substitute for Viljoen, and Kidd used their knowledge of European football well as they both scored to give City a 3-1 lead on the night and 4-2 aggregate score.

That should have been enough to see the Blues sail through, however Twente pulled a goal back and for a while City had to defend like crazy as the Dutchmen searched for an equaliser that would have eliminated the Blues. Peter Gardner: "Twente worried them with long ball tactics at which their skipper and sweeper Epi Drost was a master. Had Twente been blessed with a finishing punch and enjoyed the same sort of chances that came the home side's way, then City might well have been drawing the curtains on Europe there and then."

Kenny Clements and Gary Owen were viewed as having significant performances, although

Owen was cautioned in the 40th minute for dissent (as he had been in the first leg) and would miss the following European game as a result.

18th October 1978
Round 2 Leg 1
Attendance: 27,487

City 4-0 Standard Liege

City Goalscorers: Hartford, Kidd 2 (1 pen), Palmer
City: Corrigan; Clements, Donachie, Booth, Watson, Viljoen (Keegan), Palmer, Bell, Kidd, Hartford, Barnes

Asa Hartford scored in the 13th minute but, despite several attempts that was all that separated the clubs up to the 85th minute. A frantic late rally by the Blues saw three goals in four minutes to create a decisive and emphatic victory. All those who had left the stadium early (to get to their cars and buses) realised that no game is over until the final whistle.

The transformation was heralded as a high point in the career of Peter Barnes. He demonstrated his skills superbly as he made Liege suffer with attack after attack (below). Peter Gardner: "Twisting, turning, tormenting

and teasing the harassed Belgians, Barnes paved the way for that final three-goal fling with Kidd grabbing tow and Palmer the last. It was Barnes at his brilliant best although Hartford and Watson were also heroes on a night when City proved that patience always pays."

1st November 1978
Round 2 Leg 2
Attendance: 25,000

Standard Liege 2-0 City

City: Corrigan; Clements, Donachie, Booth, Watson, Owen, Channon, Bell, Kidd, Hartford, Palmer

Despite a warning from Tony Book, the Blues lost this game: "We won't sit back and defend that 4-0 lead. Our aim must be to go out and really finish off Liege with an early goal."

The defeat hardly mattered though, as an all-round creditable performance sealed City's place in the third round. Tommy Booth, Kenny Clements, Willie Donachie and Dave Watson impressed most as the Blues did enough to ensure the side progressed.

Sigurvinsson scored in the 63rd minute – "he bent it five or six yards" according to Dave Watson – and Liege scored a second from a penalty when Hartford was adjudged to have handled a Clemence clearance. However, the Blues did more than enough to see the side through to the next round.

Unfortunately, there was one particularly black moment when Gary Owen was dismissed in the 86th minute, resulting in a five match European ban. "Manchester City were poised to graduate with European honours... until Gary Owen failed the test of temperament. His sending off in Belgium was the one souring note of a magnificent Blues performance" read the *Manchester Evening News*.

Owen's misdemeanour, as seen by Peter Gardner, was always likely to see him sent off: "He chased fully fifteen yards to aim a flying kick at Phillipe Garot, the Belgian international defender who had fouled Hartford. Gary Should have known better. He had missed the first leg because of a one match suspension... and the authorities rightly took this into account when reaching the decision of a stiff five match ban."

The 'paper added: "Dave Watson and Tommy Booth were outstanding, flanked by the dependable Willie Donachie and under rated Kenny Clements."

Incidentally, Liege were so impressed with youngster Roger Palmer that they tried to sign him that night. He remained at City of course, finding fame later on as a cult hero for Joe Royle's Oldham Athletic.

23rd November 1978
Round 3 Leg 1
Attendance: 40,000

AC Milan 2-2 City

City Goalscorers: Kidd, Power
City: Corrigan; Clements, Donachie, Booth, Watson, Power, Viljoen (Keegan), Bell, Kidd, Hartford, Palmer.

The first leg took place in Milan's impressive San Siro stadium, but wasn't staged as anticipated. The game should have been played on Wednesday 22nd November, but the conditions were poor with thick, swirling fog forcing the referee to postpone the match. There was already a large number of supporters in the stadium and the atmosphere was incredible, with manager Book admitting that the fervour of the Italian fans shocked the City men to start with. He felt relieved when the referee ordered the game to be played the following day with a lunchtime kick off.

Not everyone was happy of course with the delay. Many Italians could not take time off work, while those City fans that had journeyed to Milan all had to hastily rearrange their travel plans or stick with the original schedule and miss the game. Some on a Supporters' Club charter had to leave the game at half time to make sure they made their Thursday afternoon flight.

City estimated the delay cost the Club over £5,000 in additional travel and accommodation costs, plus larger amounts

(top) Dave Watson, Joe Corrigan and Kenny Clements ready to face Milan.
(Bottom) Watson is uncertain of Milan's flower choice.

Corrigan was ready for anything.

Substitute Ged Keegan.

in terms of gate receipts and so on. In truth, however, it probably helped the side progress which from a supporter perspective is always a much more worthy achievement than profit.

On the Thursday lunchtime the attendance was reported as 'no more than 30,000' at time of kick off. This did increase to around 40,000 as the game progressed and, although this was significant by English standards at the time, it was much less than the previous night. This reduction helped kill the atmosphere – at least the atmosphere from the Milan fans as journalists talked of the passionate noise being generated by the Mancunians in the crowd.

The game commenced in typical European style with City captain Dave Watson swapping pennants with Milan's Gianni Rivera, although the tough City captain looked rather bemused when his opposite number also presented him with a bunch of flowers. Possibly the presentation affected City's early play with Milan creating a perfect opportunity to score in the first minute. Fortunately, full back Collovati shot wide, but for a short period Milan were in control with their number 10 Gianni Rivera proving his skill.

After the first fifteen minutes, City began to gain control with Tommy Booth and Dave Watson dominating the defence. In fact the Blues demonstrated a great deal of poise and confidence at this point and were clearly in control. So much so that after around 30 minutes the chant of 'Easy, Easy' emanated from the City fans on the terraces. This was before the Blues had even scored a goal. The chant seemed to increase the players' confidence even further.

After 38 minutes the popular Brian Kidd netted the first goal, prompting wild celebrations amongst the City fans. Hartford sent a carefully flighted cross to the unmarked Kidd, who simply headed home past two Milan defenders and goalkeeper Albertosi. It was just what City deserved, and with a further six decent goal attempts that half, as opposed to Milan's two – the opening attempt from Collovati and a shot by Buriani saved by Corrigan - the Blues were delighted with their performance.

In the 57th minute City increased their lead with Paul Power - playing his first game since injury in the League Cup at the start of October - making a long, 70 yard run into the penalty area. Once there he cut inside 18 year old defender Franco Baresi, and fired home a low left foot shot over the diving body of Albertosi. It was an important goal and gave the Blues an incredible 2-0 lead. Only two sides had defeated Milan in 52 European meetings at the San Siro, and no British side had ever defeated them there. City now seemed ready to make history. Understandably, the Blues lacked concentration immediately after Power's goal and Milan fought back.

Derek Wallis of the *Daily Mirror:* "Milan halved the lead two minutes after City scored when Albertino Bigon forced the ball over the line from Walter Novellino's cross and immediately City faced increasing pressure. Three times Corrigan was beaten, but each time the Linesman's flag was raised for offside. The decisions disgusted the crowd, some of whom took out their spite on Corrigan by pelting him with rubbish."

Other reports claimed Corrigan was hit by cans and fruit as the atmosphere turned hostile. Journalist Peter Gardner later wrote about the problems at the game's end: "Italian fans, as only they can, still caused a riot because of their own team's shortcomings and tear gas bombs were thrown to disperse the crowds."

With the viciousness of the crowd encouraging the Milan players, it was no wonder that the home side were dominant for the last 30 minutes, putting City were under great pressure. Defenders Booth and Watson once again proved their worth as they skilfully ended a number of important Milan moves. In the 83rd minute Albertino Bigon scored his second for the home side, and the game ended 2-2.

Tony Book felt the goal should have been disallowed: "I thought Milan's equalising goal was at least two yards offside, but I am extremely delighted and extremely satisfied with the result."

Everyone connected with the club recognised that a 2-2 draw in the San Siro fortress was still a remarkable achievement. Tony Book: "I can't think of a better performance in the four and a half years I have been manager of this Club. It was a truly magnificent effort by everyone. It was the best-ever given by a Blues team in Europe and we were only 8 minutes away from becoming the first British club ever to win in the San Siro stadium. The performance was magnificent. But it still took a lot of the cream from the display that we were pinned to a draw

at the finish. So we became the 10th overseas team to take a draw away from Milan - and we not only proved we have come of age in Europe but also learned a lot on the day."

"I am highly delighted at this result. More so in view of the fact that we were without Mike Channon, Peter Barnes and Gary Owen."

Kenny Clements: "We had the audacity to go two goals up at the San Siro thanks to Kidd and Power. It was a tough ground to play at. Fireworks going off and an intimidating atmosphere. No one ever beat them at home, but we were. They came back at us and it ended 2-2."

6th December 1978
Round 3 Leg 2
Attendance: 38,026

City 3-0 AC Milan

City Goalscorers: Booth, Hartford, Kidd
City: Corrigan; Keegan, Donachie, Booth, Watson, Power, Channon, Viljoen, Kidd, Hartford, Barnes

The return leg at Maine Road saw City demolish the Italians 3-0 with goals from Booth (14th Minute), Hartford (a wonderful 20 yard effort that dipped past Milan's keeper in the 31st minute), and Kidd (42nd minute). In addition to the goalscorers, the stars of that match were Colin Viljoen - who played his best game since signing - and the ever improving Paul Power.

The result put City through to the quarter finals of a European trophy for the first time since 1971, but the January UEFA draw wasn't kind as it paired City with top German side Borussia Monchengladbach. With West Bromwich Albion, Hertha, Duisberg, Dukla Prague, Honved and Red Star Belgrade all through the Blues had hoped for one of the smaller, less powerful sides. Nevertheless, the Blues were hopeful.

Kenny Clements: "We thrashed them at Maine Road in the second leg and I felt we'd made our mark as a European power. Everybody was talking about us, and we should have progressed further but we messed up."

Peter Barnes in action against Milan
(below and opposite)

7th March 1979
Round 4 Leg 1
Attendance: 39,005

City 1-1 Borussia Monchengladbach

City Goalscorer: Channon
City: Corrigan; Donachie, Power, Reid,
Watson, Booth, Channon, Viljoen, Kidd,
Hartford, Barnes

On 3rd March City defeated Bolton Wanderers 2-1 at Maine Road in the last game before the crucial meeting with the highly successful Borussia Monchengladbach in the UEFA Cup quarter final. Liverpool, in particular Bob Paisley, had spent considerable time helping the Blues prepare for this match by providing vital information on the West German side. Liverpool were the most experienced of all English clubs in Europe and had faced Monchengladbach on five occasions, the most famous was the 1977 European Cup final and the most recent being in the 1978 European Cup semi-final. Paisley told City that the game would be tough, and outlined the players to

watch. He also suggested that Dave Watson and Tommy Booth might be the key men in City's side as the Germans seemed to lack ability to attack the ball in the air.

In the 1977 European Cup final, Liverpool had defeated Monchengladbach by playing to the strengths of players like Tommy Smith and Paisley felt City should do the same. The first leg saw Malcolm Allison, who had returned to the Club in January as 'coaching overlord', perform one of his many shock moves when Nicky Reid was thrust in to the spotlight at the age of 18. Allison selected him to mark Allan Simonsen. It was an amazing selection at the time, but Reid did enough to justify Allison's bold move.

Mike Channon, who was rumoured to be unhappy at the Club, managed to give the Blues a 1-0 lead. Unfortunately, the highly disciplined Germans kept the pressure on and managed to snatch an equaliser and the often vital away goal.

20th March 1979
Round 4 Leg 2
Attendance: 30,000

Borussia Monchengladbach 3-1 City

City Goalscorer: Deyna
City: Corrigan; Donachie, Power, Viljoen, Watson, Booth, Channon, Reid (Deyna), Henry, Hartford, Barnes

Reid retained his place for the second leg (but still didn't make his League debut until eleven days later when he scored against Ipswich). He was clearly a talented player but his arrival in the heat of European competition without even making an appearance in the League did raise many questions about the way the Club was being managed. Reid went on to captain the Blues to the FA Youth Cup final the following May, and was voted City's young player of the year.

Malcolm Allison made yet another surprise selection as Tony Henry - another reserve who up to that point had only featured in two League game (once being substituted by Kenny Clements, once coming on for Asa

Hartford) - was included while experienced European campaigners Deyna, Bell, and Kidd were left on the bench with Paul Futcher.

City were very much the underdogs throughout the match and were losing 3-0 when, late on, Reid was substituted by Deyna. The experienced Pole provided City's only goal of the match, but it was too late and City were out of Europe.

Kenny Clements: "I broke my leg a few weeks after Milan so that made life a bit difficult for me, but the big problem was the return of Malcolm Allison. I know he was a great coach first time at City, but second time he really did ruin everything. All the older players told me it'd be great having him back, and then when he was back they all admitted they were wrong. I think he'd become too hung up on new ideas that he forgot about the basics. I remember he used to give us homework. He'd tell us to go home and write "I must win" or "I will win" a thousand times, then the next day he'd ask us if we'd done it.

"I always used to say 'yeah', but some of the younger, more impressionable lads would produce their lists and some would even write out twice as many lines! He insisted we drank coffee before a game to keep us alert, and brought in lots of motivational people. It didn't motivate me I'm afraid!

"By the time of the next UEFA match (Moenchengladbach) I was fit but didn't start, and then for the second leg both Brian Kidd and I had to sit it out while youngster Nicky Reid marked one of the greatest players of all time. When we were two goals down Kiddo threw his shirt at Allison in anger."

The Football Season Daily Reminder

January

1st January 1996

Two goals from Niall Quinn gave 1996 a good start as City defeated West Ham 2-1 at Maine Road (right) before a crowd of 26,024.

2nd January 1899

Local rivals and fellow promotion challengers Glossop North End defeated City 2-0 at Hyde Road with the *Glossop Chronicle* reporting: "There was evidently a determination to give the Mancunians a great surprise."

3rd January 1994

After 39 minutes City's game with Ipswich Town was abandoned with the Blues winning 2-0. The scorers were Vonk and Ingebrigtsen – his only League goal for the Blues was expunged from the records as a result.

4th January 1975

City play 'away' at Maine Road against Newcastle in the FA Cup. The tie should have been played at Newcastle but the FA ordered that the match be played at Maine Road following crowd disorder at St. James' Park the previous season. City lost the match 2-0.

5th January 1980

Allison's multi-million pound City side were humbled 1-0 at Fourth Division Halifax Town in the FA Cup.

6th January 2001

Goals from Andy Morrison, Darren Huckerby and a penalty from Shaun Goater brought City a 3-2 FA Cup third round win over Birmingham City.

7th January 1956

With the score at 1-1 City's cup tie with Blackpool was abandoned in the 56th minute after fog enveloped the ground. Four days later 42,517 attended a 2.15pm kick off on a Wednesday afternoon to see City win 2-1.

8th January 1990

Forward Wayne Clarke was signed from Leicester City while David Oldfield travelled in the opposite direction as part of the deal. Whereas Oldfield had played his part in City's history as one of the goalscorers in the memorable 5-1 victory over Manchester United in September 1989, Clarke struggled to carve out a place in the side. He left Maine Road for a variety of loan spells the following October after making only seven (plus 14 as substitute) first team appearances.

9th January 2000

Despite goals from Shaun Goater and Ian Bishop Division One City lost the fourth round FA Cup tie to Premiership Leeds United 5-2 at Maine Road.

10th January 1953

City defeated Swindon Town 7-0 in the FA Cup third round at Maine Road. The goalscorers were Hart (4), Broadis, Cunliffe, and Williamson. Exactly one year later future City full-back John Gidman was born in Garstang. Gidman went on to make 66 (plus 1 as substitute) appearances for the Blues and briefly

became a cult hero by stating that City were the only side he would leave Old Trafford for at the time of his transfer in 1986.

11th January 1977

Joe Royle ensured City progressed to face Newcastle United in the FA Cup by scoring the only goal of the Third Round replay at West Bromwich Albion. The first game had ended in a 1-1 draw at Maine Road.

12th January 1974

Denis Law and Rodney Marsh (above) provided the goals as City defeated Leicester City 2-0 at Maine Road. Four days later Law scored again as the Blues beat Coventry City 4-2 in the League Cup quarter-final replay. That game was notable as it came in the middle of industrial action resulting in power cuts across the Country. For this game to go ahead

City had to bring in an Electricity generator, which was positioned outside the ground.

13th January 1987

Peter Barnes re-signed for City from Manchester United and made his first appearance at home to Liverpool four days later.

14th January 1981

Kevin Reeves had a goal disallowed for 'illegal jumping', according to referee Alf Grey, in the first leg of the League Cup semi final against Liverpool at Maine Road. Afterwards manager John Bond claimed the referee would "never make a worse decision for as long as he lives." Liverpool went on to score a late winner but, despite a valiant effort, the Blues could only manage a 1-1 draw in the return game.

15th January 2005

Two goals from Shaun

Wright-Phillips helped the Blues defeat Crystal Palace 3-1 before a 44,010 crowd at Eastlands. The other City scorer was Robbie Fowler.

16th January 1909

Despite a hat trick from Tom Holford City lost 4-3 to Tottenham at Hyde Road in the FA Cup.

17th January 1925

Frank Roberts scored four as Liverpool were defeated 5-0 in Division One.

18th January 1913

Fred Howard scored four on his debut against Liverpool at Hyde Road. Three of those came in a 13 minute spell as the Blues won 4-1.

19th January 1991

Mark Ward scored twice as Howard Kendall's City defeated Sheffield United 2-0 before 25,741 at Maine Road.

20th January 2002

An own goal by Helguson helped the Blues defeat Watford 2-1 in Division One. The other scorer for City was Paulo Wanchope.

21st January 1976

Goals from Peter Barnes, Ged Keegan, Alan Oakes and Joe Royle in the semi-final second leg against Jack Charlton's Middlesbrough (below) guaranteed City an appearance in the League Cup final. The Blues had lost the first leg 1-0 to a Boro side that included Graeme Souness. The aggregate score was 4-1.

22nd January 1977

Brian Kidd scored four as City defeated Leicester 5-0 in the only League game featuring City to be staged during January 1977.

23rd January 1926

Manchester United were defeated 6-1 at Old Trafford by managerless City. This remains the record score in a Manchester derby match.

24th January 1981

John Bond's City defeated his former club Norwich 6-0 in the FA Cup fourth round tie.

25th January 1936

After a minute's silence (overleaf) to mark the death of King George V a Maine Road crowd of 65,978 witnessed a 2-1 City victory over Luton Town in the FA Cup fourth round.

26th January 1946

A comfortable 3-1 victory

Manchester City and Luton Town teams observing the two minutes' silence for King George at Maine-road this afternoon. Right: A section of the crowd paying their silent tribute.

for the Blues over Bradford Park Avenue in the fourth round of the FA Cup seemed certain to put City through to the fifth round. However, this first season of FA Cup football after the war saw games played on a home and away basis and the Blues were defeated 8-2 in the Maine Road return. Future England manager Ron Greenwood played for Avenue in both games.

27th January 2002

The fourth round FA Cup tie at Ipswich ended 4-1 as Kevin Keegan's side thrilled. The City scorers were Eyal Berkovic, Shaun Goater (2) and Darren Huckerby.

28th January 1961

Denis Law's six goals against Luton in the FAC were wiped from the records when the game was abandoned due to fog. City were winning 6-2, and lost the replay 3-1 (Law scored City's consolation).

29th January 1930

The fourth FA Cup tie played by City in 18 days ended in a 10-1 victory over Swindon Town.

30th January 1954

50,576 witnessed City's 1-0 FA Cup 4th round defeat by Tottenham at Maine

Road. In the previous round the Blues had beaten Bradford Park Avenue 5-2 with a hat trick from Bill McAdams.

31st January 1953

A goal from Ivor Broadis brought a 1-1 draw in the fourth round of the FA Cup at home to Luton. The match was watched by 38,411. City lost the replay 5-1.

CITY'S NUMBER ONE

THE PROFILES

45 - KEITH MACRAE

A £100,000 signing from Motherwell, Keith MacRae was signed by Johnny Hart shortly before he stood down as manager in October 1973. This was a very expensive signing at the time and it is clear that MacRae's arrival was a sign to both Joe Corrigan and Ron Healey that their opportunities at the Club would be limited. In fact in November 1973 the Club seemed keen to show that both goalkeepers were on their way out by including interviews with them both in the match programme saying that it was time to move on. This was a rather surprising move, but with MacRae the first choice of both Ron Saunders (who replaced Hart as manager in November 1973) and his successor Tony Book (who became manager in April 1974) it was inevitable that Healey and Corrigan had to consider their careers.

A League Cup final appearance came in March of MacRae's first season when City were defeated 2-1 by Wolves.

The following year MacRae started the season as number one and still seemed to be preferred over Corrigan – for example on 18th January 1975 the Blues beat Newcastle 5-1 with Corrigan hardly putting a foot wrong but MacRae still replaced him for the next game. Fate played its hand a few weeks later however as injury at Leicester on 8th March 1975 meant MacRae had to leave the field. Mike Doyle donned the green shirt for the rest of the match but, significantly for MacRae, Corrigan had to be selected for the following game. It was an opportunity the future England star would make the most of and MacRae lost his place as City's regular number one.

Occasional appearances followed before MacRae moved on in 1981 realising that Alex Williams was now regarded as Corrigan's understudy. He went to the States before a spell at Leeds United in which he made no League appearances.

Appearances: League: 56 FAC: 2 League Cup: 13

46 – ALEX WILLIAMS

Wilbraham High School pupil Alex Williams was a key member of City's youth team of the late 1970s, and appeared in two FA Youth Cup finals. Former City 'keeper Steve Fleet was involved with the youth set up at this time and he was keen to see the youngster given whatever opportunities possible. By the end of the 1978-79 season Williams' career had developed so much that he replaced Keith MacRae in the Central League.

In March 1981 he made his League debut – a 2-1 victory at home to West Bromwich

Albion - but inevitably Corrigan returned for the next game. Occasional appearances followed before Corrigan moved on in 1983 and Williams was given the Number One shirt on a permanent basis. He excelled.

During the 1984-85 promotion season Williams kept 21 clean sheets in a 42 game League – only one short of Joe Corrigan's record made in 1976-77. That consistency helped the Blues earn promotion under manager Billy McNeill, and the future looked bright for City's popular 'keeper. Sadly injury affected him and City suffered a bit of a goalkeeping crisis over the following seasons while Williams fought hard to regain fitness. Loan spells at Queen of the South and Port Vale followed. Then in January 1987 he moved to Vale Park on a permanent basis.

After 35 appearances at Port Vale Williams was forced to give up the game and he moved into community work for the Potteries club. In 1990 he moved back to City to help strengthen City's community work. Over the following two decades he worked tirelessly for the Blues, earning a MBE for his community work.

Appearances: League: 114 FAC: 2 League Cup: 9

47 – ERIC NIXON

Legend has it that Eric Nixon was working for a car valet company in Dukinfield while playing for Curzon Ashton when he turned up at Maine Road one day and asked for a trial. In September 1983 he was given his chance to shine in City's reserves and in a 1-1 draw with Barnsley he did enough to encourage the Blues to take a closer look. Three months later City signed him on professional forms and in September 1985 injury to Alex Williams gave Nixon his first opportunity to impress in the League. His debut saw City draw 2-2 with West Ham and, with Williams struggling to regain fitness, Nixon was given an extended run. In total he played in 28 League games and every cup game played by the Blues that season. This included an appearance at

Wembley in the inaugural Full Members' Cup final.

Despite Nixon's excellent season Billy McNeill was not entirely convinced and he signed Perry Suckling in 1986. Nixon went on a series of loans, and played for four different clubs in four different divisions over a five month period. He returned to the City first team for the final five League games of the 1986-87 season and re-established himself as City's first choice for the 1987-88 season.

Unfortunately, a sending off against Crystal Palace in December brought an enforced absence and the following February he went on loan to Tranmere. He signed for the Merseyside club the following July and went on to play over 300 League games for them. Spells at a variety of clubs followed and Nixon made a League appearance for Sheffield Wednesday at the age of 40 years and 11 months in 2003. Nixon was Wednesday's goalkeeping coach and came on as substitute for Kevin Pressman. According to Wednesday Nixon made several crucial saves in the goalless draw.

Appearances: League: 58 FAC: 10 League Cup: 8

48 – BARRY SIDDALL

After long spells at Bolton and Sunderland, Barry Siddall was a very experienced 'keeper. He arrived at City on loan in March 1986 as cover for Eric Nixon and Alex Williams as City were suffering a bit of a goalkeeping crisis due to Williams' injury earlier in the season. This was Nixon's first League season and it was anticipated that Siddall would help develop the younger 'keeper while also helping the Blues stabilise in Division One – remember City had been promoted the previous season.

Siddall's debut came against Liverpool at Anfield on 31st March 1986, but the match ended in a 2-0 defeat – only 9 days earlier Nixon had performed well in the 2-2 draw at Old Trafford and so most fans felt that Nixon would have offered more consistency.

Only one point was earned during Siddall's six League appearances with Eric Nixon deservedly returning to action for the final match of the 1985-86 season while Siddall returned to Stoke City. Spells at a variety of clubs followed, including Bury in 1993-94.

Appearances: League: 6

The Alex Williams Interview

Shortly after City's move to their current stadium Gary James interviewed Alex Williams. Here's a selection of questions and answers from that interview.

As a boy in Moss Side how did you view City?

I enjoyed playing football and City were naturally the club I wanted to play for, but I never really expected to get the opportunity. I came from a school which produced several good players – Roger Palmer, Clive Wilson, Eric Nixon - and I was also involved with the Manchester Boys side, so when Steve Fleet asked me to come for training two nights a week it was a great thrill, but not necessarily a great surprise. I was delighted to be at Maine Road, but when I saw some of the other guys play I felt average! There were some great players, but I was lucky because being a local lad I was available when some of the others couldn't be.

A chance came and I played for the A team against Carlisle Reserves. I did okay, and we got a good result. I still didn't think I was good enough, but I was offered a two year apprenticeship at the end of that season.

You say you were lucky, but you are clearly playing down your qualities because you started to be considered for representative honours didn't you?

Yes, I suppose you're right. I won a cap when I played for the England U-18 against Yugoslavia, and I was also picked for the U-21 squad, but I guess what I'm trying to say is that I kept my feet on the ground. I never considered myself a great player.

Others did though. I remember a piece by journalist Derek Hodgson saying you

would win more international caps than Joe Corrigan. How did that feel?

Well it was nice, but I didn't want any of that to go to my head because, as my injury showed later, you can never predict football.

How did your first League appearance come about?

Well, it was West Brom V City in 1981 and I think Joe Corrigan was injured but I had no idea I'd be playing. On the morning of the match no one said anything about it at all and then at 1.30 John Bond took me to one side and told me I was playing. Fortunately, I didn't have time to think and so I managed to keep my nerves under control. I was also very glad that my father was at the game. It meant an awful lot to him.

How did the game itself go?

I was wearing a red top because I think West Brom were wearing yellow and green stripes, and of course I'm black, so I certainly stood out! I suppose I became an easy target, but we won the match 2-1 and I was very happy. I knew I was understudy to Joe, but making that first appearance meant so much. My father was so proud. Remember his life had been hard at times. He'd come over from Jamaica and had to take on all sorts of jobs to feed the family. He used to work in Middleton and at one time in Hyde, and would do any job he could. So me playing for City was a great time for him. He was a very proud father, although I have to admit I sometimes worried about how he felt about the abuse and the bananas.

I'm glad you've mentioned that because, as a fan, I remember seeing opposition fans throwing bananas and shouting racist abuse. How did you cope?

That's a difficult one. I tried to block it out, but I kept thinking about how my dad would feel. He did suffer from Asthma and I eventually persuaded him not to come to the game for health reasons but, if I'm honest, the abuse played a part in that decision.

You were the first Black goalkeeper in the League, weren't you?

I was the first of the modern era, but there was actually a 'keeper called Arthur Wharton at the end of the 1890s who played for Rotherham and Sheffield United who was the first black player in the League. Obviously, society changed completely by the time I was playing 80 years later, so I became recognised as the first. It did bring difficulties, but to me I was a goalkeeper and, on the pitch, that's all that mattered. I received a lot of abuse at the start of the Tottenham game in 1982 but we won 2-1 and, at the end, the London fans gave me a very good ovation. That felt nice because my performance won them over.

Another difficult place for black players was Leeds but to me it was one of the best grounds to visit. Sure the atmosphere was intimidating but I thrived on it there, and always seemed to be at my best. I never lost at Elland Road and could have played there every week.

Considering you eventually took over from fans' favourite Corrigan I'd be interested to know how you felt the City fans treated you?

They were – are – always terrific. They always gave me great support. They appreciate good goalkeepers and I think I did enough in my first few games to show I had some ability. I was still a young player and when I slipped a little I was worried I'd be replaced. Then there were rumours that Pat Jennings was going to sign, but the manager told me to ignore all of that and enjoy the game. I did and the fans helped me enormously. Their support lifts you a great deal.

I have to ask you about the Luton relegation match in 1983.

Could I have stopped the goal? I've asked myself this dozens of times over the years and I can honestly say I could not have done any better. I dived and did actually touch the ball but I couldn't do anything more than that. Relegation was a major blow and I did worry again that someone else might come in, but two years later I kept 21 clean sheets in a 42 game season.

So what do you view was you greatest game?

A 1-0 victory over Chelsea at Stamford Bridge in December 1983. We were both pushing for promotion and this was a crucial result at the time. Jim Tolmie scored, but I was unbeatable that day. Speedie and Dixon battered us but nothing could get past me. I don't know how I did it. It was one of those days when you just know you can't fail. I loved it. It was great.

ATKINSON FOR ENGLAND

The second part of our excerpt from "Atkinson For England" By Gary James & Mark Brown

"Unusual in't it?" said Reg who was impressed. He liked hotels with a bit of character, and this was so unexpected that he was still behaving like a schoolboy, hopping from photo to article, from wall to wall.

"I'm not keen on that picture," said Norman, pointing at Varadi who looked a bit too much like Uri Geller for Norman's liking, "and that one scares me to death." He gestured towards the Gidman picture, but couldn't bring himself to look at it again.

"Get away," chortled Reg, "eh listen, it's past three o'clock. Get your stuff hung up and we'll find a cafe for a sarny and a pot of tea, OK?"

"Aye OK," said Norman.

After traipsing around the streets surrounding the hotel, Reg and Norman found a distinct lack of suitable establishments to provide a sandwich and a pot of tea. It seemed as though most shops were closed and as the clock approached five in the afternoon, hunger had forced them into Pizza Hut. After they had finished, Reg took himself back to his room at the Kippax for a late afternoon siesta, while Norman decided to see a few of the nearby sights.

Later that evening, the two men went out to sample some of the local hostelries. They found that a similar problem applied to the afternoon - not many pubs appeared to be open. After trying out the least offensive, Reg and Norman decided to return to the hotel for a night-cap at the bar before retiring for the night.

Dave Bayley welcomed them back with open arms. Reg and Norman took a seat at the bar while Dave prepared to serve them.

"What can I get you?" he asked.

"Couple of pints should do it," said Reg.

Dave poured two pints of bitter and told Reg and Norman that the drinks were being paid for by the FA so not to worry about the bar bill.

"Great!" Reg exclaimed, "you joining us Dave?"

"Don't mind if I do," said a delighted Dave, and poured a pint for himself.

"That's a nice touch," said Norman, pointing to a sign above the bar that read "DENIS LAW BAR".

"That came from the Kippax," said Dave, "The Kippax was the stand where I used to go when I was a kid."

"Oh right," said Reg, "The Kippax Hotel."

"Yeah, that's where the name came from," said Dave, "the stand got demolished in ninety-four. Everybody wanted a piece of it as a souvenir. Some people got bits of concrete steps, crush barriers, you know. Me, I got this." He gestured towards the bar sign.

"I played against Denis Law in his first game," announced Norman.

"Yeah?" said Dave. Reg looked on - he had not heard this before.

"Aye," Norman continued, "Christmas 1956. Denis was playing for Huddersfield and I was at Notts County then. We had to play 'em twice over Christmas and the bugger scored in the second game."

"I cannot believe that I am in the same room as somebody who played for Joe Mercer..."

"For three weeks," whispered Reg.

"...and played against Denis Law as well," finished Dave, by now in fan heaven.

"Little sod robbed the ball off me on the halfway line and before I could get anywhere near him, he'd put it in the back of the net," Norman said wistfully, "mind you, he was about twenty years younger than I was then. You could see he was going to be a good player though."

Dave remained speechless. He had a new hero.

"I retired not long after that," Norman continued, "things were getting too fast for me."

The three sat in silence for a moment, contemplating their beers.

"Tell us Dave," Reg began, "why is London shut?"

"What do you mean?" asked Dave, startled out of his reverie. He could not take his eyes off Norman who was slowly sipping his pint.

"Well," Reg continued, "we went out this afternoon for a bite to eat but everywhere was closed. Same tonight - we went out looking for a nice pub but they're all shut. I thought the capital of England would be a bit busier than this."

"That's right," Norman confirmed, "the city that never sleeps."

"That's New York," hissed Reg.

"Same thing," Norman hissed back.

"It's funny," said Dave, "but it does look like that sometimes. It's as though all the action happens in little pockets. You probably just walked through all the quiet bits."

"Probably," said Reg, unconvinced.

"So," said Dave, rubbing his hands, "big day tomorrow then?"

"Aye," said Reg.

"Nervous?" asked Dave.

"A bit," Reg replied. He had been back to his room to retrieve his briefcase. Within the case was a potted history of Reg's work, photographs of completed projects and recommendations and references from past customers. He had placed this on the barstool next to him and now opened it. As he leafed through the documents, he came across an old photograph of a boiler suited Tom Finney stood next to a young Reg with a ballcock in his hand. He handed this to Dave.

"There y'are," he said, "that's part of my football connection."

"Blimey," Dave gasped, "is that Tom Finney?"

"Aye," Reg replied, "when I left school, my Dad insisted I take up a trade and got me in as an apprentice with Tom Finney in Preston. Not many people knew he was a fully qualified plumber."

"Blimey," said Dave again, "if that had been part of City folklore, I would have been pinching that picture and putting it on a wall somewhere." He laughed.

"Have you got any pictures Norman?" asked Dave almost reverentially, "you know, of you and Joe Mercer or you and Denis Law?"

"He wasn't near any of 'em long enough," quipped Reg.

"Oy," said Norman, feigning annoyance, "I've got some pictures at home somewhere, but I don't know if I've got any of those two with me."

"Oh," said Dave, still too excited to be disappointed.

Reg continued looking through his documents: there were photographs of bathroom suites, central heating systems, Mansfield swimming baths and many instances of Reg's work.

Norman looked at Reg - he could tell the younger man was nervous. Probably the best thing, he thought, would be to change the subject of the interview to something more comfortable.

"Do you play any football, Dave?" he asked.

"Not much now," Dave said, "although I used to play for the Under Sixteen's at school. I just don't get much opportunity these days."

"Shame that," said Norman kindly, "Reg manages our pub team - The Forest Inn. Won the league last year."

"That's great," said Dave impressed, "eh, maybe you can convince the FA to give you the England manager's job while you're there tomorrow?" They all laughed which helped relieve some of Reg's tension.

Over the course of the next hour, Reg and Norman got to know Dave a lot better and the beginnings of a friendship were established. They discussed his plans for the hotel and his certainty that the quiet times were a thing of the past. Dave was investing in an Internet site and looking at the potential for marketing the hotel in different ways. Although Reg and Norman had their doubts - especially as the hotel seemed completely empty apart from themselves - they said nothing to dampen Dave's enthusiasm: after all, this was his life. It was fairly obvious he was obsessed by City and the hotel was a monument to him. Not too many visitors would understand everything; Dave had done this for himself - it was his temple.

So, they discussed football - this was the main connecting factor in all their lives. Norman recalled his own playing days in the late forties and fifties. Reg told of his father's hero worship of Stanley Matthews and the influence he had on his life. It helped relieve any anxiety Reg had for the next day and brought the three men closer together. They also discussed memories of Manchester where Reg had spent most of his school life.

Eventually, some time past midnight and half way down a bottle of Dave's best single malt, Reg remembered what he had come to London for and announced he was off to bed.

"Bloody 'ell," said Norman, "It's that time already?"

"See you in the morning Dave," said Reg, "I could keep talking all night, but like you said, big day tomorrow."

"Yeah," said Dave disappointed. He never had opportunities to talk in depth like this, with people who he considered to be the same class as himself and the same sort of background. And Norman, bloody hell, he had turned out to be someone who had rubbed shoulders with two of City's best-loved heroes. He had really enjoyed himself. He perked up again.

"'night lads," he said, "breakfast is whenever you want it. Just give us a shout OK? No time limits."

"Yeah, cheers Dave," yawned Reg. He and Norman stood up - Norman was a little unsteady on his feet. He nodded his thanks to Dave - he didn't trust himself to speak at this moment.

Reg and Norman headed for the lift. When they arrived outside their respective doors they bid each other a good night and entered their rooms. Reg was soon in bed asleep; Norman climbed under the covers of his own bed but kept looking at the picture of John Gidman which was on the wall directly facing the bed. Even in the dark, he could feel that mesmeric gaze - the eyes were boring into him.

Enough was enough – he could cope with a million bananas suspended from the ceiling, but those things on the wall... yuk! Norman clambered out of bed, switched on the light and shuffled over to the offending picture. He grabbed both sides of the frame and levered the picture around until its back was facing the room and Mr Gidman faced the wall. The back of the picture revealed an even more disturbing picture of John Bond - Norman wasn't entirely sure who it was but knew that this picture was not much of an improvement on the last. With a grunt, he took the whole picture off the wall and placed it in the wardrobe for the night.

Norman returned to bed quite happily, switched off the light and was soon asleep.

"Atkinson For England" by Gary James & Mark Brown (published in 2001) continues with Reg taking on the biggest role in football. For details on how to purchase an ebook version of the story see www.manchesterfootball.org

CITY'S NUMBER ONE

THE PROFILES

49 – PERRY SUCKLING

Bought for £50,000 plus the popular David Phillips, England youth international Perry Suckling was anticipated to be City's first choice for several years when he arrived from Coventry City in May 1986. It didn't work out that way however and by the end of December 1987 he was on loan at Chelsea. A permanent move to Crystal Palace followed in January 1988 – City received £100,000 – and after 39 League appearances that was it.

Spells for West Ham, Brentford, Watford and Doncaster followed.

Appearances: League: 39 FAC: 1 League Cup: 3

50 – BOBBY MIMMS

Despite earning an FA Cup finalists medal for Everton in 1986 Bobby Mimms knew he was always likely to be understudy to Neville Southall at Goodison.

In September 1987 he arrived on loan at Maine Road during a period of goalkeeping instability for the Blues and made three consecutive League appearances. The last of these saw City beat Leicester 4-2, but the others had ended in defeat.

On 8th October 1987 he returned to Goodison, but was soon on the move again. By the end of his career he had played League football for 13 clubs. His longest first team run coming at Spurs where he made 126 League appearances over a five year period.

Appearances: League: 3

51 – MIKE STOWELL

Another Everton 'keeper on loan to the Blues. Mike Stowell arrived at Maine Road in February 1988 and managed to stay with the Club for three months. The opening minutes of his debut suggested the 'keeper might find life at City difficult – he conceded a goal after only three minutes against Blackburn (City lost the game 2-1).

He played in 14 consecutive League games but was replaced by Eric Nixon for the fifth round FA Cup tie with Plymouth on 20th February. City won that match 3-1 but Stowell was selected for the quarter final tie with Liverpool the following month. That game ended 4-0 and many fans felt that Nixon, who had appeared in every FA Cup tie that season (and every League Cup tie which also resulted in a quarter final appearance), should have been given the opportunity.

After City, Stowell made appearances for Port Vale and Preston, but became most known for his permanent move to Wolves where he appeared in over 370 League games.

Appearances: League: 14 FAC: 1

52 – ANDY DIBBLE

Andy Dibble joined City in the 1988 close season after impressing in the League Cup final for Luton against Arsenal. In that match Dibble saved a penalty and basically helped transform what seemed like certain defeat into a Luton victory. His City League debut came in a Second Division match on 27th August 1988 against Hull. Sadly, the season's opener ended in a 1-0 defeat. A 4-1 defeat by Oldham followed and Dibble found himself in a team desperate for a win to help ease the pressure on manager

Mel Machin. That win eventually came in the fifth match of the season and, thanks to Dibble's obvious vocal encouragement, City tightened up defensively as the season progressed.

By the end of February the Blues seemed certainties for promotion and Dibble had played his part with six clean sheets in the first seven League games of 1989. Then misfortune struck as a leg injury in the game at Walsall on 25th March forced him to leave the field. Dibble missed the following six games (three of which ended in defeat) and then, when he returned, injury struck in his second match. Nigel Gleghorn went in nets, as he had done at Walsall, and the match with Crystal Palace became one of the most talked about and memorable games of the late 1980s as Gleghorn performed heroically to help City achieve a 1-1 draw (he'd also scored the opener!).

The following season Dibble was joined at Maine Road by experienced 'keeper Paul Cooper. Dibble was without doubt City's first choice, but injury caused him to miss seven games early on.

In 1990 Tony Coton was signed by manager Howard Kendall and Dibble effectively became Coton's understudy. A series of loan spells followed but with Martyn Margetson developing rapidly and Coton proving a quality 'keeper, Dibble's chances became limited further.

In 1997 Dibble impressed during a loan spell at Rangers and on 12th March that year he made a permanent move to the Scottish club.

He later returned to England and made 22 League appearances for Stockport County before a move to Wrexham in August 2002 where he shone once more.

Appearances: League: 113 (plus 3 as sub) FAC: 8 (plus 1) League Cup: 14

The Andy Dibble Interview

In February 2004 Gary James interviewed Andy Dibble while he was still playing League football for Wrexham. Here's a selection of questions and answers from that interview.

Looking at your pre-City career, it was the League Cup final for Luton in 1988 when most City fans would have first noticed you.

That was an unbelievable moment in my career, and I guess it's the penalty save from Nigel Winterburn that most people will remember. Of course, the fact the game was at Wembley meant a great deal to me. I don't care what people say about the way the stadium was in its final years, playing at Wembley was always something very, very special.

The following summer you joined City. How did that come about?

I was out of contract and my manager, the late Ray Harford – a truly lovely man - talked to me about the future. I knew City were interested and that appealed enormously. I didn't move for money – I'd have been as well off at Luton – but the glamour and history of City appealed. I'd heard a lot of positive comments about the Club and it appealed. It seemed a logical progression.

So what was your debut like?

Awful! We lost 1-0 at Hull City, and then we got beat 4-1 at home to Oldham. We had a few new players and it took some time for the team to settle, but when we did we started to push for promotion from Division Two. Our first away win of the season was at Chelsea (3-1) who, in the end, were our biggest rivals for promotion.

Which games stood out for you during that season?

Quite a few matches became crucial towards the end of the season, but I suppose the biggest test was when we beat Oxford 4-2 at the end of April. I'd been missing for about 5 weeks after injury in the match at Walsall and this was my first game back. If we'd have lost that we wouldn't have stood much chance of promotion because we'd slipped up a little during April.

The saddest part for me is that I missed out on the last two games of the season because of injury again. I think I came back a little too soon. I was fortunate that surgery eventually sorted me out but there are times as a player when you can't help but think of others like Paul Lake whose career was cut short through injury. He was a great player.

How did you find your first season overall?

Great. Apart from the injuries it was all I'd hoped for. The funny thing is this was the season when the banana craze really dominated. I loved that time. It didn't matter which ground we went to we could always see our support. The yellow bananas were so visible that we always felt as if we were the home side. I think that, together with the overall size of City's away support, helped to create an intimidating atmosphere for our opponents – even on their own ground! That support certainly helped the players.

Despite promotion, a few months into the 1989-90 season Mel Machin was dismissed as manager. How did this affect your career?

Well I was very happy with City following promotion. So much so that I signed a new four year contract. I wanted to ensure I was

City's number one for a long time. Of course Howard Kendall replaced Mel Machin and in 1990 he brought in Tony Coton – a friend of mine incidentally. Competition is healthy, but I did think at the time that I was on a par with Tony. A series of loan spells followed but I was never likely to be first choice at City on a regular basis after Tony's arrival.

As a supporter it seemed Howard Kendall found the infamous Gary Crosby goal in the game with Nottingham Forest in March 1990 difficult to accept. The player sneaked up and knocked it out of your hands before firing home. Nowadays I don't believe the goal would stand, but as the key City player involved how were you treated at the time?

That goal! Even today I get reminded about this on a regular basis. It's one of those things you can never get away from, but at the time the media attention was massive. It was shown time after time on a variety of shows. I think it was a complete fluke and I did feel very hard done by at the time. Nowadays I have no worries about it at all. In fact I can now laugh about it. Just!

Once Coton was at Maine Road was it difficult sitting on the bench?

I didn't really have to sit on the bench. Back then the second choice keeper was usually playing for the reserves. If I wasn't in the reserves or on the bench I was on loan, so I was always kept busy. It must be difficult for some of today's Premiership 'keepers to be sat waiting for their chance. For younger 'keepers it's all part of a transition, but for good quality established 'keepers it must be difficult always sat on the bench.

What was the worst moment of your City career?

My last game. It was against Oxford and we were winning but went on to lose 3-2 (November 1996). It was all very sad and the fans were far from happy that day. I'd have preferred to have left with a good win but that's history now. It's particularly sad, as I didn't want to leave the Club at all.

The loan spells had brought some great moments – play offs with Middlesbrough for example – and since leaving I've had plenty of other good memories. Playing for Rangers against Celtic alongside Gascoigne and the other great players they had at the time was awesome.

As a boy had you always wanted to be a goalkeeper?

I actually started as a left back but I remember being compared to a dressmakers dummy, so I was eventually persuaded to play in nets. My heroes were Joe Corrigan and, of course, the other great 'keepers of Clemence, Shilton and Parkes. Big Joe succeeded because of his hard work and dedication so I suppose that was something I always wanted to match. He was a good example to follow.

Finally, how did the City fans treat you during your time with the Blues?

Tremendous. I loved being at the Club and I always wanted to get out and meet the fans. I attended supporters meetings, Junior Blues events and the like. To me that was as important as playing in some ways. I am a very keen believer in meeting supporters and promoting the Club. Even now I like attending supporter events when I can.

At heart I am still a very big Blue.

SUPPORTERS' CLUB FOCUS

Today City have two official supporter organisations – the Official Supporters' Club (OSC) and the Centenary Supporters' Association (CSA) – with the oldest of these, the OSC, claiming a formation date of 1949. The CSA was created as a result of a split within the OSC during 1993 when some branches and members were in conflict with the governing OSC committee over the Francis Lee-Peter Swales takeover battle.

Since the mid-nineties efforts have been made to bring the two organisations together, however despite a close working relationship between branches and members the two organisations remain separate. It is also worth stating that other supporter organisations have existed including a Supporters' Trust during the takeover issues of the modern era.

In 2009 the OSC proudly boasted of its sixty year existence – a proud record, especially as many other clubs did not have a supporter organisation of any description until the 1960s (In 1968 it was reported that United's supporters' organisation only came into being in 1963).

Despite the OSC accepting 1949 as their formation date, it appears that one form of official supporters' club, or possibly some of the present OSC's branches, is actually much older than the organisation admits. There is evidence to say an OSC was actually formed in the 1920s.

In March 1968 a newspaper article focussed on Manchester's two leading sides and Edith Whelan was interviewed about the City Supporters' Club. She revealed that the organisation consisted of 14 branches

with an annual subscription of 3 shillings and that club ties were available at 13s 6d old money. The article added that the organisation was created in 1928, though no hard evidence was presented to say how this was known.

In 1928 City's leading supporter representative was a man called Bob Roden. Roden was a well known figure around the Blues and was recognised as the Club's first historian. It is not clear whether he was one of the founders of the first supporters' club, but he does appear to have been influential at that time in all supporter related activity. *The Topical Times* profiled him in 1928 as the leading Manchester City supporter and it seems likely that this prompted the creation of the Supporters' Club.

Despite the references to the City Supporters' Club existing pre-war it seems that the date of 1949 has been highlighted as the OSC formation date as the Brooks Bar branch, for many years the most prominent branch, was created in that year. The Brooks Bar branch became the model and template for many subsequent branches and so it seems appropriate that this should be seen as the father of many branches.

However, this downplays the history of the Supporters' Club at places such as Denton and Gorton who are known to have had vibrant branches before 1949.

Inevitably, some will say that whatever supporters' organisation was in place in 1928 it seems clear that this did not survive the war years, however this is not true. Even if all pre-war supporter organisations are ignored it is a fact that there existed several branches of an official supporters' club prior to 1949.

Match programmes carried news of supporter meetings pre-1949. For example on 13th March 1948 the City programme listed the next meeting dates for several branches under the small heading: 'Supporters' Club News'. Those branches, with the venue for their meeting in brackets, were: Longsight (Crown Hotel), Denton (Nottingham Castle), Miles Platting (King's Arms), Gorton & Reddish (The Plough), Eccles (Duke of York), Ladybarn (Talbot), Northenden (Tatton Arms) and Chorlton (Southern Hotel).

Looking at this list of branches and the frequency of their meetings (each branch met weekly!) it seems highly unlikely that the entire Supporters'

Their fan club girls are fanatics

By KENNETH MOOR

MANCHESTER City have a supporters' club which proudly boasts it is one of the few recognised by the directors of a football club.

Manchester United have a fan club—'the only one recognised by the board'.

As secretaries, both have ladies who are football fanatics. Both deplore Soccer hooliganism. Both have around 2,000 members. There the similarities end.

Manchester City Supporters' Club was founded in 1928. There are 14 branches up and down the country. Subscriptions are 3s. a year.

Dances

On match days, members are admitted to Manchester City's Social Club—claimed by manager Roy Clarke, much-capped former Welsh international, to be 'the biggest and finest of its type in Europe'—on production of their card.

The supporters' club organises dances and concerts to raise funds. They sell club ties at 13s. 6d. and half-crown lapel badges.

Secretary Mrs Edith Whelan says: 'Over the past three years we have made very favourable progress.'

She has been secretary for six years, says her husband is a football widower, and first saw Manchester City as a shawl-swathed babe-in-arms, carried to the Hyde Road ground by her father.

Mrs Whelan, a company cashier, says: 'We are proud and jealous of the name of our supporters' club. We are pledged

to expel members who are involved in trouble. This hasn't happened yet.

Objects: to support Manchester City and organise trips to away matches. To stamp out hooliganism.

Manchester United's Fan Club was founded in 1963. It has no branches. Subscriptions are 10s. a year.

There are no club functions but members receive a free 16-20 page magazine in January, April, and December. At present the club's badge, featuring a red devil on a silver background, is also free. From September, members will have to pay an extra 2s. 6d. for it.

Secretary Miss Dorothy Woolley, who puts in 30 unpaid hours a week, says: 'In the first year we had a £70 loss. Now we make a modest profit which is put aside for emergencies.'

She has been secretary for four years, is respectfully called 'Miss' by the younger members of the committee, and watched United for the first time five years ago.

Cheering

The club committee meets weekly in a hired room.

Objects: To keep supporters in 32 countries up to date with club affairs and to sell pictures of star players. More than 100 letters weekly are written giving news of United.

Some are to explain that the fan club can't arrange match tickets.

Last night, from their stand seats, Mrs Whelan was cheering the Blues, Miss Woolley the Reds.

Supporters' Club News: Next week's branch meetings: Tuesday, Longsight (Crown Hotel), Denton (Nottingham Castle), Miles Platting (King's Arms); Wednesday, Gorton and Reddish (Plough); Thursday, Eccles (Duke of York), Ladybarn (Talbot); Friday, Northenden (Tatton Arms). Kick-off 8 p.m. in each case. The Chorlton branch is holding a dance at the Southern Hotel on Wednesday night. Everyone invited.

HYDE

DO you come from Hyde? The Secretary of the Hyde Branch of the Manchester City Supporters' Club is Mr. T. Darling, 25, Albion Street, Hyde.

Club would collapse and reform within the following year or so. The Denton branch, and possibly some of the others, must surely have evolved into the present day Denton branch. However, it is known that by the end of the 1950s the Supporters' Club did include the year 1949 within their title. So what actually happened in the forties? It

seems a major shame that the OSC does not claim its history back to 1928.

The Big Book Of City would like to identify the truth about the pre-1949 supporters' organisations and would like to help document the development and extent of City's various supporters' clubs from the beginning of the Blues through to the 1940s. If you have information on the history of the branches listed above, or of the organisation during the 1920s and 30s then please email **city@manchesterfootball.org** or write to us at **The Big Book Of City, James Ward, PO Box 822, Halifax, HX1 9FX.**

CITY'S NUMBER ONE

THE PROFILES

53 – PAUL COOPER

When the experienced Ipswich Town UEFA Cup winner Paul Cooper joined City on 21st March 1989 he arrived to provide urgent support as City pushed for promotion from the Second Division. Initially he was supposed to simply provide reassurance and perhaps some coaching expertise but four days after his arrival Andy Dibble was injured at Walsall. Cooper made his debut in the next match and did help the Blues achieve promotion with eight appearances that season, including the final match of the season at Bradford. In fact it was Cooper's throw that ultimately set City up to score the equaliser via Trevor Morley.

The following season Dibble appeared in the first couple of games, but then Cooper's chance came again and he made seven consecutive appearances during a crucial period. That run included a memorable 5-1 victory over Alex Ferguson's United on 23rd September 1989.

On 20th July 1990 Cooper moved to Stockport where he made 22 League appearances for County.

Appearances: League: 15

54 – TONY COTON

Howard Kendall was keen to strengthen all aspects of the Club when he arrived during the 1989-90 season. Kendall did rate regular number one Andy Dibble however the 'keeper had suffered with injuries during the late eighties and Kendall felt there simply was not strength in depth. The new manager signed Tony Coton for a fee of around £1m during the 1990 close season and he proved to be an excellent signing.

By this time Coton had enjoyed a good career with First Division Watford and Second Division Birmingham. In fact he had hit the headlines from the moment he made his debut for Birmingham when, with only 54 seconds played of a 1980 meeting with Sunderland, he saved a penalty with his first touch of the ball.

At Maine Road some supporters found it difficult taking to Coton initially. Andy Dibble, and Paul Cooper for that matter, was a popular 'keeper and the fee seemed exceptionally high when there were still other gaps in the side that needed filling. However, none of the fans' criticisms were actually as a result of Coton's efforts. In fact the 'keeper did nothing but impress. So much so that he was voted City's player of the year in his second season. He also gained an England 'B' Cap in 1992. To many it seemed only a matter of time before a full England cap arrived but sadly it never did. Why it didn't mystified most City fans and neutrals, and some have even suggested that City Chairman Peter Swales' role on the FA international committee played a part (the rumour was that the player's contract would mean the Blues would have to pay him more if he became an international).

Coton was one of England's finest 'keepers of the nineties and should have played for the national side. The fact he didn't perhaps says a great deal about the direction of England and the FA during the immediate post-Robson period.

In 1993-4 Coton was again voted City player of the year, and he remained a very popular 'keeper, providing stability during a difficult season for the Club both on and off the field. Sadly injury affected him for a spell, but following Alan Ball's appointment as manager Coton seemed to be out of favour.

During 1996 he was transferred to Manchester United for £500,000 – at the time a record for a transfer between the two clubs. As is the norm with City a variety

of rumours circulated. These claimed that Coton had sacrificed a first team place at City for life on the bench at United, but these rumours now are widely accepted to be false. In fact Coton has revealed in recent years that Alan Ball had told him that he would not be City's first choice and that he was on his way out. Knowing how other 'star' City players, including for example Niall Quinn, were treated at this time it is clear that Coton's comments are believable. He is adamant that the move was not sought by him. The criticism he received following his transfer is clearly not justified and it's worth stating that Coton felt he could have still achieved a great deal at Maine Road when he was transferred by Ball. A point proved by the fact that six months after his Old Trafford move he had a spell at Sunderland where he did play in their first team.

Inevitably Coton moved into coaching while at United, but his love of City continued.

As a key player during the reign of four managers – Kendall, Reid, Horton, and Ball – Coton proved to be a very capable 'keeper and a firm favourite with City fans.

Appearances: League: 162 (plus 1 as sub) FAC: 12 League Cup: 16

55 – MARTYN MARGETSON

When Nicky Weaver came on as substitute on the last day of the 2004-05 season and David James moved into an outfield position it was widely reported that this was the first time two goalkeepers had appeared in a first team game at the same time, but this is not true. In fact goalkeeper Martyn Margetson was brought on as an outfield substitute in a League Cup tie against Wycombe in 1995 while Eike Immel remained between the posts. Basically, Margetson was brought on as substitute for Richard Edghill as the Blues defeated Wycombe 4-0 on 4th October 1995.

Of course Margetson was more familiar to City fans as a 'keeper. He joined the Club from school and made his debut in a goalless League Cup tie against Torquay when he came on as substitute for Tony Coton on 10th October 1990. He had to wait some time for his League debut but when it came it was by far the most high profile League game of the season – the Old Trafford derby match. Ryan Giggs made his debut for United that same day and City suffered a 1-0 defeat, but seven days later the final game of the season saw Margetson help the Blues to a 3-2 victory over Sunderland. That game relegated the Wearsiders, but the victory also meant that City finished above United for the first time since 1978.

As Tony Coton arrived during the summer of 1990 Margetson's chances became limited and in 1991-92 he managed three League appearances. The following year his only appearance came on the final day of the season but this was not a pleasant experience and he was substituted at half time as Everton tore City to pieces at Maine Road (the game ended 5-2 to the visitors).

In 1996 25 year old Margetson was brought back into the side for a run of ten consecutive League games, but even then it was clear that he was not the preferred choice. Tommy Wright was signed and Margetson's run came to an abrupt end, although the Welshman did return to the side for the final six games of the season, and the first 12 games of 1997-98.

Clearly the managerial merry-go-round of the late 1990s upset long term planning at the Club and as a result Margetson, Immel, Wright and Dibble each had spells as first choice. When Joe Royle finally brought stability to the Club in 1998-99 Margetson had already left the Blues. Spells at Huddersfield and Cardiff amongst others followed.

Appearances: League: 51 FAC: 3 League Cup: 2 (plus 2 as substitute)

SPOT THE DIFFERENCE

For this edition of *The Big Book Of City* we have trawled through our archive, photograph libraries nationwide, players' collections and through those of City supporters in a bid to find varied images. So imagine our surprise when we found these two similar – but different - images of the Blues from the late 1960s.

The images come from different collections and neither is properly dated, however it is clear that these were taken at the most one or two seconds apart. Seeing this has caused us to analyse the photos looking for differences. We believe there are at least nine facial differences. See how many you can spot.

Our nine differences appear on page 213.

CITY'S NUMBER ONE

THE PROFILES

56 – SIMON TRACEY

Sheffield United goalkeeper Simon Tracey arrived at Maine Road during Brian Horton's managerial reign. The 26 year old was brought to City as the Blues were enduring a bit of a goalkeeping crisis with injuries and suspensions forcing Tony Coton and Andy Dibble out of action.

Tracey's debut saw City defeated 1-0 by Coventry on 29th October 1994. This was a highly disappointing result, particularly as the previous match had seen Horton's side thrill against Tottenham, winning an entertaining match 5-2.

A 3-3 draw with Southampton followed the Coventry match but then the worst result of Horton's City reign came on 10th November when the Blues were humiliated 5-0 before an Old Trafford crowd of 43,738.

Inevitably Andy Dibble returned for the following game and Tracey moved on. After City Tracey managed a small number of first team appearances for Norwich and Wimbledon in other loan spells. The Norwich loan period in 1994-95 was particularly upsetting for the player as he was stretchered off in the second of three first team appearances. It is reported that during a game for Sheffield United at Norwich in 2000 Tracey made a charge out of his area to limit the danger of an attack. Unfortunately, this allowed Norwich striker and future City star Craig Bellamy to score.

Tracey ended his career in League football after appearing in over 330 League games for Sheffield United, and later became goalkeeping coach at Rotherham United.

Appearances: League: 3

57 – JOHN BURRIDGE

Highly experienced 'keeper John Burridge became the oldest player to appear in the Premier League when he made his debut for City against Newcastle on 29th April 1995. For that game Burridge was named substitute and was called into action when an injured Tony Coton was substituted at half time. Burridge helped City achieve a goalless draw.

The former Newcastle and Sheffield United 'keeper had actually been with City since December 1994 and had spent virtually all of his time as goalkeeping substitute. A frustrating role which is rarely called into action and, as many goalkeepers have said over the years, means the second choice 'keeper rarely gets match action. Something no 'keeper truly wants.

Burridge was clearly desperate to make his mark and keen on playing and so, throughout his period at the Club, supporters were entertained with the sight of Burridge warming up – often for the full length of the game! – on the touchline at the Platt Lane end of the Maine Road Main Stand. Game after game, no matter what the weather, Burridge tended to throw himself to the ground and occasionally his exploits were much more entertaining than the game itself!

As well as his debut, Burridge played in the final three games of 1994-95 and was aged 43 years and 162 days when he appeared in his final Premier League game for City against Queen's Park Rangers on 14th May 1995. At the start of the 2009-10 season this remained a Premier League record. At the time Burridge, an absolute fitness fanatic, declared: "I'm fitter now than I've ever been." No one doubted him.

Sadly, the game ended in a 3-2 defeat and was the last managed by Brian Horton. Inevitably, Burridge moved on and played for a variety of clubs, including three Football League appearances for Darlington during late 1995. He later became a coach and enjoyed spells in the middle-east. He also became a summariser for programmes focusing on the English game in the middle-east and also in Singapore.

Appearances: League: 3 (plus 1 as substitute)

58 – EIKE IMMEL

When West German international Eike Immel arrived at Maine Road in August 1995 the media immediately made comparisons with City's earlier German 'keeper Bert Trautmann. This inevitably worked against Immel – who could hope to match Trautmann? However, had 34 year old Immel been compared to other 'keepers of the period and of a similar age he would have been hailed as a City star, or at least been perceived as a bit of a cult hero.

Immel made his debut on the opening day of the 1995-96 season and became an ever present in all first team appearances that season. Alan Ball was City manager at this time and Immel was initially selected because Ball's hand was forced - Coton was recovering from injury and subsequent operation. As the season progressed Immel was preferred by Ball to Coton (who was transferred in 1996) and that impacted on the player's popularity. No matter how well Immel performed, poor results on the pitch and the fact Coton was cast aside affected the way Immel was viewed by fans.

Ignoring the baggage surrounding Immel's place in the team and the comparisons with Trautmann, it is clear that he was a very talented 'keeper.

In West Germany Immel had gained 19 caps

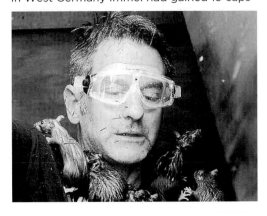

and had played over 500 league games for Borussia Dortmund and Stuttgart. He was idolised – as German visiting fans to the MCFC museum in 2008 explained – and at Maine Road City fans did admire his bravery.

Immel was first choice when the 1996-97 season commenced but a hip injury caused him several problems and after only four League games he had to withdraw from the side. Medical trips home to Germany followed and, despite suggestions he would return to league football in his home country, he was forced into retirement in 1997.

He later became a coach – in 2005 he was with Fenerbahce – and in January 2008 he hit the headlines again as a contestant on the German version of *I'm A Celebrity Get Me Out Of Here*! He finished fifth and performed two trials, including the 'Terror Tunnel'.

Appearances: League: 42 FAC: 5 League Cup: 3

59 – TOMMY WRIGHT

Northern Ireland international Tommy Wright joined City from Nottingham Forest on loan in January 1997 and despite being cup-tied and missing out on his new club's 1997 FA Cup run (City reached the fifth round, losing controversially to Middlesbrough), Tommy made a terrific impression on the fans at Maine Road and finally signed a permanent deal in March 1997. The Blues had endured a managerial merry-go-round during the early part of the season with four men taking charge of first team games before the arrival of Frank Clark as manager on 30th December 1996. With injury to Immel both Andy Dibble and Martyn Margetson had played but Clark felt he needed to bring in more experience, especially as naming a goalkeeper as substitute meant that a bigger pool of players was needed than a decade earlier.

Wright made his debut on 18th January 1997 as City drew 1-1 with Huddersfield in Division One and made a total of 13 League games

that season. It would have been more but a leg injury caused him to miss the final six games of the campaign and the start of the 1997-98 season - he suffered a torn quadriceps muscle during the club's close-season tour to Scotland. Nevertheless, when fitness returned Clark made sure Wright knew that he was the manager's first choice and the 'keeper made 18 appearances in 1997-98. Clark was dismissed in February and less than a month after the arrival of Joe Royle the new manager replaced Wright with Margetson.

The following season Nicky Weaver became City's first choice with Wright helping the young 'keeper develop. Wright went on loan to Newcastle and Wrexham, making a total of 19 appearances, in 1999 and then in January 2001 he went to Bolton where he made four League appearances.

Appearances: League: 33 FAC: 2 League Cup: 1

60 – NICKY WEAVER

The 1999 Play Off final lifted Nicky Weaver to the status of cult hero after his heroics in the penalty shoot out guaranteed City's promotion to Division One.

Weaver's £100,000 arrival at Maine Road from Mansfield owed much to the judgement of City's goalkeeping coach of the period Alex Stepney. Stepney spotted his potential immediately and at one point in 2000 he rated Weaver as better than United's £8 million signing Fabien Barthez: "I would put his worth at £16m right now. For his age, his size, his build, and his contribution you would not find many better anywhere. Any manager ought to be happy to pay that kind of money for Nick."

Under manager Joe Royle Weaver made his debut on the opening day of the 1998-99 season at the age of nineteen. He kept a clean sheet in that game as the Blues won

3-0 and he went on to miss only two first team games that season – the League match with Chesterfield in September and the Auto-Windscreens tie with Weaver's former club Mansfield in December. That meant he played in 55 first team games in his debut season – an incredible record for such a young 'keeper and playing in such an important period for the Club.

The facts of his debut season are even more remarkable when it's known that he kept 22 clean sheets in 45 League games – this equalled Joe Corrigan's 1976-77 record (although Corrigan played 42 games that season).

The following season he continued to impress, missing only one game (due to influenza) as the Blues gained a second promotion in successive years. However, as his City career progressed injury started to take its toll and the Blues were forced to sign other goalkeepers, although it seemed that Weaver was destined to have a long and distinguished career with the Club. It didn't work out like that however.

By the summer of 2002 Kevin Keegan was manager and the Blues were back in the Premier League determined to re-establish themselves as a force and it was felt the wearer of City's number one shirt had to be a recognised, quality 'keeper. Peter Schmeichel was signed; the following year David Seaman arrived, followed by David James and Weaver's chances were

virtually non-existent, although he did play in City's 2-0 UEFA Cup win at Cardiff against Total Network Solutions.

On the last day of the 2004-05 season Weaver came on as substitute to allow David James to play as an outfield player as the Blues pushed forward – it was one of those crazy 'typical City' moments!

A loan spell to Sheffield Wednesday followed and then in August 2006 Weaver played the opening game of the season, following injury to Andreas Isaksson, and he went on to be the first choice for the rest of the year.

Despite that run Weaver was signed by Charlton Athletic on 4th July 2007, and the chance to be established as City's number one ended.

Regardless of the lack of opportunity during the final 5 years of his City career, it is worth remembering that Nicky Weaver was well-loved by fans and will always be recognised for his contribution during a difficult period for the Club. Without Weaver's important performances the Blues may well have remained a third tier side.

Appearances: League: 205 (plus 2 as substitute) FAC: 16 League Cup: 15 Euro: 1

SPOT THE DIFFERENCE – THE ANSWERS

The nine facial differences we identified from page 208 are circled below. There may be others, but clearly a special mention must be made of Tony Coleman who seems totally and utterly unaffected by whatever it is that has caught Malcolm Allison and Francis Lee's eyes.

The full line up is: (back row, left to right) Alan Oakes, Neil Young, George Heslop, Ken Mulhearn, Colin Bell, Glyn Pardoe and Mike Summerbee.

(front row): Malcolm Allison, Dave Connor, Francis Lee, Tony Book, Tony Coleman, Mike Doyle and John Hart.

The Football Season Daily Reminder

February

1st February 1986

Gordon Davies and Paul Power both scored to give City a 2-1 victory over West Bromwich Albion in Division One. Exactly 28 years earlier a Bill McAdams hat trick and a goal from Colin Barlow ensured a 4-1 Division One victory over the same club.

2nd February 2005

Robbie Fowler scored an equalising penalty in the 49th minute to give City a 1-1 draw at home to Newcastle.

3rd February 1951

Despite losing 1-0 at half time the Blues secured a 2-2 draw at Luton Town in Division Two. George Smith netted both City goals before 12,087 during a promotion season for the Club.

4th February 2004

City's amazing fight back against Tottenham was the inspiration for a winning play (written by a female Spurs fan) in the Radio Five Live Short Story

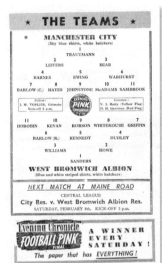

★ THE TEAMS ★

competition of 2005. The Blues had been losing 3-0 at half time and down to ten men but an amazing fight back saw City win the fourth round replay 4-3. The play was a story of commitment (it was clearly fiction – the City fan had walked out at half time!).

5th February 1964

City were defeated 1-0 in the second leg of the League Cup semi-final. This Maine Road tie with Stoke was watched by 16,894.

6th February 2005

A Stamford Bridge crowd of 42,093 witnessed a goalless draw at Chelsea. This meant City were the only side to take 4 points from the eventual Champions.

7th February 1959

Future City and Eire player Mick McCarthy was born in Barnsley on this day.

8th February 1964

City 'keeper Harry Dowd broke a finger and was moved into a centre-forward role. He scored an equalising goal as City drew 1-1 with Bury in Division Two.

9th February 2003

Shaun Goater came on as substitute against United at Old Trafford and scored an equalising goal within 9 seconds. The match ended 1-1.

10th February 2002

An important Division One game with Preston ended in a 3-2 City win. The game came seven days

MANCHESTER CITY FOOTBALL CLUB

MAINE ROAD, MOSS SIDE, MANCHESTER

FOOTBALL LEAGUE

Division One

CITY v ASTON VILLA

Saturday, 7th February 1976

Kick-off 3-00 p.m.

You are advised to take up your position
half an hour before the kick-off

BLOCK

H

ENTRANCE
ROW

H

SEAT

2377

Secretary

GRAND STAND
£1.10

TO BE RETAINED (SEE PLAN AND CONDITIONS ON BACK)

after a surprise defeat at Wimbledon had raised a few doubts over City's ability to maintain their promotion challenge.

11th February 1989

Goals from Wayne Biggins (2), Brian Gayle and Trevor Morley gave City a 4-0 Division Two win at home to Ipswich Town.

12th February 2006

Goals from Dunne, Samaras and Barton ensured a 3-2 victory over Charlton Athletic in the Premier League.

13th February 1993

A brace from David White ensured a 2-0 fifth round FA Cup victory over Barnsley at Maine Road. The win brought the belief

that this would be City's year for the FA Cup and TV pundit Alan Hansen went on to tip City for FA Cup success. Sadly, a miserable performance against Spurs in the quarter final ended the dream and Hansen's wish.

14th February 1970

Eighties Mancunian player Jason Beckford was born.

15th February 1992

Adrian Heath scored a rare City goal to help City to a 4-0 win over Luton. Andy Hill and David White (2) were the other scorers.

16th February 1974

Future City captain Jamie Pollack was born in Stockton. He went on to make 49 (plus 11

as substitute) first team appearances between March 1998 and August 2000.

17th February 1944

Former City 'keeper Jack Lyall died in the USA. He had made 44 first team appearances for the Blues between 1909 and 1911. He emigrated to North America in the inter-war years.

18th February 1984

A crowd of 41,767 witnessed a 2-1 defeat to Newcastle in Division Two. City were third prior to the match, with Newcastle fourth. Despite the Blues taking the lead via Steve Kinsey, future Blues Peter Beardsley and Kevin Keegan netted fine goals to give the Geordies the initiative. City finished the season fourth and missed out on promotion.

19th February 1961

Justin Fashanu was born in Kensington, London. Fashanu had two brief spells with City in 1989 when the Club was managed by Fashanu's former Norwich colleague Mel Machin. Despite a career that had promised much when he was at Norwich, by the late 1980s Fashanu was struggling for fitness. His time at City was an opportunity for him to prove he was once again fit for the rigours

The Football League Ltd.

6 STARKIE STREET, PRESTON

Telephone No. 4658/9

Telegrams—" League, Preston "

Date as Postmark

Dear Sir,

26 Feb 55 Manchester City v Wolverhampton W.

Please note that *R. H. Chandler* has

been appointed to officiate as Linesman in this match, vice

C. H. Hant

Kindly advise him time of kick-off in due course.

Yours faithfully,

Howarth

Secretary.

---

of English football after spells in North America. Sadly, apart from scoring 3 goals in a reserve game against United, Fashanu's time was not successful. Two first team substitute appearances were all he could manage. He later had spells at a variety of other clubs before tragedy struck in May 1998. Fashanu's body was discovered in a garage, the victim of suicide. By that time lurid stories about his sexual orientation had made their way into the tabloids.

20th February 1926

City beat Crystal Palace 11-4 at Maine Road in the FA Cup with goals from Roberts (5), Browell (3), Austin, Johnson and Hicks.

21st February 1934

City defeated Sheffield Wednesday 2-0 at Maine Road in a fifth round FA Cup replay. A remarkable Wednesday afternoon crowd of 68,614 enjoyed the match. Four days earlier Hillsborough's record attendance of 72,841 had witnessed a 2-2 draw.

22nd February 1975

Goals from Colin Bell, Joe Royle and Dennis Tueart ensured a 3-1 victory over Birmingham City in Division One before a crowd of 33,240.

23rd February 1935

City drew 1-1 with Arsenal at Maine Road but the game made history by being the highest League crowd ever (79,491).

Although that record has since gone, it remains City's highest league crowd.

24th February 1899

The great Jimmy Ross signed for City. Ross was one of football's leading names when he played for the famous Preston side that won the League and Cup double of 1889. By the time he arrived at Hyde Road, Ross had captained Liverpool to promotion and played for the Football League. At City he was influential from the start as his seven goals in the final nine games of the 1898-99 season brought the Division Two title for the first time. In the years that followed he helped City establish their name before tragedy struck in 1902. He died on 12th June that year after an illness described as "an acute skin disease and a raging fever."

25th February 1970

Shaun Goater was born in Hamilton, Bermuda

26th February 1977

City's League game with Sunderland was postponed as the Blues faced Leeds United in the fifth round of the FA Cup that day. As with many other games from that period tickets (right) were issued for the initial fixture and were used for the rearranged game. City beat Sunderland 1-0 on 9th March with a goal from Dennis Tueart.

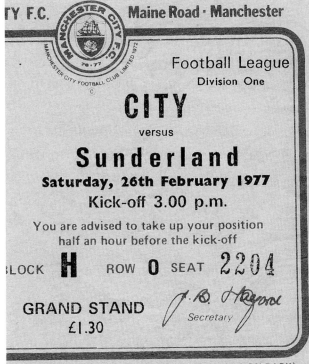

Maine Road · Manchester

Football League
Division One

CITY
versus
Sunderland
Saturday, 26th February 1977
Kick-off 3.00 p.m.

You are advised to take up your position half an hour before the kick-off

BLOCK **H** ROW **0** SEAT **2204**

GRAND STAND
£1.30

Secretary

TO BE RETAINED (SEE PLAN AND CONDITIONS ON BACK)

27th February 1993

City defeated Nottingham Forest 2-0 at the City Ground in the Premier League. The scorers were David White (below) and Garry Flitcroft. This was the last time Brian Clough managed a side against City.

28th February 2005

Goals from Robbie Fowler (2) and Antoine Sibierski gave City a 3-2 victory at Norwich City on 28th February 2005, but the most newsworthy part of the night came when Norwich's Delia Smith went on to the pitch at half time to encourage the home fans to make a bit of noise. She memorably called out: "A message for the best football supporters in the world: We need a twelfth man here. Where are you? Where are you? Let's be having you! Come on!"

29th February 1992

City beat Aston Villa 2-0 at Maine Road watched by a crowd of 28,268. The goals were scored by the ever-popular Niall Quinn and David White.

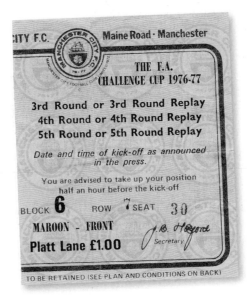

TICKET PRICES

European Cup admission prices for the Platt Lane Stand for the first ever City home European game in September 1968 were 8 shillings (40p in today's money) for an adult ticket and 4 shillings (20p) for a Junior or OAP ticket.

A ticket to sit in an uncovered section at City's first FA Cup final in 1904 cost Blues 5 shillings (25p in today's money). In 1933 City fans could expect to pay 7 shillings and sixpence (37½p) for a covered seat in the Grand Stand.

The dearest City season ticket for the 1976-7 season cost £29 if purchased before 30th April 1976. A similar ticket at QPR or Arsenal would have cost around £60 that season, while £8 would buy an adult season ticket for the Kippax.

City secretary Walter Griffiths upset fans when the Blues announced in November 1969 that tickets for the League Cup semi final with United would be at significantly higher prices than regular games. The new prices ranged from 8 shillings (40p) – uncovered terracing at the Scoreboard End – to 25 shillings (£1.25 in today's money) for a seat in the Main Stand. It would be a surprisingly high 10 shillings (50p) for a place on the Kippax terracing. For other high profile cup games 8 shillings would normally have bought a seat in the Platt Lane Stand.

Hundreds of complaint letters poured into the Club and the *Manchester Evening News* prompting Griffiths to go on the defensive. He tried to justify the increase by saying: "You don't have to move outside Manchester to watch your side in this semi-final."

CITY'S NUMBER ONE

THE PROFILES

61 – CARLO NASH

Bolton born Carlo Nash was signed by City from Stockport County on 12th January 2001 for a fee of £100,000. He made his debut against Arsenal on 11th April that year. The Gunners were absolutely superb that day and the match ended in a 4-0 Arsenal victory. They were applauded off the pitch by City fans who recognised a side that should have won the title that season.

Despite his debut scoreline, Nash remained first choice for the rest of the season, managing one clean sheet (V West Ham) in six games. City were relegated that season and Nash managed to appear in 23 Division One games the following season under new manager Kevin Keegan.

This was a much more successful period and Nash featured in the final run in, when only four points were dropped out of a possible 33 points to secure the First Division Championship.

Despite some excellent performances, Nash was replaced for much of the 2002-03 season by new signing Peter Schmeichel. He did enjoy a six game run during January and February 2003 which included a memorable 1-1 draw at Old Trafford – a game that saw cult hero Shaun Goater net City's equaliser a mere 9 seconds after coming on as substitute.

On 14th August 2003 the former Stockport 'keeper was transferred to Middlesbrough for a £50,000 profit.

After making only five first team appearances for the Riverside club Nash moved to Preston in March 2005. This proved to be a much more positive move as within months of arriving he was making some excellent saves in County's play-off final appearance. The following season he established a new record of 24 clean sheets – County's defensive record was better than champions Reading.

A move to Wigan came in 2007, followed by spells at Stoke and Everton.

Appearances: League: 37 (plus 1 as substitute) FAC: 1 League Cup: 2

62 – PETER SCHMEICHEL

After making his name with Denmark at Euro 88 and with Brondby where he won four championship medals in five seasons, Peter Schmeichel joined Alex Ferguson's Manchester United in 1991 for a fee of around £530,000. It was a significant signing and helped United become defensively strong as they embarked on a long period of success taking the Reds to a position of power in the game.

Schmeichel actually only spent eight years with the Reds but it was this period that really set the template for what followed and, although players such as Eric Cantona, David Beckham and Ryan Giggs, tend to receive a great deal of praise it is possible that Schmeichel was perhaps the most influential of all these players.

In 1999, after captaining the Reds to European Cup success, Schmeichel had a spell in Portugal before returning to England with Aston Villa in 2001. On 20th October that year he made history by becoming the first goalkeeper to score in the Premier League.

By the start of the 2002-03 season Schmeichel had joined City. Kevin Keegan had wanted to strengthen the Blues following promotion as Division One champions, and Schmeichel fitted the bill as the type of confident, experienced, respected international 'keeper Keegan desired. With the Dane in the side City's defence had to feel confident.

Schmeichel made his debut on 24th August 2002 as the Blues defeated Newcastle United 1-0 at Maine Road. A couple of

months later City faced the 'keeper's old side in the last derby at the Blues' old ground. Pre-match, much was made of the fact that Schmeichel had never been on the losing side in a derby and, sure enough, Schmeichel maintained that record as City humiliated the Reds with a 3-1 victory on 9th November.

Some great performances followed including the 3rd May 2003 game at Anfield. The match saw City defeat Liverpool 2-1 with goals from Anelka, but Schmeichel had made a breathtaking save during the match to deny Liverpool a point (the Merseyside club missed a Champions League spot by three points that season).

The 2002-03 season was City's last at Maine Road. It was also the end of the goalkeeper's playing career as he announced his retirement, and so Schmeichel became the last City 'keeper to appear in a first team competitive game at Maine Road. After both Schmeichel's and Maine Road's final game (V Southampton on 11th May) a special presentation was made to the 'keeper.

Since retiring, Schmeichel has appeared as a summariser on BBC television and on Champions League football for a Danish broadcaster. He also attended games at City to watch his son Kasper appear for the Blues. He has also been given the tribute of having a dog named after him in Granada TV's Coronation Street – Schmeichel is of course a Great Dane!

Appearances: League: 29 FAC: 1 League Cup: 1

Date Quiz 2

Here's our second Date Quiz. As before, these Manchester images have been selected as the dates hold relevance to City.

Take a look at these photographs and see if you can identify what moment in City's history these dates tie in with. Of course some of the dates may have more than one significance and so to help steer you towards the answer we're looking for we've given you three options. For each image, only one of these options is correct.

Next time you're in the city centre have a wander around and see what City related dates you can find.

Answers can be found on page 224.

IMAGE A

Although Manchester Central Library officially opened in 1934 this proudly-Mancunian date stone highlights an earlier year. What significance did this date have to the Blues? Did:

A City win the League

B City win the FA Cup

C Wear numbers on their shirts for the first time

IMAGE B

This stone marks the opening of the Manchester Town Hall Extension. Exactly eleven days before the date on this stone what feat did City achieve:

A They became the first team to be relegated the year after winning the League

B They became the first Manchester side to win the League

C They achieved the Club's record crowd of 84,569

IMAGE C

In Albert Square there are many significant dates. The statue above this plinth recognises the contribution of James Fraser, Bishop of Manchester. It was erected by public subscription in a year that's more famous to City fans as:

A The year St Mark's Church side was formed

B The year the Blues re-formed as Ardwick AFC and moved to Hyde Road

C The year Ardwick won the Manchester Cup for the first time, beating Newton Heath in the final.

IMAGE D

The fountain in Albert Square commemorates significant improvements to Manchester's water supply, but what record did the Blues achieve in October that year?:

A They scored four goals in 3 consecutive games

B They played with ten men in the Manchester derby and still beat Newton Heath 6-1

C They created a record by winning the opening seven games of the season.

IMAGE E

The Corn Exchange (modern day Triangle shopping centre) was rebuilt in this year, but what relevance does it have to City?:

A The Blues won the Second Division Championship

B City won the FA Cup beating Bolton in the final

C The Blues moved to Maine Road.

IMAGE F

The Wellington Bridge spans the divide between Manchester and Salford, but this year had other significance for the Blues. Did they:

A Beat United 5-1 in a game commonly known as the Maine Road Massacre

B Achieve promotion on the last day of the season at Bradford City

C Beat Huddersfield Town 10-1 with hat-tricks from White, Adcock and Stewart in the record score at Maine Road.

DATE QUIZ – THE ANSWERS

Here are the answers to our second Date Quiz

Image A – The significance of this date to the Blues is that (c) City wore numbers on their shirts for the first time in the 1933 FA Cup final.

Image B – Exactly eleven days before the date on this stone City became (a) the first team to be relegated the year after winning the League.

Image C – The statue was erected by public subscription in a year that's more famous to City fans as (b) the year the Blues re-formed as Ardwick AFC and moved to Hyde Road.

Image D – The fountain in Albert Square commemorates significant improvements to Manchester's water supply, but City (c) created a record by winning the opening seven games of the season.

Image E – The Corn Exchange (modern day Triangle shopping centre) was rebuilt in this year, but what relevance does it have to City?: (a) The Blues won the Second Division Championship.

Image F – The Wellington Bridge spans the divide between Manchester and Salford, but this year had other significance for the Blues: (c) Beat Huddersfield Town 10-1 with hat-tricks from White, Adcock and Stewart in the record score at Maine Road.

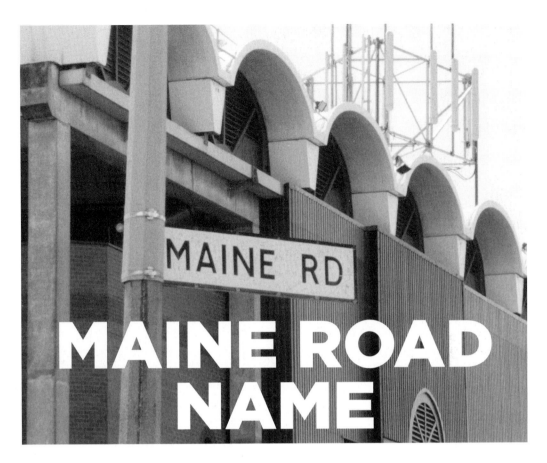

MAINE ROAD NAME

AT last, after decades of research, *The Big Book Of City* has finally managed to track down exactly how Maine Road got its name and what the name actually means.

In 2003 I wrote *"Farewell To Maine Road"* and at that time I revealed that the actual street Maine Road had originally been known as Dog Kennel Lane. The name 'Maine Road' did not appear on maps until the 1870s. At that time I questioned why the new name had been selected and how. I outlined a few theories – one focused on Mancunian soldiers who, together with members of the prominent Lloyd family, had volunteered for war in America and could possibly have fought in Maine – but I admitted: "all of this is pure conjecture, but it is known that Lloyd Street was named after the family, and it is clear the renaming of a road during this period was a very

deliberate act and there must have been a reason. It would be entertaining to discover where the original 'Dog Kennel Lane' got its name."

I also claimed to have found the earliest reference to Maine Road in a newspaper – November 1904, the *Manchester Guardian*.

Now, after much detailed research I now have the answer to both the questions: How did Maine Road get its name and where did the name Dog Kennel Lane come from? I have also tracked down earlier references to Maine Road in newsprint.

So, *The Big Book Of City* can now exclusively reveal that the Maine Road name was indirectly named after the US state of Maine but that this was, in itself, a compromise. The road was to be called 'Demesne Road' (pronounced Demain) after a farm positioned slightly south of where the Maine Road Stadium would eventually

Clockwise from top left: Dog Kennel Lane c.1890 looking south close to the eventual site of the Maine Road Directors' car park; Demesne Farm; The Temperance Billiard Hall c.1960; Main Stand during construction in 1923; The Temperance Billiard Hall c.1900; Moss Grove Farm on Maine Road 1900.

be built. The local authority did not want that, so in the end Maine Road was agreed. It ultimately had more significance as the following newspaper article shows:

"Dog Kennel Lane took its name from the kennel where hounds were kept. It stood on the right hand side at the bend about a thousand yards from Moss Lane, opposite to the road which tracked off to the left and led to Demesne Farm. The common name of this lane is so 'common' and unattractive that when the Temperance Company bought the Trafford land they asked the local board to change the name to Demesne Road, and the subject was compromised by calling it Maine Road out of compliment to the Temperance principles of the petitioners."

It's important to explain this. The Temperance movement had been growing since the 1850s and, as with so many other areas, Manchester played a lead role. The idea of the movement was to discourage people from drinking alcohol. After a series of campaigns of voluntary abstinence failed in the States the Temperance movement changed its approach.

On 2nd June 1851 the State of Maine passed the first recognised prohibition law, and two years later the United Kingdom Alliance was founded in Manchester, calling itself a legitimate political party and pledging to badger Parliament to outlaw liquor in England.

The 'Temperance Company' mentioned in the article was actually part of the movement and had bought some land at the top of Dog Kennel Lane – this area is covered today by the buildings on the western side of Maine Road, close to the junction with Moss Lane East, and stretching to Princess Road. They wanted to create a better standard of living and within that area they erected buildings in keeping with their approach to life, such as the Temperance Billiard Hall. However, the 'Dog Kennel Lane' name was clearly an issue and so the selection of the name 'Maine Road' was made. Maine, due to the State's role in the

Temperance movement, was a significant name.

So the name Maine Road does not refer to the American War of Independence but it does refer to the US State and the part that Maine played in the Temperance movement.

Initially, only the top section of the road was renamed but gradually as housing was developed southwards the new name replaced Dog Kennel Lane.

Research for this book has also managed to identify earlier information on the land that ultimately became City's ground. The land was owned by the Chadwick family, sometimes they were referred to as the Chaddock family. In 1760 all of the Maine Road ground site, plus most of the area east of Dog Kennel Lane/Maine Road down to Demesne Farm and across to Heald

Place was part of 'Chadwick's Tenement' – described as 49.5 Lancashire acres of farm land.

The family were believed to have owned this land from around 1500 to the early 1800s. By 1857 the land was owned by someone called Mr Broadie but within the following few years areas were sold off until by 1903 all that was left was a farm house, Moss Grove Farm, on the corner of Moss Lane East and Maine Road. That was demolished shortly afterwards and by 1910 terraced housing covered the site.

The earliest media reference to Maine Road identified to date is 3rd January 1903 in the *Manchester City News*, but the road was marked on maps before this time.

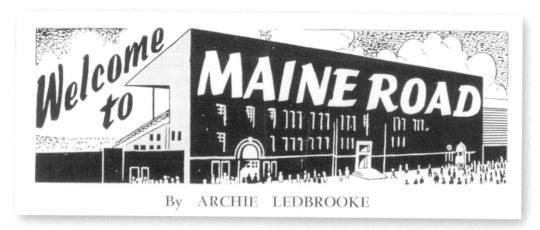

By ARCHIE LEDBROOKE

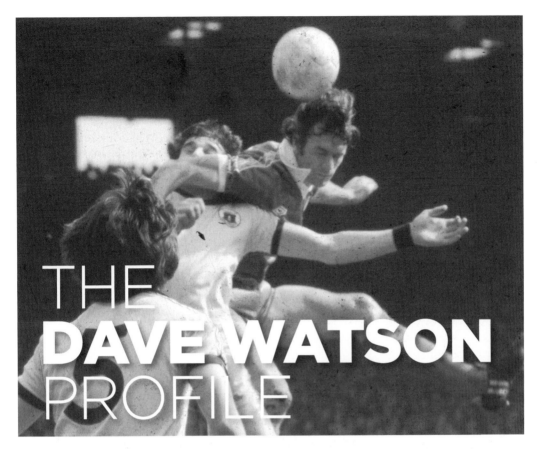

THE DAVE WATSON PROFILE

Centre-half Dave Watson joined the Blues in June 1975 and made his first team debut on 2nd August 1975 at Blackpool in the Anglo-Scottish Cup. He stayed at Maine Road until June 1979 after making 190 first team appearances for the Club. During that time he became a tremendous hero to thousands of Blues, including the author of this book, and so when the decision was taken to select a player for a profile in this book the selection was an easy one. Dave Watson achieved a great deal at City and, hopefully, this article will explain why he remains a significant Blue hero.

DAVE WATSON was one of City's - and England's - greatest central defenders of all time, some would say the greatest. He was a granite-like figure who simply made it impossible for his opponents to play.

He was born in Stapleford on 5th October 1946 and joined his local League side Notts County in January 1967. At that time he was playing as a centre forward but the following year he joined Rotherham United where, under the management of Tommy Docherty, he became more of a utility player. In December 1970 he transferred to Sunderland where his career really came alive.

At Roker Park he gained the first of his 65 England caps and became a popular member of the side that defeated Leeds in the highly memorable 1973 F.A. Cup Final. Sunderland were then a Second Division club and their Wembley success made the rest of football sit up and notice their star players. Within a year City had signed Dennis Tueart and then in June 1975 the Blues obtained the brilliant defender for a fee later valued at £275,000. Wisely they signed him on a six year contract.

In 2003 I interviewed Watson for a feature on Maine Road and his views on why he chose City at this time are worth repeating. He told me: "From the moment I arrived at City I loved the place. In fact once I knew I was leaving Sunderland there was only one place I wanted to go to. I had friends who were City fans so felt privileged to know what the club was about before I'd even got there.

"Prior to City I'd been at Sunderland and I have to be honest the Roker Park atmosphere was special because it bellowed from the Kop behind the goal, but at City there was no Kop so the atmosphere was different. Instead of the fervour coming from one end, it came from the entire side. It was a huge sound and they certainly knew how to support their team."

Watson's recognition of what City was about was typical of the way players from the Seventies felt about the Club. Players were much closer to fans in those days and activities such as the Junior Blues, the Social Club and of course the close relationship with the Supporters' Club ensured the players were accessible. As a result they developed a special bond. Watson had that bond and as a result has retained his love of City ever since.

Within weeks of arriving in 1975 Watson became one of the club's most popular players with fans admiring his rugged qualities and fighting spirit. Often the media liked to portray Watson as having a negative style of play, but the truth was that he was simply determined. He was keen to see the Blues succeed and he always gave his all, as the 1976 League Cup Final proved. Few fans will ever forget the sight of Watson helping the Blues to victory while blood poured from his head. The ITV cameras also filmed him receiving stitches in the dressing room after the match while Brian Moore was interviewing him. Watson's comments that afternoon suggested the wound was nothing more than a scratch, but the television viewers knew the truth, and Watson's tough guy image grew.

The 1976-7 season saw him deservedly voted City's player of the year. He was also the Junior Blues player of the season. Then the following year he became captain and continued to perform exceptionally well for both City and for England despite the additional responsibility. It was during this season that Watson scored a goal that will

DAVE WATSON'S CITY RECORD

	LEAGUE		FA CUP		FL CUP		EUROPE		OTHERS*		TOTAL	
	App	Gls	App	Gls	App	Gls	App	Gls	App	Gls	App	Gls
1975-76	31	1	1	0	7	1	0	0	3	0	42	2
1976-77	41	2	4	0	1	0	2	0	2	0	50	2
1977-78	41	0	2	0	6	0	2	0	0	0	51	0
1978-79	33	1	2	0	4	0	8	1	0	0	47	2
TOTAL	146	4	9	0	18	1	12	1	5	0	190	6

*Others includes appearances in the Anglo-Scottish Cup and Tennent-Caledonian Cup both of which were viewed as first team competitive games at the time. Friendly, reserve, testimonial games and similar have not been included.

Member of the 1976 Football League Cup winning side.
Supporters' Club Player of the Year 1976-77.
League debut: V Norwich City, 16th August 1975.

Dave Watson V Alan Gowling at Bolton

forever be remembered as one of the most significant moments of his City career. The goal was a wonderful, powerful header from around the edge of the penalty area.

Watson described his goal to me in 2003: "My best memory has to be the goal I scored against Ipswich in April 1977. It was such an important goal and so many fans over the years have discussed it with me. City and Ipswich were second and third in the League, and were both putting considerable pressure on Liverpool. We couldn't afford to lose, and Peter Barnes sent a great ball in. I met it about eight feet in the air and headed it in from about twelve yards out. Mick Mills said that I'd rose up and headed it in before he'd even had chance to move. It gave me a lot of satisfaction and, of course, we won the match 2-1. We also ended up runners-up that year to Liverpool, missing the title by a point."

The following October an injury sustained against Luxembourg in an international once again proved his determination. Tony Book: "Dave played in Luxembourg without being 100% fit. It was not possible for him to have been in peak condition because he had limped out of training on the day prior to the international complaining of injury.

It was highly improbable for the damage to have healed overnight. Of course, he wanted to play for England, just as every Saturday he wants to play for City. The man is made that way - he does not want to give in to injury, he always wants to play. The outcome is now well known. Dave limped out of the international in the 70th minute and returned to us bound for the treatment table. On Saturday I took him out to Nottingham to check the injury. Dave was prepared to play, just as he was in Luxembourg."

In the end Book refused to let Watson play at Nottingham Forest on 15th October 1977, but the player was still keen to appear.

Despite his many abilities, Watson did not survive the Malcolm Allison purge of 1979 when experience seemed to count for nothing, and he was transferred to Werder Bremen on 26th June 1979. Watson didn't want to leave: "Maine Road holds so many memories for me. Most of them are good and I have to say that when I left City in 1979 I just did not want to go. I hated leaving and it hurt enormously. People always say it was a wrench leaving but it truthfully was. I wanted to stay. So much so that in the years that followed I continued to keep in touch with Peter Swales. I used to speak with him often, and would discuss City's future with him. I know he had his critics but you couldn't take away the fact that he was a Blue through and through. I know he wanted the club to succeed and so did I. There's a great passion about the place."

Watson's time in Germany was not particularly long and he returned to England the following October to join Southampton. Nevertheless, Watson was liked by Werder Bremen supporters. In 2003 Werder fan Arnd Zeigler dedicated four pages to Watson in the excellent German language history of the club "Das W Auf Dem Trikot."

Watson later had spells with Stoke and Vancouver Whitecaps, before returning to England again with Derby County. During the mid eighties he played for Fort Lauderdale, Notts County, and Kettering Town.

While at Stoke in 1982 he set a record by becoming the first man to make England international appearances while on the books of five different clubs, and it was that same year that he made the last of his 65 international appearances, at the age of 35. Amazingly for a central defender he managed to score four international goals (V Northern Ireland February 1979, Northern Ireland May 1979, Bulgaria June 1979, and Bulgaria November 1979). He also captained England on three occasions during 1981 (V Romania, Wales & Scotland). During his Maine Road career he made thirty England appearances and, at the time, this made him second only to Colin Bell in the number of international appearances he made while with the Blues.

The muscular and effective Watson is regarded by many as England's premier central defender. He was a rock in defence, and a vital member of Tony Book's impressive side from 1976 to 1979. City struggled to find a defender to replace him and many fans still believe the Club has yet to sign Watson's equal.

Watson had a great career at City and will always remain a true Blue hero. He continues to visit City and attend games.

To read more about Dave Watson's career check out "My Dear Watson: The Story of a Football Marriage" by Dave's wife Penny. Unusual for the period it was produced (1981), this was the story of Dave's career as seen through the eyes of his wife. The book came out in 1981 (ISBN 0-213-16814-6) and provides plenty of information on Dave's time at City.

Watson challenges against a brown shirted Coventry City.

CITY IN EUROPE

2003-04

Competition: UEFA Cup
Reason For Qualification: Qualification via Fair Play League
Manager: Kevin Keegan

14th August 2003
Qualifying Round Leg 1
Attendance: 34,103

City 5-0 Total Network Solutions

City Goalscorers: Sinclair, Wright-Phillips, Sun, Sommeil, Anelka
City: Seaman; Sun, Tarnat (Tiatto), Sommeil, Distin, Bosvelt (Barton), Wright-Phillips, Berkovic, Anelka, Fowler (Wanchope), Sinclair

The first European game since 1978-79 was also the opening competitive fixture for the new City Of Manchester Stadium. It's difficult to accurately portray the atmosphere of the period but it is fair to say that qualification for Europe, no matter how it came about, gave the Blues a great deal of positivity and optimism, particularly after the move from Maine Road and the distressing news of Marc-Vivien Foe's untimely death.

For significant periods during the Eighties and Nineties City had struggled and underperformed, however resurrection came under the astute stewardship of Chairman David Bernstein and Managing Director Chris Bird. Sadly, both men had moved on by the time the Blues actually moved to Eastlands

Substitutes Tiatto (top) and Wanchope (bottom, watched by Sinclair).

but their legacy was that a firm base had been created to build on. With manager Kevin Keegan – absolutely adored by the majority of fans at this time for the excitement of his first two seasons – the future looked bright.

Inevitably, a return to European competition prompted fans to dream of the opponents the Blues could face in the latter stages, but before that could happen City had to progress through the Qualifying Round. The opponents were progressive Welsh side Total Network Solutions whose manager, Ken McKenna, was delighted with the draw: "It's a great story. A village team against Manchester City. If you made it up they would lock you up."

TNS owner Mike Harris was equally excited: "This is fantastic, the best draw we could possibly have had. I am confident we can go up to Manchester and get a good result and then really put the pressure on them in the second leg. If we get the right result I will be looking to relocate the game to the Millennium Stadium - why not?"

The general tone from a media perspective was typical of the usual giant-killing style stories that surround the third round of the FA Cup. "Would TNS be the plucky underdogs who upset the Premier League giants?" was the type of story being written which, unfortunately for City, meant that the British media were hardly supportive. In the end City dominated the first leg so comprehensively that the giant-killing stories would have to wait.

Daniel Taylor, writing in *The Guardian*, accurately summed up: "Doubtless TNS and the clutch of boisterous sightseers who had followed them from mid-Wales harboured aspirations of inflicting similar humiliation upon their opponents, but the threat never really materialised. Instead the Welsh Premier League side managed only two shots all night, neither of which required David Seaman to muddy his knees, and traipsed sheepishly off at the final whistle after sieving four goals in the second half to add to the one that had scarcely reflected City's domination throughout the opening exchanges."

Focusing on the fairytale nature of the match Taylor added: "This was not a night for the romantics. With City emphasising the gulf in status from the first minute, the side with nine Englishmen in their starting XI (TNS) were never a serious match for the team with four (City), especially when one of that quartet, Trevor Sinclair, opened the scoring 14 minutes into an uncomfortably one-sided opening half."

City should have increased their lead, but after the initial goal the Blues seemed to hold back. In fact it wasn't until five minutes into the second half, when a speculative shot from Shaun Wright-Phillips entered the net, that Keegan's side could make it 2-0. TNS 'keeper Gerry Doherty was far from happy that the ball managed to sneak under his body.

Substitute Sun Jihai netted the third after Robbie Fowler chased what looked to be a lost cause before crossing for Sun to head home from close range. David Sommeil added a vital touch to a shot from Joey Barton, a 54th minute substitute for Bosvelt, shot to make it 4-0. Nicolas Anelka made it 5-0 three minutes from time.

Despite the emphatic win Kevin Keegan felt the result could have been even more impressive: "We could and should have scored more goals."

28th August 2003
Qualifying Round Leg 2
(at Millennium Stadium)
Attendance: 10,123

Total Network Solutions 0-2 City

City Goalscorers: Negouai, Huckerby
City: Weaver; Flood, Tiatto, Dunne, Wiekens, Bischoff, Bosvelt (Whelan), Negouai, Huckerby, Macken (Wright-Phillips), Berkovic (Barton)

With the Recreation Field at Llansantffraid holding a capacity of around 2,000, TNS decided to switch the second leg to the Millennium Stadium in Cardiff. This meant that City's first two UEFA Cup ties of the new Century would be played in Britain's two newest and most impressive venues.

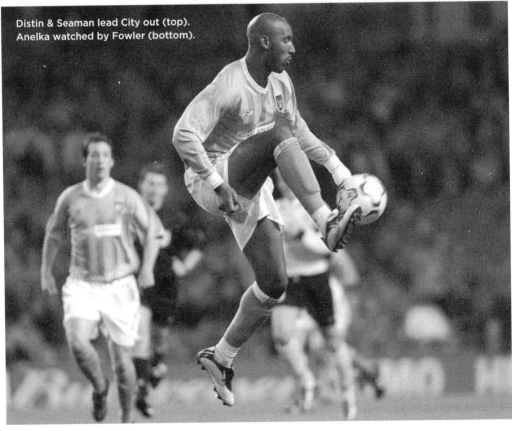

Distin & Seaman lead City out (top).
Anelka watched by Fowler (bottom).

Although the attendance was significantly greater than the Recreation Field would have allowed, the Millennium Stadium felt relatively empty. The first leg scoreline had clearly had an effect and limited the number of neutrals looking for a giant killing. As did the fact that Keegan rested the majority of his first team.

Only two who started the first leg, Eyal Berkovic and Paul Bosvelt, were involved from the start. 18 year old Willo Flood made his debut at wing-back. As a result the game was closer than the first. In the 37th minute Richard Dunne preserved City's lead when he deflected a drive from TNS's Naylor on to the post.

Despite that scare the Blues still controlled the game and two minutes before half time Christian Negouai, the Martinique-born midfielder who was playing his first competitive game in 18 months, stroked the ball passed 'keeper Williams for the first goal. Nine minutes from time Darren Huckerby made it 2-0.

Afterwards TNS received much praise. Journalist Phil Shaw: "The Welsh Premier Leaguers fought tenaciously, almost scored the goal of the tie through Gary Brabin and denied City the third goal that would have equalled their biggest aggregate win in Europe. Not that Kevin Keegan cared, City having confirmed a place alongside Liverpool, Newcastle, Roma and Barcelona in the first-round draw."

24th September 2003
Round 1 Leg 1
Attendance: 29,067

City 3-2 Lokeren

City Goalscorers: Sibierski, Fowler, Anelka
City: Seaman; Sun, Tiatto (Dunne), Sommeil, Distin, Bosvelt (Wright-Phillips), Sibierski, Reyna, Anelka, Fowler, McManaman

What was seen as an easy tie in the build up to the match became quite difficult as the Blues allowed a sixth minute lead to be thrown away by half-time. Antoine Sibierski had opened the scoring with a free kick, after Anelka had been bundled over on the edge of the area. However, only seven minutes later Sun Jihai attempted to head a relatively aimless Lokeren attempt back to David Seaman but instead he sent the ball high into the air. Lokeren's Patrick Zoundi latched on to the loose ball, sending his half-volley flying over a surprisingly hesitant David Seaman and into the net.

Five minutes before the break Lokeren took the lead when Distin miss-kicked a clearance and the ball fell to an unmarked Runar Kristinsson, whose first-time shot beat Seaman.

In the second half Robbie Fowler (below) managed to poke home an equaliser after 77 minutes, and then two minutes later the Blues took the lead. City had been awarded a penalty after a foul on Sun Jihai with Nicolas Anelka netting the spot kick.

It was not a great, convincing home victory, but at least it was a City win in European competition.

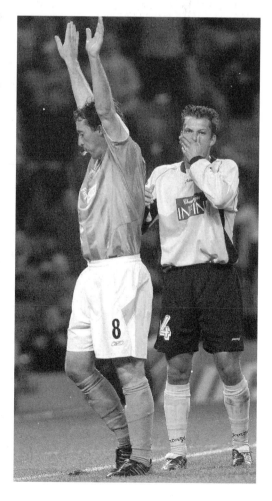

15th October 2003
Round 1 Leg 2
Attendance: 10,000

Lokeren 0-1 City

City Goalscorer: Anelka (pen)
City: Seaman; Sun, Tarnat, Sommeil, Distin, Bosvelt, Wright-Phillips, McManaman, Anelka, Wanchope (Reyna), Sinclair (Barton)

Around 4,000 supporters travelled to Lokeren for this nail-biting tie. With Lokeren netting two away goals, the Blues knew they had to be defensively tight if they were to progress.

The opening moments saw Lokeren looking keen, however Wanchope and Anelka combined fairly early on to give City the first real chance of the match. Anelka's resulting shot went over the bar. Nevertheless, it demonstrated City's intentions and was soon followed by an attempt by Wright-Phillips which was saved by the Lokeren 'keeper.

After nineteen minutes City did take the lead. A foul on Wanchope gave City a penalty which Anelka coolly scored from.

The two goal cushion seemed to give City confidence and during the second half Wright-Phillips shone, however as the match progressed the Blues seemed to hold back. They appeared happy with the lead and seemed intent on killing the game. This worried the fans who demanded the Blues search for a second goal on the night.

As City held back Lokeren seemed to run out of ideas and the match ended 1-0. Kevin Keegan defended the style of the win: "We have done what we had to do here. It was not exciting, it was a workmanlike performance. We were fortunate to get a penalty. If it had been given at the other end, I would have been disappointed. I think there was an infringement but you don't often get penalties for something like this. Lokeren made it very difficult for us. They pressed us in midfield. They are a good team and I cannot understand why they are bottom of the league. They took the Belgian League by storm last year but they have lost a striker - if they had someone up front they could be a real handful. This was always going to be a difficult game after we

won 3-2 in the first leg. But we're in the hat for the next round and we'll meet stronger teams than them now."

6th November 2003
Round 2 Leg 1
Attendance: 32,506

City 1-1 Groclin

City Goalscorer: Anelka
City: Seaman; Sun, Tarnat, Dunne, Distin, Barton, Wright-Phillips, Reyna (Bosvelt), McManaman (Tiatto), Anelka, Fowler (Wanchope)

The optimism of playing European football during the new stadium's first season was disappearing as this game came to a close. Pre-season there had been a belief that City had almost catapulted themselves forward to a level in keeping with the Club's tradition, but the truth was that on the playing front the Blues were clearly not ready to challenge in Europe.

The game opened brightly with an attempt from Claudio Reyna going over the bar in the first five minutes. This was quickly followed by Anelka chipping the 'keeper to score the opening goal after a Fowler pass had set the Frenchman up.

Further attempts followed with Anelka forcing Groclin 'keeper Liberda to race off his line to save. Gradually, however, the Polish side began to appear confident and they began to create opportunities for themselves rather than react to City's attempts.

David Seaman was forced in to action to make a couple of quality saves as Groclin began to look dangerous on the break. City still had chances, but it was becoming obvious to all that the game would not be a walkover for the Blues.

In the 64th minute, with the crowd showing their frustration, Kevin Keegan took the understandable decision to replace a rather ineffective Steve McManaman with the more recognised City battler Danny Tiatto.

Unfortunately, despite the change proving a good one, two minutes after the substitution

Groclin scored from a set-piece strike twenty yards from goal.

Despite noteworthy efforts from Wanchope and Tarnat the game ended in a draw.

27th November 2003
Round 2 Leg 2
Attendance: 5,500

Groclin 0-0 City

(City lose on away goals rule)
City: Seaman; Sun, Dunne, Sommeil, Distin, Barton, Wright-Phillips (Reyna), McManaman, Anelka (Macken), Fowler (Wanchope), Sinclair

Despite the home result City were still hopeful of progressing. They knew it would be tough, but pre-match manager Kevin Keegan and other Club officials made all the right noises, however two successive 3-0 League defeats (Leicester & Newcastle) suggested City would struggle. Shaun Wright-Phillips had been missing for those games due to a three match domestic ban, and it was abundantly clear the side had missed his enormous talent. Even though the player had appeared in the previous leg against Groclin, the perception was that Wright-Phillips' return would be enough to ensure victory.

In the 12th minute Wright-Phillips sent a cross to Trevor Sinclair. Unfortunately the Manchester born player's resulting header was fairly weak, but nevertheless it showed City's determination. There were other attempts during the opening fifteen minutes and the 1,000 or so City fans at the stadium did feel that a City goal would be forthcoming.

Unfortunately, City's optimism faded as the game progressed. Chances were squandered and in the 73rd minute Keegan substituted both Anelka and Fowler hoping that Jon Macken and Paulo Wanchope would find the much-needed breakthrough. It was not to be however and City were eliminated from Europe on the away goals rule.

Being knocked out of Europe was a bitter blow but with League form poor some suggested the defeat ultimately helped City survive that season – the Blues finished fifth from bottom. The majority of fans felt differently believing that a decent run in Europe – or at least surviving until after Christmas – would have given confidence to the Club.

Whatever the views, it has to be remembered that City's chance to play in European competition came via the Fair Play League. Viewed in that way, it should be seen as a nice bonus until the day comes when the Blues qualify for Europe on merit.

CITY QUOTES

"Supporters have urged the Club to sign this or that star or have been less specific and have called for a signing in any one of several positions. At no time has the Club made any secret of its willingness to spend money, and spend big, for any player or players they believe will strengthen the team. But a willingness to spend does not always coincide with a willingness by other clubs to part with the player desired. That has been the experience of City recently in inquiries that have been made with a view to improving the first team. Our failure so far to get what we want is equally disappointing to the Club as it is to supporters but we will not slacken our efforts."

Match programme editorial from 12th March 1960 outlining City's determination to buy the best.

***

"City have been winning everything, but now I feel it's our turn."

Wilf McGuinness (Manchester United), August 1970

***

"Francis Lee is one of Europe's top twenty stars."

Bobby Moore, January 1971.

Actually Francis Lee had been voted 14th in the European Footballer of the Year poll. German Gerd Muller was first with Bobby Moore (second) and Gordon Banks (8th) being the only British players to finish higher than Lee.

***

"People say George Best was the greatest Irish footballer, but the greatest was Peter Doherty. He was better than even Pele or Di Stefano, but he did not make such a big impact because there was no big TV sport then."

Irish hero Danny Blanchflower talking about City star Doherty during the late 1970s.

***

"The greatest player I've ever seen and a truly great man."

Former United goalkeeper Harry Gregg commenting on ex-City star Peter Doherty.

***

"Every second person you meet tells you he is going to see the final.
City have a fine opportunity of setting up a record in being the first to bring the Cup to Cottonopolis."

The Manchester Weekly Times, 22nd April 1904, comments on the 1904 FA Cup final.

***

"Homecomings are becoming monotonous"

Malcolm Allison 30th April 1970 talking of City's second homecoming parade in two months.

***

"Success is becoming monotonous"

Vice-chairman Frank Johnson 30th April 1970.

***

"It is wrong of the English Football Association to place a permanent touchline ban on Allison. That is where he should be, guiding the men he has trained and coached throughout a week's work. Why make him anonymous by placing him out of reach high in the stands? I merely get fined. Perhaps a £100 every so often, but it is worth it to be with my team when they might need me during a match."

Schalke's coach Rudi Guttendorf talking about Malcolm Allison's touchline ban, April 1970. Guttendorf was the highest-paid coach in Germany at the time with a salary of around £13,000 a year.

***

"It was a very good season for the Club, but I wasn't too happy with my performances. I was dogged by injuries. I only managed to find my old form towards the end of the season."

Neil Young talking in August 1970 about the 1969-70 season.

***

"I've lived near Franny most of my life. We knew each other as schoolboys when he lobbed the odd centre for me. I know most of the City team, in fact. But in League football, you don't stop to think that you're playing against friends. They're opponents."

Everton's Alan Ball talking about City in August 1970.

***

"Malcolm never worries me. He's fanatically keen about the game and naturally gets carried away at times. He'll mature with the years. He's got the main things that I want. Heart and real feeling for the game. He likes to make things happen. He's a very mild fellow underneath that so called tempestuous facade of his. Whatever faults he may have he's okay with me."

Joe Mercer talking about Malcolm Allison, February 1971.

***

"I rate goalkeeper Joe Corrigan highly. At over 6ft 4 inches and 15 stone, Corrigan might not have the agility of other 'keepers, but is excellent when dealing with high crosses. In addition to his physique, the lad also has a sound temperament."

Johnny Giles gives his views on Joe Corrigan in April 1972.

***

241

"Now that was entertaining! There must have been twenty shots at goal in the first quarter of an hour. Normally, in League football today, you're lucky if you see twenty shots in the whole match."

Fifties Cup final goalscorer Bobby Johnstone talking about the enjoyment he got from seeing the 1986 FA Youth Cup final second leg in which City beat United.

***

"Manchester City will always be number one with me. The crowds we were getting even when we were struggling made Manchester City supporters the best in the Country in my view. I have a great feeling for Maine Road and would love to be still there."

1981 Cup finalist Gerry Gow talking of the power of City in 1984.

***

"Most people know I'm not too clever with my left foot and I could do with being five yards faster, especially when marking Ian Rush!"

A frank assessment from City centre-half Mick McCarthy shortly after the Liverpool-City goalless draw in August 1986

***

"I have been a Manchester City fan, man and boy as they used to say, for more years than I care to remember. It began back in 1934. I was a kid of eight, one of the stars in the local wolf-cub team. We were at summer camp in Donaghadee. As a special treat, the football team was taken to a tiny cinema to see fleeting glimpses of Manchester City winning the FA Cup on the newsreel. Those were the days when Matt Busby was a good wing-half and when Manchester United were just another humble club on the other side of the railway track. They were good years of allegiance for a growing boy."

Spurs and Ireland legend Danny Blanchflower talking about his love of the Blues on 11th March 1973.

***

"We have encouraged the bananas here. They're tremendous. They have made a better atmosphere with a lot of comedy."

City secretary Bernard Halford comments on the banana craze in 1989.

***

"The best £400,000 I have ever spent."

Joe Royle commenting on his bargain buy of Shaun Goater.

***

"I still have a lot of special memories about my time at City. The year we got promoted under Joe Royle was tremendous and you don't realise until you play for City how much of an honour it actually is. You could never play at another club like it."

Danny Glanville

The Football Season Daily Reminder

March

1st March 1969

Tottenham were defeated 1-0 in the FA Cup quarter final at Maine Rd.

2nd March 1973

City fan and player Trevor Sinclair born in Dulwich.

3rd March 1934

84,569 spectators paid to watch City's FA Cup quarter-final victory over Stoke City. This remains the highest crowd for a provincial match in England.

4th March 1969

The first City League game for almost seven weeks saw the Blues defeated 2-1 at Burnley. Poor weather, combined with FA Cup weekends, created this long gap for the reigning League Champions.

5th March 2006

City raced into a two goal lead against Sunderland when Samaras scored two goals in two minutes (9th & 10th minutes). In the 25th minute Kyle scored for the Wearsiders. The game played at Eastlands ended 2-1 before a crowd of 42,200.

6th March 1963

Due to an exceptionally snowy winter, City's appearance in the FAC was delayed until this date. The Blues beat Walsall 1-0 in the 3rd round. 7 days later they beat Bury (1-0) in the 4th round and then lost to Norwich (2-1) on 16th March in round 5.

7th March 1993

City's quarter-final tie with Tottenham should have been a day of major celebration but instead the Blues failed to deliver. The game eventually ended in a 4-2 defeat but that scoreline does not give a fair reflection of how the match was actually played out. Frustrated fans invaded the pitch.

8th March 1924

City played out a goalless fourth round cup tie with Cardiff before a Maine Road crowd of 76,166. At the time this was the largest attendance for any footballing fixture (including three FA Cup Finals) in Manchester.

9th March 1968

Coventry City were defeated 3-1 at Maine Road as Joe Mercer's City began to be recognised as

MANCHESTER CITY F.C.

MR. J. B. HALFORD, Secretary
MANCHESTER CITY F.C. PLC
MAINE ROAD, MOSS SIDE, MANCHESTER M14 7WN

WHERE APPROPRIATE, THIS TICKET IS FOR THE SEAT STATED ONLY.
PLEASE TAKE UP YOUR POSITION AT LEAST 45 MINUTES PRIOR TO KICK-OFF

OFFICIAL CLUB SPONSORS
brother
The future at your fingertips

DIAL-A-SEAT 061-227-9229 | RETAIN THIS PORTION OF TICKET FOR FUTURE APPLICATIONS | CITY CLUB CALL 0898-12-11-91

F.A. CUP 6TH ROUND
M.C.F.C. v TOTTENHAM HOTSPUR
SUN 07 MAR 1993 KICK OFF 03:05 P.M

UMBRO STAND BLOCK Y
ROW SEAT PRICE
23 106 £11.00

JAMES 250293 15:23:41 D

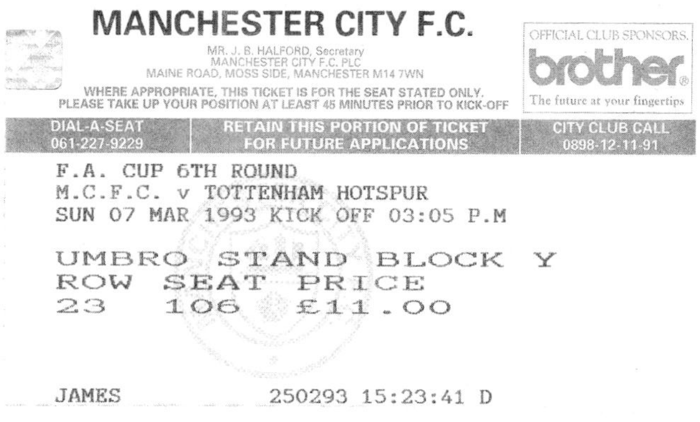

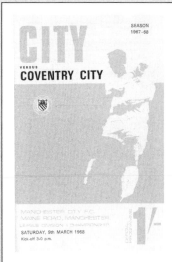

SEASON 1967-68

CITY

VERSUS

COVENTRY CITY

MANCHESTER CITY F.C.
MAINE ROAD, MANCHESTER
LEAGUE DIVISION 1 CHAMPIONSHIP
SATURDAY, 9th MARCH 1968
Kick-off 3.0 p.m.

1/-

14th March 2004

The first Manchester derby at Eastlands ended in a 4-1 City victory over United.

15th March 1960

Denis Law signed for City (right) from Huddersfield for £55,000 - £10,000 more than the previous British transfer record fee.

16th March 1996

Georgi Kinkladze made the headlines with two goals one after an absolutely outstanding run – against Southampton at Maine Road.

17th March 1956

A solitary goal from Bobby Johnstone was enough to see City beat Spurs in the FA Cup semi final at Villa Park.

serious title challengers. The goalscorers were Colin Bell, George Heslop and Francis Lee.

10th March 1971

A crowd reported as 100,000 at the time witnessed a 2-0 City defeat at Gornik in the ECWC quarter final first leg.

11th March 2005

Stuart Pearce took on managerial duties after Kevin Keegan's departure. Exactly 25 years earlier the Blues paid a figure claimed at the time to be £1.2m for Kevin Reeves.

12th March 1932

The FAC semi against Arsenal ended in a 1-0 last minute defeat.

13th March 1948

Two goals apiece from Roy Clarke and George Smith gave the Blues a 4-1 victory over Burnley in Division One (right).

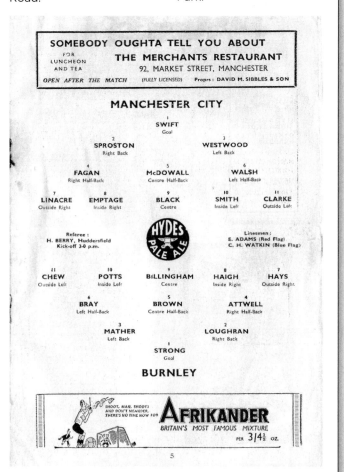

SOMEBODY OUGHTA TELL YOU ABOUT
FOR LUNCHEON AND TEA
THE MERCHANTS RESTAURANT
92, MARKET STREET, MANCHESTER
OPEN AFTER THE MATCH   (FULLY LICENSED)   Proprs: DAVID M. SIBBLES & SON

MANCHESTER CITY

1
SWIFT
Goal

2
SPROSTON
Right Back

3
WESTWOOD
Left Back

4
FAGAN
Right Half-Back

5
McDOWALL
Centre Half-Back

6
WALSH
Left Half-Back

7
LINACRE
Outside Right

8
EMPTAGE
Inside Right

9
BLACK
Centre

10
SMITH
Inside Left

11
CLARKE
Outside Left

Referee:
H. BERRY, Huddersfield
Kick-off 3-0 p.m.

Linesmen:
E. ADAMS (Red Flag)
C. H. WATKIN (Blue Flag)

HYDES PALE ALE

11
CHEW
Outside Left

10
POTTS
Inside Left

9
BiLLINGHAM
Centre

8
HAIGH
Inside Right

7
HAYS
Outside Right

6
BRAY
Left Half-Back

5
BROWN
Centre Half-Back

4
ATTWELL
Right Half-Back

3
MATHER
Left Back

2
LOUGHRAN
Right Back

1
STRONG
Goal

BURNLEY

SHOOT, MAN, SHOOT!
AND DON'T MEANDER,
THERE'S NO TIME NOW FOR
AFRIKANDER
BRITAIN'S MOST FAMOUS MIXTURE
PER 3/4½ OZ.

5

SECRETARY AND PUBLIC RELATIONS OFFICER:
ALAN HARDAKER, O.B.E.

REG. NO. 80612 ENGLAND

ALL OFFICIAL CORRESPONDENCE
MUST BE ADDRESSED TO THE
SECRETARY.

THE FOOTBALL LEAGUE LIMITED

REGISTERED OFFICE
LYTHAM ST. ANNES
LANCS.
FY8 1JG.

TELEPHONE:
ST. ANNES 729421
(STD 0253)

TELEX:
67675

TELEGRAMS.
"LEAGUE" ST. ANNES

21st March, 1977

14/F

The Secretary,
Manchester City   Football Club.,

Dear Sir,

West Ham Utd. v. Manchester City
12th March,   1977.

    I am in receipt of your letter dated 18th March, in connection
with a discrepancy on your Team Sheet for the above match.

    I have to inform you, however, that in accordance with the Management
Committees' instructions notified to you on the 21st August, 1973, a fine
of £5.00. is imposed on your club for this error.

    I look forward to receiving your remittance for this amount in due
course.

Yours faithfully,

A. Hardaker

Secretary.

18th March 1933

Derby County defeated 3-2 in the FAC semi-final.

19th March 2005

Stuart Pearce managed the Blues for the first time following the resignation of Kevin Keegan. The game with Spurs ended in a 2-1 defeat with Reyna scoring for City at White Hart Lane. Pearce's side went unbeaten for the rest of the season after this match.

20th March 1976

A penalty from Dennis Tueart and a goal each from Mike Doyle and Ged Keegan gave City victory by the odd goal in five against Wolves at Maine Road. City ended the season eighth while Wolves were relegated alongside Burnley (their last appearance in the top flight until 2009-10) and Sheffield United.

21st March 1984

After a glittering career with Everton and Liverpool, striker David

Johnson joined the Blues. Despite a reputation as a lethal striker - and hard evidence of real achievement – Johnson's time at Maine Road was not particularly successful. After one goal in four (plus two as substitute) games Johnson moved to play soccer in North America in May 1984.

22nd March 1969

Tommy Booth scored the only goal of the FA Cup semi final for City against Everton at Villa Park. The game was watched by 63,025.

23rd March 1986

The day after drawing 2-2 at Old Trafford in the Manchester derby, City were defeated 5-4 by Chelsea in the inaugural Full Members' Cup final. The match was played at Wembley and, although the competition hardly registers today, the final was watched by 68,000 – that season's FA Cup final only attracted 14,000 more – and brought wild celebrations for Chelsea (it was their first cup success since 1971).

24th March 1994

Peter Beagrie signed for City from Everton and soon established himself as a hero. With his trademark somersaulting goal celebrations Beagrie scored 5 goals in 58 (plus 7 as substitute) appearances, but his contribution to the exciting style of play enjoyed under Brian Horton was much more impressive than those statistics suggest.

25th March 1998

Cult hero Ian Bishop returned to Maine Road for his second spell.

26th March 1955

The FA Cup semi against Sunderland ended 1-0 to City thanks to a Roy Clarke goal (left).

27th March 1926

The first FA Cup semi-final between City and Manchester United ended 3-0 to the Blues. The match was played at Bramall Lane. The Blues were managerless for this game – Vice-Chairman Albert Alexander senior took on most of the manager's duties between November and April.

28th March 1932

City beat Birmingham 2-1 at Maine Road and the following day beat the same side 5-1 at St. Andrew's.

29th March 1924

City's 2-0 defeat to Newcastle in the FA Cup semi-final brought an end to Billy Meredith's playing career. Remarkably Meredith (below) was over 49 when he played this match.

30th March 1973

Salford born Barney Daniels officially signed for City on this day, but the date also has significance as it saw Malcolm Allison resign as manager.

31st March 1971

In Copenhagen City defeated Gornik 3-1 in the ECWC quarter final replay.

GOLDEN GOALS

Kevin Horlock

1999

v Gillingham

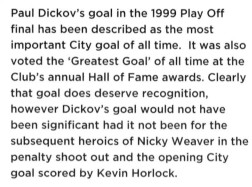

Paul Dickov's goal in the 1999 Play Off final has been described as the most important City goal of all time. It was also voted the 'Greatest Goal' of all time at the Club's annual Hall of Fame awards. Clearly that goal does deserve recognition, however Dickov's goal would not have been significant had it not been for the subsequent heroics of Nicky Weaver in the penalty shoot out and the opening City goal scored by Kevin Horlock.

The late 1990s had been a very difficult period for City and Horlock's goal came at a moment when all hope that the Club could resurrect itself seemed to have vanished. This goal was obviously important as it gave City hope and ultimately that transferred into achievement.

The idea of this 'GOLDEN GOALS' feature is to remember a significant or spectacular goal from yesteryear. The Big Book Of City's hope is that modern day supporters will learn more about some of these goals. If you would like to nominate a goal for possible use in a future 'Big Book' then email: city@manchesterfootball.org with details of game, goalscorer and date.

Match Stats

Date: 30th May 1999
Score: City 2-2 Gillingham, City won 3-1 on penalties
Venue: Wembley Stadium
Scorers: Kevin Horlock (89) & Paul Dickov (90+5); Carl Asaba (81 mins) & Robert Taylor (86 mins)
Attendance: 76,935

City Team: Weaver, Crooks (Taylor), Edghill, Wiekens, Morrison (Vaughan), Horlock, Brown (Bishop), Jeff Whitley, Dickov, Goater, Cooke

Pre-Match

Third placed City missed out on automatic promotion by five points, but defeated sixth placed Wigan 2-1 on aggregate in the play-off semi-final. This earned them the right to appear in the promotion decider against Gillingham. Pre-match City were regarded as favourites, due to their final League position, form and stature in the game. It was anticipated by the media that the Blues would sweep aside Gillingham with ease. Fans of course knew this was a time when the side often displayed its 'Typical City' qualities, but even City couldn't make a mess of this, could they?

Arguments over ticket allocations had given the game a bit of an edge – City pointed to the Club's enormous and loyal support while Gillingham argued this was the biggest day in their history. The fortunate Mancunians who had managed to get tickets to the game viewed anyone wearing a brand new Gillingham shirt as suspicious, particularly as those encamped close to the ramps on Wembley Way were singing songs glorifying Manchester United, and Millwall, with only occasional chants of 'Gillingham'.

Those favouring Gillingham colours mainly congregated around the twin towers area and their chanting was abruptly ended when a small group of City supporters lightened the atmosphere by marching through the middle of the Gills chanting: "Wem-ber-ley, Wem-ber-ley, it's that sh*tty place in London that we thought we'd never see!" Everyone laughed, and it said much about the City fans approach.

The pre-match entertainment was not particularly inspiring with two London based DJs pretending to support Gillingham and City, and then sing songs connected with the clubs. The 'City DJ' chose to sing Oasis songs, surely Blue Moon would have been more appropriate at this point? And even the arrival of Moonchester couldn't save the DJ from embarrassment.

Eventually, the players were brought out on to the pitch for the commencement of play. They were greeted by smoke, fireworks, and inflatable Nationwide Building Society men.

The Game

It has to be said that when play commenced City were not the great force the media expected, instead they slipped their way across a wet surface and relied on the 20 year old Nicky Weaver to keep Gillingham at bay, particularly in the 9th minute when he palmed away an effort from Galloway.

Confidence did grow as the match progressed and in the 26th minute a downward header from Kevin Horlock was superbly saved by Gillingham's Bartram.

Mixed play followed, but City should have taken the lead in the 75th minute when Shaun Goater hit the post. Nerves started to increase for both sides as the game progressed, but it was Gillingham that seemed most equipped to deal with the situation.

Only nine minutes from time City were dealt a tremendous blow when Carl Asaba toe-poked a shot into the roof of City's

net. Worse was to follow for City as Robert Taylor made it 2-0 in the 86th minute. Two thirds of the stadium fell silent, then many, many Blues decided enough was enough and left for home. Supporting City through the late 1990s had been extremely tough and many felt humiliation at Wembley was the final straw. Had the Blues failed then the entire existence of the Club would have been in doubt. This is no exaggeration and every member of City's staff, management and the Club's owners must never forget that City fans kept the Club alive during some very dark days. This is something the Chairman at the time David Bernstein knew well.

Radio Five commentator Alan Green told his listeners about the plight of the thousands of City fans silent at Wembley adding: "That many fans go to every home game. Why do they do it?"

The situation looked exceptionally bleak and then, with a mere 17 seconds of normal time remaining, Kevin Horlock scored the goal that helped to bring life back to the Club.

The goal itself was not the most spectacular but it was highly significant. Gillingham supporter Haydn Parry described it and its impact on his side perfectly: "Horlock drilled home a desperate defensive clearance for a scrappy but well-taken goal. The bloke behind me muttered it was merely their consolation goal. Yet an invisible shockwave of tension spread rapidly around the Gillingham end of the stadium."

The BBC website focused on how City were forced into an attacking frame of mind after the two Gillingham goals which, let's face it, were fairly late in the game themselves: "Those two strikes left City with no option but to attack, and the pressure caused the first cracks in the Gillingham defence, with

Horlock driving a left-footed shot through a crowd of players."

Conrad Leach writing in the *Independent*: "Gillingham had scored their goals after 81 and 86 minutes and City were looking down the barrel of another season in the Second Division, but the game was transformed in the 89th minute - as good a time as any to score - when Kevin Horlock drove in a low shot from 18 yards to make it 2-1. It just seemed like a consolation goal and the supporters continued to leave but would come to regret it. To give City further heart, the fourth official then held up his board indicating there would be four minutes of stoppage time."

Greg Struthers, the *Times*: "With a minute remaining of the 90, Kevin Horlock latched onto a loose ball and drove it into the Gillingham goal to give City some hope at 2-1. The Gills fans began whistling for full-time when five minutes of stoppage time began, but the drama was not over."

Over time the focus from City fans has been on the goal that followed this, however it has to be stressed that Horlock's goal was the turning point even if none of us thought this at the time. Some fans obviously saw the goal on the day as being significant and loved the hope it brought but others simply saw it as a consolation effort. Interestingly, Gillingham fans recognised that the entire balance of play was altered by this goal. City held the upper hand and, according to Haydn Parry, one Gillingham supporter with a macabre outlook gave a fair assessment of how Horlock's goal made Gills feel. It was akin "to watching a car crash in slow motion, unable to move and knowing full well who would be leaving the scene in a bodybag."

The momentum did switch to City and four and a half minutes into injury time

Paul Dickov fired an equaliser into the top corner. The impact of those two goals was enormous. Extra time followed, and then came penalties. The City players huddled together as a team, showing the unity that previous sides had clearly not enjoyed. This unity helped City win the penalty shoot out 3-1.

Man Of The Match

Extremely difficult to pick a man of the match because of the drama of the entire day. Today people automatically assume Dickov was the star, and he was certainly worthy of the acclaim, but all the penalty takers – including the much maligned Richard Edghill – deserve the praise. As does Kevin Horlock. Nicky Weaver's goalkeeping exploits were of course highly significant.

Post Match

The game was crucial as it brought promotion to Division One – still lower than history dictated should be City's rightful position – and allowed the Club to move forward. Had City failed the consequences would have been horrendous to even contemplate. City captain at the time Andy Morrison admitted: "It was a fantastic feeling. We had put in so much effort and needed to win because we didn't have

City fans celebrate behind a disconsolate Vince Bartram.

a Plan B. Every game during the season felt like a cup final for the teams we were playing. There were 26,000 fans for my debut and we filled our allocation of away supporters wherever we played. You have to give credit to them; they followed the team everywhere even though we were in the Second Division. They can never be accused of jumping on the band-wagon."

That comment on support was highly appropriate and was recognised throughout the Club from Chairman David Bernstein through to Chris Bird, who soon became the Blues' Managing Director. They were both Blues and fully understood the importance of the fans.

Bernstein admitted this was not the end of City's struggle, though: "This is only the first stage. We will clear our heads and take it from there. I'll be working even harder to raise finance, which I've got to say will be easier now we are in the First Division."

Manager Joe Royle was delighted, although it's fair to say he looked absolutely worn out when he made it into the dressing room after the celebrations. In a rather down to earth manner he told the media: "We're not getting too excited about this. A club this size should not be too euphoric about getting out of the old Division Three. And even though we won today, I still think the play offs are a joke. After 46 League games it comes down to a lottery."

Moving on to the performance Joe added: "My players were magnificent, and I never once thought we were beaten. We have now lost just twice in our last 27 matches and I think that tells you everything about their fighting spirit. We have played 49 cup ties this season and this is a very hard division. When fans are hanging off the rafters for you at places like Colchester, it all adds to the pressure. These lads will be better players for this experience and the strong nucleus in this side will go forward.

"I think we have gone a long way to curing Man City-itis. We can handle the big games now, even though we weren't at our best today."

Promotion was significant and it helped develop a mood about the Club that resulted in a second promotion the following season. This finally brought to an end City's four season exile from the Premier League – City's longest spell out of the top flight since their first promotion in 1899.

Elsewhere

The impact on City is well known and the transformation under Chairman David Bernstein, Chris Bird and Joe Royle paved the way for the Club's move to the new stadium. None of those men were actually at City when the Blues moved stadium and, to some extent, they were never appropriately acknowledged for the work they did. The same is true for some of the players, including Kevin Horlock.

This game – and to some extent the Horlock goal – is significantly more important to Manchester's history than simply its impact on City's own history. Had City failed at Wembley in 1999 it is highly unlikely the City Of Manchester Stadium would have been erected to the size and scale it was. In fact it seems highly likely that a much smaller permanent stadium would have been built and, subject to City's own progression, it may have been that the Blues remained at Maine Road. It has to be remembered the agreement between City and the Council was signed after promotion was assured and not before.

The 2002 Commonwealth Games were a huge success and helped lift Mancunian spirits – again that may not have been the case had the stadium been of a less significant design. In addition the success of the Games helped play an important part in the selection of London for the 2012 Olympic Games.

So, Horlock's goal paved the way for so much more than simply a Second Division promotion.

TO BERLIN

"I am not going to pretend that English football teams making tours of Continental countries do not have a very pleasant time, but at the same time these tours are not picnics. You are there to play serious football, and you have to go about it in the ordinary businesslike way."

Sam Barkas, City Captain, 27th May 1937

As Sam Barkas hinted, sometimes end of season football tours are not the fun experience a lot of fans think. Sometimes the tour takes on a whole different meaning. This is certainly true for the May 1937 tour to Germany.

The Blues, as Champions of England, were invited to play a series of high profile matches across Germany and its neighbouring States. Although this was a major honour for City it has to be stressed that the whole concept of the tour, as far as Germany's Nazi rulers were concerned, was to promote Germany's sporting prowess against the best England could offer.

Within days of their first championship success, City set off on their tour. By this time some games planned to take place in Austria-Hungary had been cancelled as City claimed the travel commitments were simply too great.

The first tour game was played in Duisberg a mere five days after the final League game of the season, however Mancunians reading the *Manchester Evening News* would have been rather worried that no news came back on the Club's progress for some time. Fans were concerned but, with Britain in the middle of coronation fever, few non-royal stories seemed to make the news.

On 13th May the *Evening News* finally carried its first snippet: "Old habits die hard, and Manchester City are still keeping up their practice of letting their opponents establish a lead before they bring out their best form. The latest victims of this tantalising peculiarity are the German eleven who were met at Schweinfurt on the City's continental tour.

"Two goals in front after twenty minutes the Germans must have had wonderful visions of defeating the Football League champions, but the rally that brought a 3-2 win for the Maine Road team was as sure and decisive as it was against many opponents in the First Division. Percival (bottom) scored two of the goals, a prolific scoring rate which is rather new to him."

This game was actually the third of the tour, but it's worth noting that the opponents – a German XI – were predominantly leading German international stars. In fact, although team line-ups are hard to come by it is clear that each side the Blues faced on this tour included international players from all over Germany. As City were a domestic rather than a national side, it is hard to describe any of the sides as a pure German national team, however they were certainly of a greater quality than perhaps City had anticipated. Many German sources claim City's opponents were basically the international team, or a version of it at least. Official Blue records are clearly inaccurate as they show the games as being played against:

■ **'A Duisberg XI'** - yet that match is known to have included several internationals, including at least two from Schalke (one of which was the German captain Szepan). This is recorded in Germany as a friendly between a German national XI and the English champions. In addition, goalkeeper Klodt was on the verge of a full international debut (it came the following season) and this was seen as being a test of his quality in the same way as England used to use B internationals.

■ **SV Wuppertal** – again this is recorded as a German XI V Manchester City in Germany.

■ **Schweinfurt** – really another German XI.

The Duisberg game was watched by a crowd recorded as 45,000 and ended goalless, prompting some criticism in Germany of the home side. The *Manchester Guardian* carried some material: "Both sides had some promising attacks, and Swift had to make several good saves, but there was no score at half-time."

Later goalkeeper Frank Swift saved a penalty, and was put under further pressure: "The Germans missed an open goal after Swift had run out, and a few minutes later he was called upon to save from a corner. Towards the close, excitement became intense. The Germans attacked hotly in an endeavour to score a goal to beat the English Champions, and Swift made several fine saves. Apart from Swift and Klodt the best players on the field were Toseland, Herd, Urban, Szepan and Elbern."

At Wuppertal in the second match, the Blues achieved a 1-1 draw before 30,000. The home goalkeeper Juerissen was the undisputed star of the match.

On the 19th May the *Manchester Evening News* reported: "Very little has been heard so far of the tour of the Football League Champions Manchester City in Germany, and they are due back a week today.

"Mr. Fred Jolly, one of the directors, forced to remain at home through demands of business tells me, however that Mr. R. Smith, the Chairman, has written to him to say that they have been delighted by their reception at all parts of the tour. They have proved to be an attraction."

After the German XI were defeated at Schweinfurt, City's next game took place exactly one week later. However, this was by far the most significant match and the most high profile as it was to be staged in Berlin's Olympic stadium. When the players returned to England at the end of the month Captain Sam Barkas (top, opposite) explained that in the build up to this match the Blues acted as English ambassadors. On the days without games they typically went down for breakfast at 9am before spending the morning on official visits – meeting local dignitaries, visiting factories, schools and

members of the public. Some afternoons the players would be free to wander around the towns on their own, but more often than not further ambassadorial style visits would be organised. During the evenings there would be official engagements. However, the Club would try to insist all players went to bed between 10 and 11pm.

This was all a bit too much of an effort for some of the players, and the formality of it all seemed stifling at times. Inevitably, some of the players tried to laugh and joke whenever possible. On arrival at one ground Frank Swift, City's main comedian, jumped off the team coach and immediately performed an exaggerated Nazi salute to the large crowd waiting. They believed it to be genuine, while the City players were creased with laughter.

While City waited for the Berlin match, the German public were keen to see how their side was performing elsewhere. Sepp Herberger had been given the role of coaching the German national side after an embarrassing performance at the 1936 Olympics. Herberger's task was to create an all-conquering powerful national side and May 1937 was to be a significant period for the Germans. A series of high profile friendlies – including the games with City – were arranged and it was anticipated that Herberger's side would end the month as proud representatives and ambassadors of the country.

City inside forward Peter Doherty (left) recognised the importance of the tour when he wrote his biography several years later. He claimed that the German players had been "sent away to special camps to prepare for the games. They played like demons, and gave us a very hard time of it."

He also said: "The German teams we played were trained to perfection."

There is a great deal of truth in what Doherty said. Herberger had taken his players to special camps and had worked hard to make them gel as a unit. This is why the significance of the tour increased game by game. The German public were watching

their national side take shape. There were high expectations. This became apparent three days before the City game in Berlin when Germany played another friendly in Herberger's series. This time they faced the Danish national side. Denmark had been unbeaten for over a year before that game but Herberger's side managed an 8-0 victory in the then German city of Breslau, Lower Silesia (now Wroclaw, Poland).

Amongst the 40,000 crowd there that day were the players and representatives of City. Doherty: "The Germans won very easily. We were guests at an elaborate banquet after the game, and everyone treated us with the utmost kindness."

The German side became known as the 'Breslau Elf' (the Breslau Eleven) after restoring pride and their next match, the 19th May friendly with City in Berlin, was

256

described what City did next: "We were expected to give the Nazi salute at the line-up before the match started; but we decided merely to stand to attention. When the German national anthem was played, only eleven arms went up instead of the expected twenty-two!"

When England played Germany in the same stadium the following May the F.A. encouraged the players to perform the salute, here the City men themselves decided not to bother. No doubt Frank Swift would have performed a rather exaggerated 'Basil Fawlty' style salute if he'd have been forced!

Inevitably, the match was a difficult one for the Blues, and within the first couple of minutes Swift had to pick the ball out of the net after Germany's opening goal. The sun had been in Swift's eyes according to the *Guardian*, but the 'keeper was angry with himself.

Doherty scored an equaliser but the Germans seemed more determined as a result. *The Manchester Guardian* reported: "The Germans played up strongly after this, but Swift, with his sure and capable hands, proved a stumbling block. Six minutes after scoring their first goal, the City went ahead through Brook, who scored with a hard, long shot."

Giving City the lead stunned the German public. They expected the 'Breslau Elf' to tear the Blues apart. Surely, an English domestic side could not be a match for the German national side?

The Guardian reported that the Blues started the second half brightly: "At this point Manchester City looked the better team and appeared likely winners, but after sixteen minutes the Germans equalised. Siffling, the inside-right, shot from a short distance, Swift was unable to catch the ball properly and let it slip from his grasp, and Hohmann ran up and scored."

Again Swift was disappointed with himself, however this was clearly a tough match, played in front of a large partisan crowd. Hohmann had not played against Denmark

viewed as being of huge significance. For City this was going to be a real test and it was also going to be a major cultural shock. Doherty: "The whole place was peppered with armed Nazi guards, and getting past them to reach the dressing rooms was an ordeal."

It was clear the Germans wanted to put in an exceptionally good performance against the best English side in the nation's capital. This match was not merely a football friendly, this was a game of pride for the Germans. The Denmark international had been seen as a major landmark moment, and now they had to beat the English champions. It has to be remembered as well that only a few days earlier German pride had been battered when the Hindenberg airship burst in to flames in one of the World's most high profile disasters.

The significance of the game at the time was so high that British Movietone sent a film crew to the stadium to capture the action. Around 40 seconds of play still survive today, but because of its significance this footage is known to have been shown in the USA as well as Britain during May and June 1937

City, the first English side to play at the Olympic Stadium, entered the arena to the cheers of over 70,000 spectators. Doherty

but Siffling had scored five of Germany's goals in that match.

As the game progressed Germany attacked relentlessly, and eighteen minutes from time Hohmann scored his second and Germany's third. Doherty remembered the moment well: "I remember very clearly the enthusiasm shown by the German forward who scored the winning goal. He was so delighted that he returned to the centre of the field turning perfect cartwheels all the way!"

The game ended 3-2 to a very powerful German national side. *The Guardian* recognised the strength of City's opponents and claimed the score could have been much greater: "It was only the brilliance of Swift that prevented the Germans from scoring again."

Swift was again City's greatest player in their final match – another 3-2 defeat to another German XI this time played in Stuttgart. A report from the press agency Reuters read: "Although conceding three goals in the first half, Swift played a fine game for the visitors. As a result Manchester City Football Club were rather unlucky to lose the last match of their German tour here today."

The *Manchester Evening Chronicle* was extremely positive in their praise of the Blues: "Though Manchester City have lost their unbeaten record on the Continent, the supporters of the Champions have no need to spend any sleepless nights worrying about the 3-2 defeat in Berlin. No doubt Manchester fans hoped to see the City return undefeated, but no disgrace was attached to such a narrow reverse. The City fans can take the defeat calmly. No need to get 'hot and bothered'."

At the game in Berlin the Blues had been presented with a Nazi pennant on the pitch and another one in the Directors' area (above). It is believed the one received on the pitch was destroyed by Club officials at the outbreak of war, while the other one was thrown into a box of souvenirs by vice Chairman Albert Alexander senior

on his return to England from the tour. It remained there until around sixty years later when Albert's grandson Eric Alexander (Chairman of City during the early seventies) rediscovered it. He believes his grandfather had forgotten all about the pennant and is certain he would have destroyed it in 1939 had he remembered it existed. Fortunately, it survived as a powerful symbol of how football can often be inappropriately used to promote political messages.

After a tiring tour, City returned to Manchester to find the city recovering from celebrating King George VI's coronation – trams and buses had been illuminated and the streets, most notably Piccadilly and King Street, had been decorated with huge banners and buntings – many City fans felt the celebrations belonged to their Championship success.

The surviving British Movietone footage can be viewed on their website: www. movietone.com. It is recorded as story number 5389 and has the following description: Elevated shot of group in Germany, Berlin. Shots of the game. Close shot of crowd yelling. Game. Germany win. Crowds wave.

CITY'S NUMBER ONE

THE PROFILES

63 – DAVID SEAMAN

Former England international David Seaman joined City on 4th June 2003 at the age of 39. Schmeichel had retired and manager Kevin Keegan still wanted a recognised 'keeper to inspire the Blues.

Seaman's debut came in Eastlands' first competitive fixture as the Blues defeated Total Network Solutions 5-0 in the UEFA Cup qualifying round and, inevitably, he was also the first choice for the opening League game at the stadium when Portsmouth managed a 1-1 draw.

Unfortunately, Seaman's City career did not last long and, following a shoulder injury, the 'keeper announced his retirement in January 2004. Almost immediately he was consulted by Kevin Keegan on possible replacements and Seaman encouraged the Blues to make a move for his England successor David James.

Since retirement Seaman has appeared on television in a variety of programmes, including quizzes and reality shows.

Appearances: League: 19 FAC: 1 League Cup: 1 Euro: 5

64 – KEVIN STUHR ELLEGAARD

After developing his skills in Danish football Kevin Stuhr Ellegaard signed for City on 26th October 2001 for £750,000 and had to wait until 9th November 2003 for his first team debut. That game ended in a 3-0 defeat to Leicester and Seaman returned for the following game, however Ellegaard came back for the next home game – a 1-0 defeat by Middlesbrough – and the 3-1 League Cup defeat on 3rd December.

On 10th January 2004 Ellegaard was part of a small bizarre piece of history for City when he came on as substitute for the injured Seaman. This was Ellegaard's last League appearance for the Blues which meant that both goalkeepers ended their City League careers with an appearance in the same game.

Ellegaard did appear in FA Cup matches after that final League match, including the 3-1 victory at Leicester on 14th January 2004, but his City career was never likely to develop further once David James was signed.

At the end of 2004 the 'keeper went on loan to Blackpool where he made three first team appearances.

He was released by City in June 2005 and spent a period at Hertha Berlin, before moving back to Denmark in 2007 with Randers. At Randers he made a good start and became established as the side's first choice goalkeeper.

Appearances: League: 2 (plus 2 as substitute) FAC: 2 League Cup: 1

65 – DAVID JAMES

England international Goalkeeper David James joined the Blues from West Ham in January 2004 after injury had led to David Seaman retiring mid-season. Whereas Seaman was always seen by supporters as a short term signing (as to some extent was Peter Schmeichel) James was viewed differently and, as a result, he immediately proved popular with supporters. It helped of course that he was still regarded as an international player, if not England's automatic first choice, and would continue to appear for the national side in the years that followed his transfer to Eastlands.

The 'keeper made his debut on 17th January 2004 as the Blues drew 1-1 at home to Blackburn and over the course of the rest of the season James' confidence and assured handling helped the Blues enormously. As with Corrigan and Swift before him, the City & England 'keeper did make the occasional slip, however his overall brilliance while with the Blues easily surpassed any occasional blips. Inevitably, he saved a couple of penalties during the season (V. Wolves & Leicester) and this always helps a 'keeper establish a place in the hearts of City fans.

On the last day of the 2004-05 season James demonstrated another exciting

aspect of his play when manager Stuart Pearce played him for the final significant period of the second half as a striker. Substitute Nicky Weaver was brought on and went in nets while James changed his shirt and played in attack. It was an interesting and exciting period and thanks to James' persistence it also led to a penalty for the Blues. Unfortunately, Robbie Fowler missed the penalty – and City's chance of European qualification – and many supporters felt that James should have been given the opportunity instead.

The following season his consistency impressed again and he was selected as part of the England squad for the 2006 World Cup in Germany, but his City career was soon to end. In August 2006 he moved to Portsmouth and with the south coast club he won the FA Cup in 2008.

On 14 February 2009 James became a record breaker when he made his 536th appearance in the Premier League, surpassing Gary Speed's record. Interestingly Portsmouth's opponents at Fratton Park that day were City.

Appearances: League: 93 FAC: 6 League Cup: 1

The Football Season Daily Reminder

April

1st April 1916

Future City defender Dick Neilson was born at Blackhall. Neilson only managed 16 first team appearances during the 1930s but his career, like so many others, was cut short by World War Two. Neilson made 130 wartime appearances. In later life he became a City coach and was one of the Club's longest serving staff members when he retired at the age of 64.

2nd April 1923

Hyde Road's last victory saw City defeat Sunderland 1-0 (interesting note: Maine Road's last victory was against the same club on 21/4/2003).

3rd April 1965

City beat Malcolm Allison's Plymouth 2-1 before a pitiful Maine Road crowd of 10,929. Allison, wearing a Cossack hat for the match, was already entertaining Mancunians after outlining his footballing aims in the *Football Pink* earlier in the season. Little did anyone present realise that within four months Allison would be helping to transform City.

4th April 2004

An 82nd minute equaliser from Sylvain Distin ensured the Blues gained a point at Aston Villa.

5th April 2003

Gerard Wiekens played his last League game for City at Bolton. The game ended in a 2-0 defeat.

6th April 2002

City defeated Barnsley 5-1 to guarantee the Division One League title. Promotion had been assured the previous day when Wolves were defeated by Millwall. Those results meant that for the first time since 1997 City knew which division they would be playing in the following season prior to the last match.

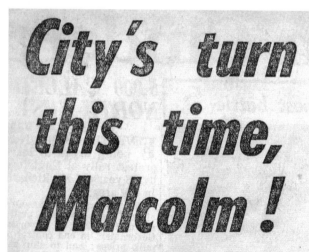

City's turn this time, Malcolm !

BY PETER GARDNER

MALCOLM ALLISON, the manager who flouts authority, is back to square one in his efforts to put Plymouth on the soccer map.

7th April 1992

A Keith Curle penalty, in front of an Old Trafford crowd of 46,781, helped City to a 1-1 draw in a controversial Manchester derby. The game was viewed as being highly significant in the title race as only four days earlier the Blues had beaten title-hopefuls Leeds 4-0 at Maine Road. Leeds ultimately won the title, with City finishing fifth (8 points behind 2nd placed United).

8th April 1977

Two goals from Brian Kidd gave City a 2-1 victory over Leeds at Maine Road. A crowd of 47,727 witnessed the game as the Blues challenged for the League title.

9th April 2005

A 90th minute goal from Musampa - his first for the Blues - at the northern end of the stadium gave City a 1-0 home victory over eventual European Champions Liverpool. This was Stuart Pearce's first league victory as City manager.

10th April 1937

A game viewed as being the title decider saw City defeat championship rivals Arsenal 2-0. The game, played in front of a Maine Road crowd of 74,918 (still not the highest for a City-Arsenal fixture at Maine Road) swung the advantage to City and ultimately the title came to Manchester.

11th April 1974

Despite bold statements from new Chairman Peter Swales at the time of his appointment, manager Ron Saunders was dismissed after less than five months in the role. In March Saunders' City had been defeated 2-1 in the League Cup final against Wolves.

12th April 2004

A 25th minute goal from Anelka helped City to their fourth successive draw under the temporary stewardship of Arthur Cox. Manager Kevin Keegan was absent due to instructions from his doctor to rest his bad back. The game with Spurs ended 1-1 on Easter Monday.

13th April 1894

A Memorandum of Association was signed creating Manchester City FC. The first aims of the Club were to promote football, cricket, lacrosse, lawn tennis, hockey, bicycle & tricycle riding, running, and jumping.

14th April 1990

Adrian Heath scored his first goal for City as

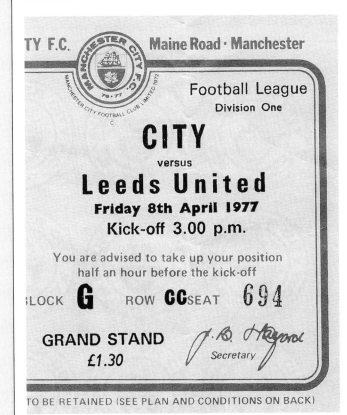

TY F.C. · **Maine Road · Manchester**

MANCHESTER CITY FOOTBALL CLUB LIMITED 1972 · 79·77

Football League
Division One

CITY
versus
Leeds United
Friday 8th April 1977
Kick-off 3.00 p.m.

You are advised to take up your position half an hour before the kick-off

BLOCK **G**   ROW **CC** SEAT **694**

GRAND STAND
£1.30

Secretary

TO BE RETAINED (SEE PLAN AND CONDITIONS ON BACK)

Sheffield Wednesday were defeated 2-1 at Maine Road. Two days later he scored his second, but sadly he would score only two further League goals during his City career.

15th April 1970

German side Schalke 04 were defeated 5-1 in the ECWC semi-final second leg at Maine Road.

16th April 1977

Brian Kidd's City popularity continued to rise as the former United star scored in the 2-0 victory over West Bromwich Albion. Kidd ended the season with 21 goals from 39 appearances.

17th April 1893

Ardwick (City) ended their first season of League football with a 3-1 win over Lincoln. This gave them a fifth placed finish in Division Two.

18th April 1972

A disappointing 2-1 defeat at Ipswich caused the Blues to stumble in their title challenge. They ended the season fourth - a point behind Champions Derby.

19th April 1980

Kaziu Deyna, Michael Robinson, and Dennis Tueart scored as Bristol City were defeated 3-1 in the top flight game.

20th April 1985

Kenny Clements and Jim Tolmie helped City to a 2-0 home victory over Sheffield United in Division Two. That victory kept the promotion challenge alive, although a few nerve-wracking moments came during the final weeks of the season.

21st April 2003

Foe scored twice as City defeated Sunderland 3-0. This was the last City win at Maine Road.

22nd April 1899

City became the first side to gain automatic promotion when they won the Second Division title.

23rd April 1904

The Blues became the first Manchester side to win the FA Cup as they defeated Bolton 1-0 via a Billy Meredith goal at the Crystal Palace.

24th April 1937

City celebrated winning their first League championship by defeating Sheffield Wednesday 4-1 at Maine Road.

MATCH MAGAZINE

TODAY'S MATCH IS SPONSORED BY

SAAB
MANCHESTER

Philips Major Appliances
Official Club Sponsors

PHILIPS

SATURDAY
APRIL 20, 1985

MANCHESTER

KICK OFF 3PM
AT MAINE ROAD
MANCHESTER

CITY

VERSUS **SHEFFIELD UNITED**

CANON LEAGUE DIVISION **2**

MANCHESTER CITY F.C.

Hon. President : L. W. FURNISS.

Directors : R. SMITH (Chairman), A. ALEXANDER, J. P. (Vice-Chairman).
Dr. J. B. HOLMES, F. R. JOLLY, W. M. SHAW and H. WOOD.
Secretary Manager : W. WILD. Registered Office: MAINE ROAD GROUND

CLUB GOSSIP
WILL TO-DAY BRING US THE CHAMPIONSHIP ?

TO-DAY we bring our season to an end so far as our home League engagements are concerned, and we are hoping it will be the happiest wind-up we have ever had in the sense that it will consummate our first Championship year.

Two points from the match with Sheffield Wednesday this afternoon and the prize for which we have striven so long and which would complete for us the full round of honours in the game, will be ours.

We have had the F.A. Cup and the Championship of the Second Division of the League, but never the trophy which is now within our grasp.

WE are not counting our chickens before they are hatched. We recognise that we are up against a desperate opposition. The match is of the utmost importance to the Wednesday, to whom defeat might mean the loss of their position, and they are sure to make a tremendous fight.

When we were at Hillsborough in December they inflicted upon us the heaviest defeat we have sustained throughout the season. They had what we should say was their very best day.

They beat us by 5—1, after we had run through six successive matches without a reverse and, except in the following game with Grimsby Town, six

27th April 1895

James Alphonso Mulligan, known as Jimmy to City fans, was born at Bessbrook in Ireland. Mulligan joined City shortly after Belfast Celtic disbanded, and made his City debut in April 1922. Capped for Northern Ireland while playing in City's reserves, Mulligan only managed 3 first team appearances. In later life he became headteacher of Mount Carmel school in Blackley and chairman of the Manchester Schools FA.

25th April 1967

Alan Kernaghan, who became manager Brian Horton's first signing in 1993, was born at Otley, West Yorkshire.

26th April 1969

Tony Book lifted the FA Cup (below) following City's triumph over Leicester City.

28th April 1934

Fred Tilson scored twice to give City a 2-1 victory over Portsmouth in the FA Cup final at Wembley

29th April 1986

Steve Redmond lifted the FA Youth Cup following City's 2-0 victory over Manchester United in the second leg of the final at Maine Road. An official crowd of 18,164 witnessed City's success.

30th April 1977

Nicky Reid signed apprentice forms for the Blues. He later made 250 (plus 6 as substitute) first team appearances including the 1981 FA Cup final.

The UEFA Cup and the European Cup Winners' Cup on display at the City museum in April 2008.

CITY IN EUROPE

2008-09

Competition: UEFA Cup
Reason For Qualification: Qualification via Fair Play League
Manager: Mark Hughes

17th July 2008
Qualifying Round 1 Leg 1 (at the National Stadium)
Attendance: 5,700

EB Streymur 0-2 City

City Goalscorers: Petrov & Hamann
City: Hart, Onuoha, Dunne, Richards, Ball, Ireland, Hamann (Fernandes), Johnson, Petrov, Jo (Evans), Vassell

Staging the UEFA Cup Final in 2008 had presented the Club with all the evidence they needed that European football was something the Blues had to strive for. Fortunately they didn't have to wait long for the chance to prove what they could do.

Qualification for the final season of the UEFA Cup (the competition was to be rebranded Europa League for 2009-10) was achieved via the Fair Play League and, as with 2003-04, City had to progress via qualification rounds. This time however, competition started much earlier for City with games played in July. It is also worth noting that the Blues had to travel to the remote Faroe Islands for their first match in the tournament.

While most club's exploits in European competition tend to focus on the players

and the games themselves with City the focus, as far as many areas of the media were concerned, was on the fans. In particular the journey to the Faroe Islands by a group of intrepid City explorers who hired a trawler.

In terms of the team itself, the Streymur game was to be Mark Hughes' first competitive fixture as City manager and the debut game for £19m record transfer Jo. At the time, this was viewed in a remarkable way as the media highlighted the fact that never before had such a significant signing made his debut at such a remote venue. As the season progressed of course the transfer fee was eclipsed significantly.

The early play was predominantly in City's favour. After only three minutes Darius Vassell saw a close-range header saved at the foot of a post, and then in the ninth minute Stephen Ireland sent a ball towards Vassell who pushed forward down the right. Vassell sent a cross which was dummied by Michael Johnson before Martin Petrov slammed the ball into the top corner of the net.

Further attempts came City's way with new signing Jo sending a left-footed shot over the bar. Then, after 28 minutes, the experienced European campaigner Dietmar Hamann volleyed City's second goal of the tie.

The game ended in a comfortable and confident 2-0 victory. So much so that after 74 minutes Mark Hughes replaced the new signing Jo with young Welsh international Ched Evans, while Gelson Fernandes came on for Hamann.

31st July 2008
Qualifying Round 1 Leg 2 (at Barnsley)
Attendance: 7,344

City 2-0 EB Streymur

City Goalscorers: Petrov & Vassell
City: Hart, Corluka, Dunne, Richards, Ball, Fernandes (Hamann), Johnson, Elano, Petrov (Etuhu), Vassell, Sturridge (Evans)

This game made history as it was the first occasion the Blues had played a home European tie outside of Manchester. Previously City had played home European games at Maine Road and at the City Of Manchester Stadium, but work at Eastlands following a concert by Bon Jovi prevented the Club from staging the game at home. The decision was taken to stage the match at Barnsley.

City comfortably won the game 2-0 with goals from Petrov three minutes into the second half and Vassell in the dying seconds, however there was some criticism in the media. Graham Chase, writing for *The Times*, claimed: "Another European win in July, but as with the first-leg victory over this amateur team from the Faroe Isles two weeks ago, Manchester City again looked very much a side working their way through pre-season as they overcame EB/Streymur at Oakwell last night through goals from Martin Petrov and Darius Vassell.

"This tie has only ever been an inconvenience to Mark Hughes and, while his team again failed to shine, the new manager is pleased to be in today's draw for the UEFA Cup second qualifying round with no new injuries to concern him.

"Not that opportunities were in short supply. City had 36 efforts on goal, but their finishing was poor and René Torgard, the EB goalkeeper and a garage mechanic, was in impressive form, making fine saves, particularly from Vassell and Daniel Sturridge. Even when Torgard was beaten, the woodwork denied Vedran Corluka and Petrov."

14th August 2008
Qualifying Round 2 Leg 1
Attendance: 17,200

City 0-1 FC Midtjylland

City: Hart, Corluka, Richards, Dunne, Ben-Haim, Johnson, Fernandes, Petrov, Elano (Etuhu), Sturridge, Caicedo (Bojinov)

The Blues were anticipated to manage an easy victory over Danish side Midtjylland but the game didn't start as planned and after only fifteen minutes City were losing 1-0. Danny Olson sent a blistering shot from the edge of the area which Joe Hart had no chance to save.

The goal seemed to spur the Blues into action and almost immediately Martin Petrov had a terrific opportunity to equalise, but his attempt was blasted over the bar. Other attempts, most notably from Sturridge just before half time whose effort hit the bar, followed.

Sadly, despite City being the better side, the much-needed equaliser failed to materialise and City suffered only their second home defeat in Europe (the first was in 1971 in the semi-final of the ECWC to Chelsea).

CITY v EB/STREYMUR

01

★★★

MCFC Official Programme
Price £2.50

Manchester City

Thomas
Cook.com

UEFA Cup
1st Qualifying Round 2nd Leg

at Barnsley FC, Thursday 31st July 2008, 8pm
v EB/Streymur

le coq sportif.

Thomas
Cook

28th August 2008
Qualifying Round 2 Leg 2
Attendance: 9,460

FC Midtjylland 0-1 City

City won 4-2 on penalties

City Goalscorer: Califf (own goal)
City: Hart, Corluka, Ben-Haim (Hamann), Dunne, Ball, Ireland, Richards, Johnson, Petrov, Elano (Sturridge), Jo (Evans)

The Danish side were clearly on top for much of this game however the match proved to be one of those great, typically City matches where the Blues somehow manage to succeed against all the odds. James Ducker, writing for *The Times*, explained: "Outplayed over the two legs of their UEFA Cup second qualifying round tie against FC Midtjylland, City somehow emerged with their reputation intact and a place in the first round proper secured after their little-known Danish opponents proceeded to shoot themselves in the foot.

"Thomas Thomasberg, the Midtjylland coach, refused to blame Collins Babatunde, but only the Nigerian striker will know how the game stayed goalless before City forced extra time with a last-minute goal that, in itself, owed much to good fortune, Danny Califf turning the ball into his own net from Michael Ball's cross after the slightest of touches from Ched Evans."

That goal gave City the initiative and, although extra-time failed to bring a winner, the Blues were clearly the more confident as they entered a penalty shoot-out to determine the winners. Ducker: "With luck like this, Manchester City must have every reason to believe that this is the season when their 33-year wait for a significant trophy ends. When the game went to penalties, the momentum was with City. Joe Hart was the hero, the 21-year-old England Under-21 goalkeeper saving twice in a 4-2 shoot-out victory. Vedran Corluka, the Croatia defender, converted the decisive penalty with what may prove to be his final contribution for the club, with a move to Tottenham Hotspur looming."

Ducker's comments about the search for a trophy and the potential Corluka move are interesting as this game was City's last in Europe before news of the Abu Dhabi takeover was released. By mid-September the entire world seemed to be focusing on how the Blues were suddenly transformed, however it has to be stressed that many Blues did actually believe the UEFA Cup offered a real opportunity for the side before the takeover. Everyone knew it would be tough but with players like Kompany already at the Club and Shaun Wright-Phillips due to arrive the morning after this UEFA Cup tie there was real hope that City could compete. The takeover took this to another level of course.

18th September 2008
Round 1 Leg 1
Attendance: 15,907

AC Omonia 1-2 City

City Goalscorers: Jo (2)
City: Hart, Zabaleta, Dunne, Richards, Garrido, Ireland, Kompany (Fernandes), Elano (Hamann), Wright-Phillips, Jo (Sturridge), Robinho

City had plenty of chances to score in this game with the first of note coming from new signing Robinho. David Anderson, writing for *The Mirror*, entertainingly reported that chance: "Record £32.5m signing Robinho has got more tricks than Paul Daniels and he forced Antonis Georgallides into making the first save after 95 seconds when he beat Hamad Ndikumana with a lovely shimmy."

Other efforts, including several for Jo, proved City had control of the match if not the lead, but four minutes into the second half the home side went ahead following a free-kick twenty yards out. The lead lasted about ten minutes before City's dominance and opportunities finally brought a goal. Anderson reported: "On 59 minutes, Wright-Phillips robbed the inept Charalambous on the left to set up Jo for a tap-in that even he couldn't fluff."

After 72 minutes Jo made it 2-1 when, as Anderson reported: "he beautifully controlled Pablo Zabaleta's deep cross on his left thigh before firing an angled drive into the far bottom corner, giving Georgallides no chance to give City a vital edge going into the second leg."

Afterwards Mark Hughes gave his views on Jo's performance: "He worked really hard for the team and I'm glad he got his reward. They were two good finishes that should settle him down. It's important you get off the mark when you join a new club, especially when you're a striker, and he's done that now."

2nd October 2008
Round 1 Leg 2
Attendance: 25,304

City 2-1 AC Omonia

City Goalscorers: Elano & Wright-Phillips
City: Hart, Zabaleta, Ben-Haim, Richards, Garrido, Wright-Phillips, Ireland, Kompany (Hamann), Elano, Robinho (Petrov), Jo (Evans)

With a first leg away victory it was clear this game was easily within City's control, and sure enough the Blues progressed. It wasn't until the second half that City managed to increase their aggregate lead. Goals from Elano (48 mins) and the ever popular Wright-Phillips (55 mins) ensured City progressed. Chris Bailey, writing for the *Manchester Evening News*, expertly reported the goals: "Marcello Pletsch made a complete hash of an attempted clearance, and Robinho strode forward down the left before pulling back to Brazil team-mate Elano whose superbly hit, low right-footer skidded beyond the despairing dive of Antonis Georgallides.

"Seven minutes later it was all over as a contest after Robinho slung a long pass out to Zabaleta who set Wright-Phillips in motion. He bundled his way into the box and then confidently lashed in his fourth goal since returning from Chelsea."

In the 78th minute the Cypriots managed a headed consolation goal, but the tie ended in a comfortable 4-2 aggregate win providing City with qualification for the group stage of the tournament.

6th November 2008
Group Stage
Attendance: 21,247

City 3-2 Twente

City Goalscorers: Wright-Phillips, Robinho & Benjani
City: Hart, Zabaleta, Dunne, Richards, Garrido, Wright-Phillips, Vassell (Elano), Fernandes, Ireland, Robinho, Jo (Benjani)

As the first game in the group stage this match was very important. In some ways it was the first truly significant test of whether Mark Hughes' side could compete on the European stage. The earlier ties had been fine, but this stage saw stronger opponents enter the competition. Thanks to Shaun Wright-Phillips the Blues did not have to wait long to make their mark as he worked well with Jo to produce the first goal after only two minutes.

City thoroughly deserved the lead but only fifteen minutes later they suffered as Twente equalised in controversial fashion. Elia won the ball in a move that looked as if he came close to kicking Pablo Zabaleta in the face. City expected a free kick but the referee allowed play to continue and the Twente player managed to rifle a shot past Joe Hart.

The Blues remained the better side and scored their second after 57 minutes thanks to the popular Robinho. Benjani made it 3-1 five minutes later. Twente made it 3-2 in the 65th minute. Mark Hughes later commented: "We were quite comfortable at 3-1 up but we just switched off on a set play and gave them a lifeline."

The game ended 3-2 and afterwards Mark Hughes praised his side, in particular Robinho: "We had some great opportunities, and Robinho could have had a hat-trick. But we were grateful for the strike for the second goal. He has fantastic ability to manoeuvre the ball in those tight areas. He is one of the best players I have seen in that position to be able to manipulate the ball and create things inside the box. Because of his ability, players know they cannot dive in on him in those areas - because he can deflect the ball from them in an instant."

Mark Hughes' opposite number, the former

England coach Steve McClaren, said: "We are very disappointed about the result, because we felt we should have got something from the game. We certainly had chances. It was an open game, which must have been great for the neutral - but for both managers it was edge-of-the-seat stuff."

27th November 2008
Group Stage
Attendance: 54,142

Schalke 0-2 City

City Goalscorers: Benjani & Ireland
City: Hart, Richards, Kompany, Dunne, Garrido (Ball), Wright-Phillips, Vassell, Hamann, Ireland, Sturridge, Benjani (Jo)

Seen by many as the biggest threat to date, Schalke were a recognised European force. However, City proved to be at their absolute best as they completely and utterly convinced all fans and many neutrals that this side was capable of progressing with confidence and style. Goals from Benjani (32nd minute following a great cross from Daniel Sturridge), a cult hero following his 2008 Old Trafford derby goal, and the ever-improving Stephen Ireland (67th minute) secured the points.

The victory placed City top of the Group with two games left to play. This meant that a solitary point would be enough to see the Blues reach the knock out stage.

Mark Hughes was delighted: "This week was a great week. We beat Arsenal comprehensively and we came here knowing it was a very difficult game on paper. But we coped with the game quite easily. We were always in control and strong on the break. I'm very pleased with the manner of an excellent performance.

"People possibly thought this might be beyond us, but I know the quality in this squad, and we were a threat all night. We haven't had that many excursions into Europe recently, so it's important for us to make our mark. We've got six points now and it would be very surprising if we didn't go through."

Off the pitch, as with the first game of the UEFA Cup campaign, City supporters generated a great deal of positive coverage. This time they played their part in trying to help a fellow fan and his family after an appalling accident. 44 year old City fan Carl Ramsbottom had been travelling back to his hotel after the Schalke game when he got caught in a crush at Düsseldorf railway station. Losing his footing he fell 15ft down a staircase. As a result he suffered severe head injuries and spent several weeks in an induced coma. It wasn't until shortly before Christmas 2008 that he opened his eyes.

Inevitably, the medical care and the fact he was being treated in Germany caused an already difficult and worrying situation to be much worse. Various supporter groups raised the profile of Carl's plight and as a result significant support came from appeals and other initiatives. A great many City fans deserve to be praised for their part in the Carl Ramsbottom Appeal and how they managed to raise publicity, finance, and support for the cause.

3rd December 2008
Group Stage
Attendance: 25,626

City 0-0 Paris Saint-Germain

City: Hart, Zabaleta, Ben-Haim, Dunne, Garrido, Elano (Benjani), Vassell (Hamann), Kompany, Ireland, Jo (Evans), Sturridge

Pre-match the talk was of City pushing for victory to ensure they won the Group stage and get an easier draw in the following round, however after resting several players the Blues were unable to score. It says much about how City were progressing that a draw against Paris St-Germain was viewed as a failure but, as far as the media were concerned, this was a failure. It seemed ridiculous – two years earlier a draw with PSG in a major competition would have been heralded a tremendous result.

Mark Hughes put it all in perspective with his post match comments. He made it clear that City remained the team in control: "We are guaranteed at least second and we are still in good shape. We are growing with every game we play in Europe. We want to avoid

Champions League teams in the next stage and, if we get a better result in Santander than Twente get in Paris, then we will. We are still in the box seat."

18th December 2008
Group Stage
Attendance: 18,360

Real Racing Club Santander 3-1 City

City Goalscorer: Caicedo
City: Schmeichel, Zabaleta, Richards, Ben-Haim, Garrido, Vassell, Fernandes, Hamann, Elano (Kompany), Robinho (Ireland), Evans (Caicedo)

City had already qualified by this stage and the result actually had no bearing on progression as results elsewhere allowed City to win the group. However, the Blues did receive severe criticism in the *Manchester Evening News* for their failure to excite the travelling fans. In the end Caicedo netted a last minute consolation tap-in for the Blues, providing the 950 fans who travelled with something to cheer. Even though the result brought criticism it has to be pointed out that Santander had never conceded more than one goal at home in a UEFA Cup game in any case.

The qualification table ended:

UEFA Cup Group A

Pos	Team	Pld	W	D	L	Pts
1	Manchester City	4	2	1	1	7
2	FC Twente	4	2	0	2	6
3	Paris St Germain	4	1	2	1	5
4	Racing Santander	4	1	2	1	5
5	Schalke	4	1	1	2	4

19th February 2009
Round of 32 Leg 1
Attendance: 30,159

FC Copenhagen 2-2 City

City Goalscorers: Onuoha & Ireland
City: Given, Richards, Dunne, Onuoha, Bridge, Zabaleta, Kompany, Ireland, Wright-Phillips, Robinho (Caicedo), Bellamy

Twice City went ahead in Copenhagen only to see the home side come back to snatch a draw in freezing conditions. The Blues should easily have won this game but sadly they seemed unable to kill off the match. The Danish side's second equaliser came in the 90th minute. Nevertheless a 2-2 away draw was a creditable result and as Mark Hughes accurately summed up after the game: "Beforehand we would have taken a positive result like this, with away goals. When you allow your opponents back into it right at the death it is very hard to take. We certainly had chances to put the tie beyond them. But it has put us in a good position."

26th February 2009
Round of 32 Leg 2
Attendance: 26,018

City 2-1 FC Copenhagen

City Goalscorers: Bellamy (2)
City: Given, Zabaleta (Elano), Onuoha, Dunne, Richards, Wright-Phillips, Ireland, Kompany, Bridge, Robinho, Bellamy.

Craig Bellamy gave City victory with goals in the 73rd and 80th minutes to put the Blues through to the last sixteen. The player had suffered a personal tragedy the previous day and it said much about his interest in helping the Blues progress that he made it on to the field at all. He later admitted: "I lost my cousin, one of my closest friends, yesterday morning. Today was a hard day for me, for my family and his family. I'll miss him dearly and I'd like to dedicate this game to him and the goals as well."

The player received praise from Mark Hughes after the game: "Whatever people say about him, he has a fantastic work ethic, no little skill and outstanding pace and we needed those qualities. For me, he has been outstanding with Wales and at Blackburn but here he is at another level."

Hughes felt the game itself had been an important test: "We were a little bit off the pace in the first half but, in the end, we won it comfortably and created a lot of chances. We've got a group of players who understand the demands that are going to be placed on them now and in the future. The expectation levels have been way ahead of any Manchester City team probably in the history of the club and we're dealing with it. A lot of teams have gone out by all accounts so let's see how far we can go. Further progression in a top European competition can only be good for us."

12th March 2009
Round of 16 Leg 1
Attendance: 24,596

City 2-0 FC Aalborg BK

City Goalscorers: Caicedo & Wight-Phillips
City: Given, Richards, Onuoha, Dunne, Bridge, Wright-Phillips (Etuhu), Zabaleta, Ireland, Elano, Robinho, Caicedo (Evans).

City turned on the style with a thrilling and entertaining performance at Eastlands which seemed certain to place the Blues in the next round. Of course, City being City, it's always a little unwise to feel confident, but even the Club's most cynical fan had to feel positively about the Blues progression.

City were in control from the start and were unlucky not to have been awarded a penalty when Robinho was hacked down in the area after displaying a few Brazilian skills. Mark Hughes entertainingly gave his view as to why it wasn't given: "I think Robbie's feet were too quick for him. The referee was mesmerised and forgot to look for the tackle."

Robinho played his part a little later however when the Blues took the lead. Journalist Daniel Taylor wrote for *The Guardian*: "Robinho began the move that led to the opening goal, gliding in from the left and playing the ball into Caicedo's feet on the edge of the area. Thereafter, it was all about the Ecuadorian's body strength. Caicedo is built like a backstreet bouncer and, having received the ball with his back to goal, he shrugged aside his marker, Michael Jakobsen, before prodding the ball past the goalkeeper Karim Zaza. The second goal was even more impressive – a classic Wright-Phillips run, starting on the right before darting inside, twisting and turning into

space to find a shooting opportunity. Patrick Kristensen, Aalborg's left-back, was left trailing and Wright-Phillips struck his shot with the outside of his right boot so that it curled away from Zaza into the top corner of the net."

19th March 2009
Round of 16 Leg 2
Attendance: 10,735

FC Aalborg BK 2-0 City

(City won 4-3 on penalties)

City: Given, Richards, Dunne, Onuoha, Bridge (Garrido), Wright-Phillips, Zabaleta, Kompany (Elano), Ireland, Robinho (Caicedo), Evans.

City were comfortably looking to a quarter-final appearance when two goals in the final five minutes forced the tie into extra time. There was some controversy about the two goals – for the first scorer Shelton looked to control the ball with his arm while the second was a penalty awarded after the ball hit Ched Evans' hand – but it was another important European lesson for the Club.

After the away goals rule and extra time failed to find a winner, the game entered penalties with City winning the shoot out 4-3.

Mark Hughes commented afterwards: "Maybe lady luck smiled on us, maybe that's a good sign. You scratch your head and wonder how that situation developed, but we've made it through to the next round. Knowing Shay was in goal for us gave the real confidence taking their kicks. I think they had a real belief that Shay would play a hand."

9th April 2009
Quarter-finals Leg 1
Attendance: 50,500

Hamburg SV 3-1 City

City Goalscorer: Ireland
City: Given, Richards, Dunne, Onuoha, Bridge (Garrido), Wright-Phillips (Fernandes), Zabaleta, Ireland, Sturridge (Benjani), Bellamy, Robinho.

Everyone expected this to be an extremely tough tie for City, and so the majority of fans

The return of Shaun Wright-Phillips brought added excitement to City's UEFA Cup run. Here he scores against Aalborg in the first leg of the round of 16.

both in the stadium and watching at home simply tried to enjoy the build up without thinking too much of how the game itself would pan out. Everyone was hopeful of course, but as the game kicked off most expected Hamburg to dominate. They were in for a shock as City took the lead thanks to Stephen Ireland after a mere 35 seconds.

That goal gave everyone a great deal of hope but sadly Hamburg equalised only eight minutes later. Then in the second half a 63rd minute penalty put Hamburg in the driving seat. The Blues were still hopeful but eleven minutes from time Hamburg increased their lead.

Afterwards Mark Hughes recognised that progression would be tough: "We have to pick ourselves up. It'll be hard but we're not going to concede that the tie is over – because it isn't. We have players who can cause Hamburg problems at our own ground."

16th April 2009
Quarter-finals Leg 2
Attendance: 47,009

City 2-1 Hamburg SV

(Hamburg won 4-3 on aggregate)
City Goalscorers: Elano (penalty) & Caicedo
City: Given, Richards, Onuoha, Dunne, Bridge, Zabaleta (Fernandes), Kompany, Ireland, Elano (Sturridge), Robinho, Caicedo.

Knowing they needed to win by two clear goals as a minimum the Blues, supported by an extremely passionate crowd, came on to the pitch with a determined air. They relentlessly pushed forward in the opening period and had a great early opportunity from Micah Richards saved.

Despite the pressure though it was Hamburg who scored first with a low cross from Pitropia finding its way to Guerroro, who fired home past Shay Given in the tenth minute. It was a significant blow and, in years gone by, would probably have completely knocked the stuffing out of the Blues. But this City performance was different and, around five minutes after the goal, a twenty yard effort from Elano was adjudged to have been handled by Trochowski in the area. The resulting penalty made it 4-2 on aggregate.

City were back in with a chance and seemed determined to progress but, despite a great deal of attempts which included a powerful Elano free kick rattling the crossbar, it wasn't until the 50th minute that City's second goal came. Ireland, by this stage recognised as one the Club's most outstanding performers of the season, provided Caicedo with a wonderful pass on the edge of the area. After some neat footwork Caicedo then fired a low shot passed Hamburg's 'keeper Rost to make it 4-3 on aggregate.

Five minutes later Elano hit the post again from another free kick as the Blues looked more likely to score than Hamburg. That pressure continued, even when Richard Dunne was dismissed for his second bookable offence, but inevitably the extra Hamburg man made the going tough at times.

In the final minute substitute Daniel Sturridge sent a shot into the side netting, and shortly afterwards City's dream of UEFA success was over. Nevertheless, the 2008-09 season had proved that the Blues were able to challenge in Europe. City were the last of the British sides left in the UEFA Cup at quarter-final stage and they had played more European games than any of the British sides that entered European competition in 2008-09, including the European Champions League finalists. They may not have won a trophy but they were certainly impressive British representatives.

THE TRAWLER TWELVE

The first UEFA Cup tie of the 2008-09 season saw City face a side from the Faroe Islands. The islands are fairly remote with few transport links and so to ensure they reached their destination a group of City fans decided to work together and charter a trawler. This story became the first major talking point of the Club's season and, as with the banana craze and many other positive stories, it demonstrated the determination of City fans to enjoy their support of the Club.

The Big Book Of City has tracked down one of the intrepid group who took part in the journey. Dave Scally, whose journey took an even more dramatic turn, tells his version of the story.

When City were drawn against EB/ Streymur of the Faroe Islands, my first reaction was where were the Faroes, and secondly I wondered how I was going to get there?

It soon became apparent that getting to the Faroes was going to be either very difficult or very expensive. I'd almost given up hope of going when a post appeared on a City forum advertising the "trip of a lifetime", it was organised by a City fan called Leighton Gobbitt. The basic plan was to drive to Aberdeen, get the overnight ferry to the Shetlands, then charter an old fishing trawler to take us the remaining distance, arriving in the Faroes on the morning of the game.

As the trip neared, the publicity around the trip increased. *Four Four Two* magazine were going to send a reporter and photographer to cover the trip; there were small snippets in newspapers and radio stations started to mention the trip.

We left the City of Manchester Stadium on the morning of Tuesday 15th July. We all gathered outside the main entrance, 12 strangers bound together only by the quest to make this adventure for a football match. After a quick interview for *Radio Manchester*, we set off in three different cars to Aberdeen. On arrival at Aberdeen ferry terminal, we found a pub to wait for the ferry. Our chatting soon stopped when we saw on the TV in the bar, a live interview with the skipper of our trawler. *Sky Sports News* was covering the story, and it soon dawned on us that this trip was making national headlines. I looked around at us, strangers, sat around a table having a pint, this was us, this was the Trawler Twelve!

Plenty of drinking was had on the overnight ferry and on the Wednesday morning we awoke in the bar to the sound of Leighton's mobile, it was Radio Manchester wanting an update at 7am. We disembarked and made our way to the harbour on the Shetlands. We saw the sky blue 'Seven Sisters' trawler and our skipper gave us the bad news. The weather and seas were too bad. We couldn't go.

We were gutted. We knew that this could have been possible, and it was a risk we took. But hearing the news we felt flat. The only thing to do was head to the nearest pub to drown our sorrows. After an hour or so a man came in with an ITV jacket. "Are you the lads from Manchester?" he asked in a strong accent. "Yes" we replied, "can I do an interview by the harbour?"

We agreed. We could either stay in the pub or do something to try and get saved. We did an interview by the harbour, and the reporter told us there was a daily flight from the Shetlands to the Faroes taking the mail. We headed to the Post Office to make enquiries. Amazingly the post master knew who were we were, he told us he'd seen us mentioned in the paper review feature on the news that morning! He asked the charter company, but they were going to charge us several thousand pounds to charter their flight.

We carried on doing interviews in the afternoon, and three of us were sat on the bridge of a trawler making a plea for anyone to help when the rest of the group returned from the pub "Get your bags lads, we're going to the airport" shouted Leighton. We didn't know

what was going on, but jumped in a taxi and headed to the airport. On the way Leighton told us that our pleas had been heard, and that the national airline of the Faroes, Atlantic Airways was sending a plane to pick us up. It wasn't any old plane, it was the charter plane that had just taken the City team to the islands, it had just dropped the team off and was turning around to pick us up.

We were still in shock when the plane arrived at Lerwick Airport. The owner of the airline, Magni Arge stepped off the plane and shouted "Come on lads, welcome aboard." Reality had left us behind as we took off on a 90-seater jet, with twelve City fans, a reporter, photographer and the owner of the airline.

We touched down in the Faroes, and found out that Thomas Cook had paid for some accommodation in a hostel.

We watched the game with the rest of the City fans who'd made the trip over. All of whom had paid a lot of money to get there, we felt guilty that we'd got there on the cheap. All credit to them though.

We were on the islands until Sunday, so on the Saturday we hired a minibus to take us to EB/Streymur's old ground, which was right on the coast, about 3 metres from the Atlantic Ocean! We had a kick about on the astro turf, on a pitch surrounded on three sides by mountains

and the open sea on one side. I believe this is the greatest football ground in the world. Someone asked what time it was, I looked at my watch and it was 3pm. 3pm on a Saturday afternoon! We couldn't have been in a better place!

On the Sunday afternoon we were due to fly back, but all night Saturday and Sunday morning I'd been feeling really ill, so ill I felt I had to see a doctor for some pain killers. I asked where the nearest doctor was, and was told it was in the hospital down the road. My mate Mike came with me and I was seen within minutes. I described the pain, the symptoms and was told it was suspected appendicitis, and they would operate immediately. I was taken into the next room, changed into a surgery gown and had to stop the surgery preparations so I could ring my family. The hospital was so quick I was almost in surgery before I'd been able to tell my family.

I'd told Mike and the rest of the group to fly back on their free flight, as I'd only be a day or two in hospital. On Sunday evening I was recovering well from surgery, and was expected to be flying home in a day or two.

Then, I gradually got worse and started to get severe pain in my stomach. The pain was so bad that I was put on morphine and was sent for a CAT Scan. I was on my own, in a foreign country in immense pain. As I went for my CAT Scan, I was very low. The porter could see it, and in broken English told me he'd arrange for a friend of his to come and see me.

On the Friday my brother John had flown out to see me, as we still didn't know what was wrong with me and I'd been on my own in hospital for six 6 days. My brother had only been with me a few hours when a group of people walked into the room "Where's Dave? Are you Dave? Hey, I'm Siggi, the manager of EB/Streymur".

He thrust a signed EB/Streymur shirt into my hands and a photographer started taking pictures. A reporter jotted down the conversation and a club official smiled politely in the background.

Siggi asked how I was going to get back to Manchester. I told him as soon as I was better

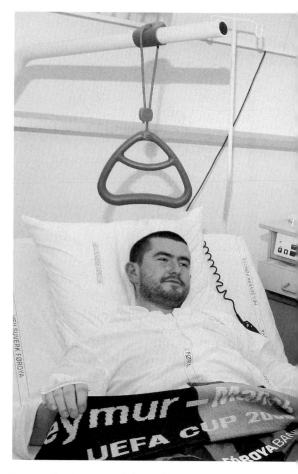

I was going to go straight to the airport and get the first flight out. He told me the EB/Streymur team was flying direct to Manchester on the Monday and that me and my brother were welcome to fly back with them! I couldn't believe my luck. We exchanged numbers and Siggi said he'd be in touch. For the next few days I gradually recovered, and even got a visit from Magni, the owner of Atlantic Airways who brought me some books, including The Hobbit, the story of Bilbo Baggins, who travels to far off lands. In fact, Magni signed the book "To the Bilbo Baggins of the Faroes".

The reporter and photographer who came to my room were from the national newspaper, and on the Saturday my picture filled the entire front page of the Faroese national newspaper! I'd become a bit of a celebrity on the Islands, as that weekend was the national day of the Faroes, St Olaf's day. My brother and I wandered into the town on the Sunday

afternoon and all the locals recognised me as "the man from Manchester" and asked how I was!

Siggi visited me again on the Sunday to discuss travel arrangements. We had an amazing chat about the forthcoming return leg in Barnsley. We talked about their players, our players, who they were wary of and their tactics. It was a weird experience talking to the opposition manager in this way.

On the Tuesday morning, Siggi picked us both up from the hospital and drove us to the airport where we met the rest of the team, who recognised me from the newspapers.

After a short flight we landed back in Manchester, and after two weeks in the Faroes I was glad to be home.

A few days later was the return leg at Oakwell. I sat amongst the City fans in my EB/Streymur shirt, cheering on EB/Streymur. After the game we went to see the EB/Streymur team. After losing 2-0 and getting knocked out of the UEFA Cup, you'd have thought they'd have been upset. But no. This was a tiny team of amateurs who'd played a Premier League team. The atmosphere was amazing, they'd done themselves proud.

As I bid farewell to the team, I gave the manager a present. It was a City shirt with his name and a number '1' on the back. He loved it, and put it on straight away, conducting his post-match interviews in his new City shirt.

My trip to the Faroes was always going to be memorable even before we set off from the City of Manchester Stadium. But it turned out to be one of the most amazing experiences of my life. I have many people to thank for that, and I will never forget the generosity of so many people, especially the people of the Faroes and EB/Streymur.

CITY'S NUMBER ONE

THE PROFILES

66 – JOE HART

Joe Hart kept City's great goalkeeping tradition alive when he made his debut for the full England side on 1st June 2008 against Trinidad & Tobago. He came on at half time for David James and kept a clean sheet, during a match England won 3-0. By this time Hart had become a regular for the England under 21 side and, of course, had appeared for City's first team.

Hart joined the Blues for an initial fee reported as £600,000 in May 2006 from his home town club Shrewsbury Town. His first team debut for the Shropshire club came in April 2004 – the day after his seventeenth birthday. In 2005 he became the club's first choice 'keeper and, with Shrewsbury back in the Football League (they were in the Conference when he made his debut), he began to be noticed by bigger clubs. Stories of Everton, Arsenal and Chelsea all making enquiries appeared in Shropshire newspapers.

In March 2006 the PFA announced that the young 'keeper had been voted into the League Two Team of the Year by the PFA's members.

Tim Flowers, by this time a goalkeeping coach with City, was seen at several Shrewsbury games during 2005-06 fuelling speculation that a move to Manchester was on the cards at the season's end. That speculation proved correct and the following October he made his City debut in the goalless Premier League match with Sheffield United. It was his only City appearance that season however, to gain valuable match experience, he went on loan to Tranmere Rovers in January 2007. He made six appearances for the Merseyside club.

A successful loan spell at Blackpool followed in April and Hart's performances in the five games he played helped the seaside club reach the end of season play-offs.

Hart was gaining many positive headlines and seemed to impress the leading coaches in the Country. He returned to City for the 2007-08 season and made his first appearance of the campaign in the fourth match of the season – a League Cup tie at Bristol City. On 29th September 2007 he made his first League appearance of the season, when City beat Newcastle 3-1 at Eastlands. Afterwards manager Sven Göran Eriksson talked of Hart's qualities and added that he was one of the biggest talents in the Country.

Hart became Eriksson's number one choice and remained City's preferred 'keeper when Eriksson was replaced by Mark Hughes during the 2008 close season. The young 'keeper went on to appear in all but two of the first 33 League, cup and European games of the season (making him second only to Corrigan in the number of European games he has kept goal in for City). However the run was brought to an end when Shay Given was signed in the January transfer window.

City were criticised severely by the media. Although the move was hard on Hart it is clear that Mark Hughes, like Kevin Keegan before him, wanted an experienced 'keeper to provide the defence with confidence as he attempted to develop a side for European glory. The criticism, however, was not really about Hart's career, it was more about England's chances in the 2010 World Cup. The view was that Hart needed first team football to develop his skills in time for England's bid for their first overseas World Cup success.

The criticism was part of what seemed like a media campaign to make City's new found wealth responsible for all the ills in the game. The fact that all the leading Premier League clubs each possessed at least one non-English player performing a key role and thereby limiting the opportunity for the development of potential England stars of the future was not considered. No. Quite simply, as one newspaper put it, City would be responsible if England failed to win the World Cup! At least the Blues weren't held responsible in 1970, 1974, 1978...!

During June 2009 the young 'keeper moved to Birmingham City on loan. Manager Mark Hughes recognised Hart needed the opportunity to play competitively on a regular basis: "His contribution to the team prior to Shay Given's arrival was fantastic, but by loaning him to Birmingham, he will add invaluable experience to that already gained here at City. I know he will relish the prospect of regular Premier League action, which is vital at this stage in his career."

Hart commented: "It's frustrating, but there's only one person can play in goal and Shay's doing that at the moment. I've had to deal with it the best I can. It's not been ideal, but it's not the end of the world. That's what [Capello] has been saying, that you need to be playing. That's what everyone wants to do anyway, regardless of whether it gets you in the England team or not. Everyone wants to play for their country and I've got more chance of playing in goal than anywhere else! So that's the role I'm pushing towards. You have to do well at club level, do well when you get opportunities."

Hart is clearly a talented 'keeper and, with the right guidance, support and opportunity he may well become England's permanent number one. His performance for England in the semi-final of the Under 21 European Championship was outstanding, even if the yellow card he received during the penalty shoot out ultimately robbed him of an appearance in the final.

Appearances: League: 50 FAC: 4 League Cup: 3 Euro: 9

67 – ANDREAS ISAKSSON

After spells with his home town team Trelleborg (Sweden), Juventus and Djurgården (Sweden), Andreas Isaksson signed for French club Rennes in July 2004. While at Rennes he impressed and in August 2006 he signed for City for a reported £2m. By that time he had also performed well in three games during the 2006 World Cup.

Unfortunately, his first months at Eastlands were not as successful as he had hoped. Knee and ankle injuries, as well as spells on the subs bench, meant his appearances were limited.

He made his debut on 9th December 2006 when he came on as substitute for an injured Nicky Weaver in the 46th minute of the Manchester derby at Old Trafford. Weaver returned for the following game but the Swedish international gained another opportunity in March. He ended the season by playing the final ten matches of the campaign and kept four clean sheets.

During the 2007 close season new manager Sven Göran Eriksson played Isaksson in the majority of the Club's pre-season games, however he fractured his thumb in a training session. This caused him to miss the start of the new season and, with further aggravating injuries, it wasn't until October that his chance to impress came again. During November and December he appeared in four consecutive League games but injury struck again. After that Isaksson was very much City's reserve.

His last appearance came on the final day of the season. It was a nightmare game and ended in an 8-1 defeat at Middlesbrough. On 2nd July 2008 he moved to PSV Eindhoven.

Appearances: League: 17 (plus 2 as substitute) League Cup: 1

68 – KASPER SCHMEICHEL

As the son of famous Danish international and City star Peter it was inevitable that Kasper's goalkeeping career would be closely watched, particularly as he arrived at Maine Road in 2002 while his father was City's first choice.

By the end of 2005, the young Schmeichel had impressed in City's reserves and it was clear that he was ready to gain first team experience. As opportunities at City were limited Schmeichel went on loan for most of the second period of the 2005-06 season, and made his first team debut for Darlington against Peterborough on 14th January 2006.

A three month spell at Bury followed from 23rd February. Schmeichel made 15 appearances for the Gigg Lane club and proved popular with fans as he helped the side move clear of the relegation zone. Another period at Bury followed in 2006-07, and then in January 2007 he joined Falkirk on loan. Again he impressed and was voted man of the match for the game with Rangers on 18th February 2007.

By the start of the 2007-08 season Schmeichel's loan experience proved invaluable when he was given his City first team debut on the opening day against West Ham. Schmeichel kept a clean sheet and he kept his place for the six League games that followed. That run included the Manchester derby which City won (1-0) and much was made by the media of Schmeichel's role, particularly as his father was spotted in the Directors' Box watching his son.

The following week Schmeichel saved a penalty from Robin Van Persie in the game with Arsenal at the Emirates Stadium, and shortly afterwards a new four year contract was agreed.

Schmeichel moved on loan to Cardiff City on 25th October 2007 as competition at Eastlands meant that Schmeichel would be unlikely to make further City appearances in the foreseeable future. Initially, Sven Göran Eriksson said the youngster could stay at Cardiff until the end of the season to gain valuable experience, however not long after the manager named Joe Hart as City's first choice Isaksson asked for a permanent transfer away from the Club. This forced Eriksson into limiting the loan to a couple of months. Schmeichel came back to the club in January 2008, although he subsequently went on loan to Coventry City.

Schmeichel is a very talented young 'keeper and throughout the 2008-09 season it was frequently rumoured that a permanent move was needed. Media reports claimed that the 'keeper and his father were keen to see him play as first choice at another club. These rumours intensified when Shay Given arrived at Eastlands.

On 14th August 2009 Schmeichel became a Notts County player when he was signed by former City manager Eriksson in his new role as Director of Football at Meadow Lane. The fee was reported as a County record.

The goalkeeper told reporters that Eriksson had been influential in his decision to move to Nottingham: "Sven was ever so helpful and told me the plans for the club. He gave me my chance at Manchester City and I enjoyed working with him, and I am looking forward to training and playing again."

Schmeichel made his debut on 22nd August 2009 and kept a clean sheet in the 3-0 victory over Dagenham & Redbridge.

Appearances: League: 7 (plus 1 as substitute) League Cup: 1 Euro: 1

69 – SEAMUS 'SHAY' GIVEN

Recognised for several seasons as one of the best 'keepers in the Premier League, Shay Given arrived at City on 1st February 2009 for a fee reported as £8m. Prior to this Given had made his name with Blackburn Rovers and Newcastle United – at both clubs he was signed by manager Kenny Dalglish. He had also had a spell at Celtic, though he never made a first team appearance, and loan spells at Sunderland and Swindon.

Eire international Given made his City debut on 7th February 2009, keeping a clean sheet in the 1-0 victory over Middlesbrough. He had replaced the popular Joe Hart but immediately impressed fans with his comments about the Club: "I felt that I should be at a club where we should be challenging for honours. You have a short career, and I didn't want to finish my career and later think that I regret it not taking this opportunity in joining Manchester City". He also admitted that he was convinced the Blues would develop: "the club [will] definitely take off and be going places over the next few years, and I am just honoured that the manager picked me to be part of this"

Given started the 2009-10 season as City's regular first choice.

Appearances: League: 15 Euro: 6

All appearance details are calculated up to the beginning of the 2009-10 season.

The Football Season Daily Reminder

May

Well, here is the final section of the Big Book Of City's Football Season Daily Reminder. As we said earlier, we don't highlight every anniversary, but this section completes our aim to provide one snippet for every single date in the period 1st August through to 31st May.

1st May 1937

League Champions City extended their unbeaten run to 22 as they drew 2-2 at Birmingham City.

2nd May 1960

65,981 witnessed a 2-1 defeat by Burnley. Burnley's win guaranteed them the League Championship.

3rd May 2003

Anelka scored in the 74th (penalty) and 80th minutes to ensure a 2-1 victory at Liverpool.

4th May 1966

A goal from Colin Bell (below) guaranteed promotion at Rotherham.

5th May 1978

City finished fourth to Nottingham Forest after a goalless game at Chelsea.

6th May 1924

Winger Billy Austin joined City from Norwich for a fee of £2,000. He went on to appear in the 1926 FA Cup final but was blamed by some for City's relegation

that same year when he failed to score a penalty in the final match of the season at Newcastle.

7th May 2005

Goals from Shaun Wright-Phillips and Kiki Musampa brought a 2-1 win at Aston Villa, and left the Blues needing victory over Middlesbrough in the last game to earn a UEFA Cup place (sadly, the Boro game ended in a draw).

8th May 1993

The first Premier League season ended with City a disappointing ninth. 17 points had been dropped during the final eleven games – another six would have ensured fifth spot.

9th May 1981

The 100th FA Cup final ended 1-1 between City and Spurs. The replay 5 days later saw Spurs win 3-2.

10th May 1947

A solitary goal from Alec Herd was enough to give the Blues promotion. The attendance for this game was recorded by the media at the time as 67,672 but official records reviewed almost sixty years later show that City actually recorded the attendance as 69,463.

11th May 1968

A 4-3 win over Newcastle United (below) gave City the League title.

12th May 1967

Darren Richard Lorenzo Beckford was born in Manchester. Although he only made seven (plus five as substitute) appearances for the Blues in the 1980s, he was a very popular player with supporters who had followed his career through the youth team and reserves.

13th May 1989

An agonising day ended in delight as the Blues drew 1-1 with Bradford City to guarantee promotion. Trevor Morley netted City's equaliser.

14th May 1995

Despite a goal from Niall Quinn (overleaf) and a

penalty from Keith Curle the Blues were defeated 3-2 by QPR on the final day of the season. City ended the season 17th in the Premier League and Brian Horton was dismissed. The Blues had to wait until 2003 before they finished higher than this.

15th May 2004

Paulo Wanchope scored his fourth goal in three consecutive games as he helped City beat Everton 5-1.

16th May 1887

Defender George Uttley was born at Elsecar. England international and FA Cup winner Uttley was first watched by City scouts in 1913 when he was at Barnsley. The Blues continued to keep tabs on his career until 20th September 1922 when they eventually signed him. Obviously in his latter stages of his career, Uttley only appeared in one first team game for City (28th October 1922 V Preston) before he moved into coaching at Bristol City.

17th May 1964

1990s midfielder Alfons Groenendijk was born at Dutch university city Leiden.

18th May 1911

Left back Eli Fletcher (below) was signed from Crewe for £300.

19th May 1937

League Champions City became the first English side to play in the Berlin Olympic stadium.

20th May 1987

After making 157 first team appearances Eire international Mick McCarthy left City for Celtic.

21st May 1905

Romiley born Julius Gregory signed for City. Gregory, described by the *Athletic News* as "very useful", only managed 3 first team appearances – the first two ended in defeat but his last match was a 5-1 victory over Sunderland on 21st April 1905.

22nd May 1973

Attacking wing-back Danny Tiatto was born at Werrobee, Melbourne, Australia.